Church-Shaped Children's Ministry

Constance Dever

manufacturers of active minds, noisy joy, and prayerful hearts since 1997

Curriculum for preschool and elementary age children,
training tools, music and other resources
are available for download or to order at:
www.praisefactory.org

Table of Contents

Other Children's Ministry Resources:

Church-Shaped Children's Ministry

Your Ministry IS Children's Ministry

Sometimes Children's Ministry might seem like the "desperate girlfriend" of your church. Always wanting more attention. More oversight. More volunteers. More money. Whine, whine, whine.

And all for what? To take care of a bunch of sniffly-nosed, wiggly kids, who would much rather be out on a playground than sitting in a classroom learning about Jesus. Yes, it provides a service that helps keep families happy and coming back; but man, what a pain!

Yet, maybe this desperate girlfriend is a little smarter than she looks. You might be surprised to learn that Children's Ministry impacts your entire church in a far more significant way that you might first imagine. I'd even go as far to say that your ministry IS children's ministry. Here's four observations why.

Why Your Ministry IS Children's Ministry: Four Observations

1. Children comprise the highest numbers non-Christians in attendance at most churches. The 4-14 window is the most common age of conversion. It is also unfortunately the time when kids are very prone to accept Christ as their Savior just to please the adults they love and respect, rather than out of true conviction. They may lead to false conversions--terrible for both the children and the church.

How will you reach these with the gospel while they are young?

Yet on the other hand, How will you look for true conversion before you baptize, for the sake of the children and the sake of the purity of the church? You don't want to wind up with baptismal statistics without the believing life to back it up. You don't want to encourage people to think they are Christians, but their lives clearly show that them are not.

2. Everyone who attends your church is or once was a child. Your current leaders and members WERE all children in the past. Your future leaders and members ARE all children now. Childhood is time of curiousity, open-heartedness, and lasting memories.

How can you fortify these future members/leaders now, helping them be a stronger part of the future church?

3. Most people who attend your church are or will be parents or grandparents. They are called to be the primary care-givers of their kids, including their spiritual nurturing. This will be one of their life's biggest, most time-consuming, challenging callings. No matter how many programs you have at church to teach their kids, the amount of time their kids spend with their parents, observing them and learning from them, dwarfs in comparison to anything the church can offer within its doors.

How can you equip this majority of your congregation for their major role in spiritually raising their children? How can you help their own life be a better witness to the truth of the gospel at work in the heart of sinners?

How can you help equip them for this job? How can you pour truth into their lives? How can you help them learn how to take that truth and feed it to their children?

4. In most churches, more members, miss more adult teaching times and services, because of taking care of their own kids, or volunteering to take care of other's kids, than any other ministry of the church. More members typically volunteer in children's ministry than any other ministry of the church. Most volunteers are not trained pastors or teachers. Yet there are usually more souls being taught by them in children's ministry than any other venue of the church, outside of the preaching from the pulpit.

How can you balance providing child-care and Bible classes for children that help support parents at church, with protecting the spiritual well-being of your members who volunteer to care and teach? How can you make sure that they do not over-serve and miss too much of the teaching that they, themselves, need on a regular basis?

Pastors are responsible before God for the soundness of all the teaching that takes place in the church. How can you make sure that the teaching these volunteer teachers provide, (and take in themselves, as they teach), is sound?

Common Scenarios that Have a Big Impact on the Church

Still not convinced of the impact of Children's Ministry on the church, present and future? Consider these all too common scenarios and how they impact the core of the church's concerns:

• Non-Christians come to church with their children. Non-Christian children come to church without parents. *--Conversion, Sound Doctrine, the Gospel, Expositional Preaching*

• Parents are new converts and have no idea how to parent as children. *--Discipleship, Sound Doctrine, Expositional Preaching*

• Teachers downstairs in the green, cinder-block wall classrooms teaching creative, but moralistic lessons while upstairs the parents are receiving sound, life-changing, expositional preaching from the pulpit. *--Sound Doctrine, Expositional Preaching*

• Poor teaching as a child that lingers into adulthood, affecting their view of God, the gospel, the Bible, and the Church. *--Sound Doctrine*

• Teachers who go online Saturday night to find an easy lesson to teach to the kids at Sunday School, not aware of the unsound doctrine it includes. *--Sound Doctrine*

• Church plants that over-stretch their few volunteers to try to have the full "wishlist" of children's programs that will attract future members *--Shepherding the Whole Flock Well*

• Churches with a growing membership that use any resulting increase in Children's Ministry volunteers to keep on expanding the programs they offer, without first using the increase in volunteers to relieve over-worked volunteers in their current programs. *-- Shepherding the Whole Flock Well*

• Parents who put pressure on pastors to immediately baptize their child who just prayed the sinner's prayer. *-- Conversion, the Gospel*

• Fluctuations in numbers of children or demographics that change what support would be most helpful to parents and children. **—Conversion, Discipleship**

• Number-hungry statisticians who pressure confessions, while creating false conversions. **—Meaningful Membership, Conversion**

• Members who come to church to serve in child-care but rarely attend the worship service. **—Meaningful Membership, Shepherding the Whole Flock Well**

• Members who leave the church, burnt out from over-serving. **-- Meaningful Membership, Shepherding the Whole Flock Well**

• No one is willing to take on the position of Children's Ministry Administrator (CMA) because it is too burdensome and thankless. It requires too many hours of work. They rarely get to enjoy a worship service or can be spared to take vacation time. They feel the pressure to fill volunteer shortages, themselves. They are left to field all program criticisms and put out all fires from disgruntled parents. **--Shepherding the Whole Flock Well**

• Fiefdoms of power arising from lack of shepherding. Someone other than the pastors assumes too much authority over a program for too long. They become offended when asked to change something they are doing. **-- Church Leadership**

• Families who have no family worship time because they/their kids are so busy in church programs many nights of the week **--Shepherding the Whole Flock Well**

• Difficulties between parents that show up as troubled behavior in their children. **--Shepherding Well the Whole Flock**

• Fluctuations in volunteer numbers that lead to over-working of volunteers to keep the same programs running as usual. **-- Shepherding the Whole Flock Well**

Evangelism, sound doctrine, conversion. Meaningful membership, discipleship, shepherding the whole flock well...these are all core issues of critical importance. Do you see how Children's Ministry takes on a significant role in all of these? Children's Ministry is not just a service on the side. It affects every single person in your church, one way or the other.

Your ministry IS children's ministry!

Children's Ministry, Past and Present

Let's take a look back at the progression of children's ministry through recent history up to today. There's nothing like looking back to look for wisdom for going forward.

Children's Ministry, as we think of it, started in the 1758 by Robert Raikes as an outreach to non-Christian children in the slums of Gloucester, England. These first "Sunday School" classes were held on Sunday because this was the only day off for these children who worked in factories the other six days of the week. Children from Christian families were not targeted for these classes, assuming their parents would educate their children in these biblical truths at home and grow under the preaching of the Word at church.

At Raikes' Sunday School, boys and girls were not only taught a catechism of Bible truth and taken to church but were also taught how to read (and write). This would be the only formal instruction many of these children would ever receive. Though controversial among Sabbatarians who saw these schools as work, rather than an act of mercy and an aid to worship, the classes were nonetheless hugely successful and spread throughout the rest of Great Britain. By 1831 it is estimated that over a million children attended Sunday School weekly—a staggering 25% of the population.

Public Education Brings Changes in Church Outreach

In 1870, public education for all children was legislated in Great Britain. From this time, Sunday Schools gradually came to focus only on Bible teaching, as well as increasingly included the children from church member families, more like what we find in churches today.

The four goals were to provide with children with:
- a testimony of life with God in the lives of their teachers
- to share the gospel that the lost might be saved
- to make disciples of all who trust in Christ
- to leave a legacy of Bible truths and knowledge of Scripture in the minds
- to prepare them to gather together well with the members of a local church

Children's Ministry Today

The goals of those 1870's Sunday Schools remain largely the same today, though some, like the importance of gathering together with the whole church body, may have retreated to the background or at least not not be as clearly articulated. Churches still invite children from non-Christian to take part in their programs. They still hold out the gospel to all, that they might be saved and grow as Christ's disciples. They still hope to leave a legacy of Bible truths in their minds and heart.

But now, in most churches, Children's Ministry often spends far more time on programs and resources for Christian parents and children (perhaps this is because they are spending less time on outreach to children). And most notable of all, most churches have expanded to many more programs than the original Sunday School Bible classes and church attendance. Now, they frequently include safe nursery-care for babies, so parents can go to their own Sunday School classes. They may be recommending resources for parents to use at home with their children; and, they may have added a host of of other, now-classic, peripheral programs (such as youth group, children's choir, AWANAs, After school Good News Clubs, Mother's Day Out, Sunday night missions programs, Bible camps, Vacation Bible School, and even Children or Youth Church that caters to a particular, homogenous age group.)

All of This Growth Has Led to Mixed Results

These intentions, and even some of the fruit, of these increased programs of today's typical Children's Ministry has been good. But sometimes the burgeoning list of programs has lead to serious fallout for parents, children and the volunteers who people these activities. The motto of "If you make the children happy, then the parents will stay" might bring more families to church, but it can unintentionally lead to malnutrition. Parent can begin to lose their sense of calling as primary, spiritual caregivers, or at least struggle to find time to fulfill it. Children may become so used to being catered for in a custom-fit, homogenous-group style that they lose their taste for the more important influences of family time and/ or gathering together to worship with the whole church body. Overused volunteers may struggle with burn-out and suffer from neglect of their own spiritual nourishment at church.

More at Any Cost?

"More is not just better, but necessary" is the even uglier step-sister motto that frequently accompanies the "If you make the children happy, the families will stay" motto. This line of reasoning exacerbates the problems mentioned above, in every size church.

Small, churches and church plants frequently face the frustrations of not enough man-power to keep open the children's programs that visiting families are seeking. Or, even if they do manage to have all the "wishlist" programs in place, they often tend to rely too heavily on too few volunteers. These tireless, big-hearted servants often sacrifice their own spiritual needs, week after week, to make sure the children's programs stay running.

Medium and large churches facetheir own version of these same problems. As the number of children and volunteers expands, the tendency is for churches to expand their program offerings, instead of first seeking healthier volunteer service limits with the programs they have. This plethora of programs can perpetuate the volunteer crisis. Yes, there are more able volunteers, but now so many more are needed to maintain the large number of programs.

Churches with more pocket money than volunteers find a solution by hiring care-givers who aren't members of their church. Others are tempted to enlist people who aren't really qualified to teach, choose a curriculum because it's an easy fit, even though it lacks biblical soundness; or, "fudge" on safe caregiver-to-child ratios to fit in more children.

And, if parents are not urged to be discerning, their children's schedules may so fill up with programs that the very families you hoped to serve with all these activities, can't find time to just be a family.

Pastors may be so overwhelmed with other aspects of ministry that they leave oversight of these matters in the hands of others who should be helpers, rather than shepherds over this segment of their church's growth.

Enter Church-Shaped Children's Ministry

Church-shaped Children's Ministry is a humble, finite approach to caring well for the families in the church. It acknowledges parents in their role as primary spiritual care-givers of their children and in encourages them in ways that are in keeping with the spiritual well-being of all of its membership. It looks to its pastor-leaders to set priorities for the spiritual support of parents and children; and, to carefully assess what resources (volunteers, finances, facility space, hours, etc.) the church has to offer towards those priorities. They prayerfully consider the best fit for the good of the whole church, and to the glory of God. Then, they lead the members in carrying it out.

Let's explore what Church-Shaped Children's Ministry looks like.

Church-Shaped Children's Ministry Overview

Church-shaped Children's Ministry is led by the church leaders, so that:
- it feeds parents and children from the pulpit.
- it decides what programs the church offers parents and children, other than from the pulpit.
- it lives out the leaders' vision and echoes their teaching priorities for the whole church.
- it reflects the resources of the church (financial, facilities, spiritually-healthy serve limits for volunteers).
- it keeps the people involved in children's ministry (families, children, volunteers, staff) under their guidance and care.

Church-shaped Children's Ministry desires:
- to provide children with a faithful testimony of life with God in the lives of their parents, teachers and other members.
- to share the gospel with children that the lost might be saved.
- to make disciples of all children who trust in Christ.
- to leave a legacy of Bible truths and knowledge of Scripture in the minds of the children.
- to prepare children to gather together well with the members of a local church.

Church-shaped Children's Ministry:
- acknowledges that parents are called by God to be the primary, spiritual caregivers of their children.
- it understands that good parenting (discipline style, biblical training methods, schooling choices, etc) often looks different from family to family and helps parents to respect each others' differences.
- also understands that parents are not Christians, alone, but are members of the local church, who encourage and build one another up, including encouraging and helping each other to spiritually nurture their children well. It supports and complements, not usurps parents' nurturing of their children.

That's why Church-shaped Children's Ministry enlists the members of a local church:
- to help equip each other in caring well for their children, at home and at church.
- to prepare them to be, Lord willing, future members of the church.
- but within limits that care for the spiritual helath of childrens' ministry workers/teachers, as well as support parents' well.

And includes programs that:
- support, not replace, parents.
- that are seen as opportunities for children's spiritual growth, but not requirements.
- don't get in the way with family time.
- help prepare the children to gather together well with the congregation.
- are sustainable, in terms of finances and volunteers required.
- will look different in each church and even within each church, as needs within the church grow or lessen, and as famiy demographics and volunteer pool change.

For the good of the whole, local church, and to the glory of the Head of the Church.

Let's take a more in-depth look at what Church-shaped Children's Ministry looks like for pastors, parents, children, programs, member volunteers and Children's Ministry leaders.

Pastors Take the Lead in Shaping Children's Ministry for the Good of the Whole Congregation

Your Ministry IS Children's Ministry

Church-shaped Children's Ministry starts with the pastors. How pastors lead their church in ministering to children is of huge importance. As we've said earlier, childhood is a ripe time for conversion and for growth.Pastors help make sure these young Christians grow on good teaching and in the presence of a mature and godly witness through their parents and through the local church. Even more sobering, pastors are accountable before God for sound teaching in their local church, even for sound teaching in Children's Ministry.

Pastors teach and encourage parents in their role as primary, spiritual care-givers of their children. They pray for families, and equip them through the preaching of God's Word. They think about how to care well for the chidlren who come to church without parents.

They provide pastoral oversight of families, programs and Children's Ministry volunteers. They are known as the church's leaders of Children's Ministry, and take responsibility for it. They lead by providing teaching priorities; approving program and curriculum choices; and, setting healthy limits on volunteering. They encourage, advise, and support the Children's Ministry team through regular meetings. They protect children and volunteers through a child protection policy.

How Pastors Can Lead

- Feed parents and children from the regular preaching of God's Word.
- Teach and encourage parents in their calling to raise their children in the nurture and the admonition of the Lord.
- Set wise guidelines for the baptism of children, membering into the church, and their partaking of the Lord's Supper.
- Realize that many of the church's future members and leaders are in their midst now as children. Setting teaching priorities to train today's children well can help prepare a stronger church of the future.
- Decide on a healthy, sustainable number of classes/programs to offer, balancing needs with available budget and volunteers.
- Establish volunteer serving limits to ensure that all volunteers are also being well-fed themselves.
- Create an effective child protection policy to keep children and volunteers safe. Abuse scars children and destroys a church's ministry.
- Appoint a like-minded administrator/team mplement the pastors' vision.
- Choose one elder/pastor as liason, overseer and encourager of Children's Ministry and its leadership. He receives regular updates on families, volunteers, programs, curriculum changes, and arising issues. He takes charge of difficult situations and bears the burden of enforcing unpopular but needful actions. He reports back to the other pastors, so they can pray, advise, and care well for those involved, too.

Note: Pastoral leadership does **NOT** mean that pastors; will not need guidance to make good decisions regarding children's ministry. The best leaders are humble learners. Pastors will need the wise insights of the Children's Ministry team, parents, teachers, and others to make the best decisions for the whole church. With many advisers, come the best decisions!

Parents Are the Primary, Spiritual Care-givers of Their Children

Church-shaped Children's Ministry recognizes parents as the primary, spiritual caregivers of their children. The Bible is filled with passages encouraging parents to raise up their children in the nurture and admonition in the Lord (Ephesians 6:4; Deuteronomy 4:9, 11:19; Isaiah 38:19; Joel 1:3; Psalm 78:4). Men being considered for roles as elder, deacon and pastor must first be good leaders of their families and children in the home (1 Timothy 3:4). God clearly takes the call to teach our children His ways very seriously, for the children's sake and for the sake of His Church.

Spiritually caring for children is no easy task. God equips parents for it through His Word, read at home and taught at church. They parent by the power of the Holy Spirit, and with the help and encouragement of the pastors and fellow members of their local church.

But just because parents are the primary spiritual caregivers, does not mean they have to spiritually care for their children alone. As members of a local church of covenanting believers, Church-shaped Children's Ministry seeks to encourage parents in this daunting task in ways that support, without usurping their special calling. Every family is different. This support is respectful of differences in approach parents may have for taking care of their children's spiritual needs. It is also sensitive to the different needs of different families. Some parents are younger Christians or single parents. These may need the most support of all.

Supporting parents can take on various forms: from honest sharing, advice-giving and prayer among members; to recommending resources for parents to use as they train their children in gospel-truths at home; to providing safe child-care while parents attend classes or workshops; to preaching to them from the pulpit; as well as offering Bible classes and youth group for the children, themselves.

Your Ministry IS Children's Ministry, as the local church raises up and equips those who will be primary, spiritual care-givers of children.

- Most of those who attend your church are, or will be, parents at one point in their lives. Parenting will be one of their greatest, God-given callings... and challenges.
- Parents help their children take part in the church services. They help them understand the prayers, music, ordinances, and the reading and preaching of God's Word. Frequently, a parent's attention is divided between training their child and focusing on the worship service. This requires much patience.
- Parents vary in their own Bible and parenting knowledge. Some are better equipped than others to spiritually nurture their children. Everyone needs help and encouragement!

What Churches Can Do:

- Fill your parents with solid teaching that they can pass on to their kids.
- Remind parents from the pulpit of their calling as the primary, spiritual care-givers of their children. Provide parenting workshop/classes or mentoring relationships to encourage parents, especially new parents.
- Encourage members to honestly share, pray, and seek advise from the pastors and from each other their parenting needs and struggles.
- Recommend resources that can help children engage in the worship services (bulletins, notebooks, etc). Provide Sunday School take-home sheets for parents to reinforce these truths at home. Provide a booklist of great books parents can use to teach their children about God.
- Provide child care for babies and toddlers during adult teaching times, so parents can listen well themselves.

- Offer Bible classes for children. These can provide helpful support to parents' teaching, as well as allow the children to see the work of God's grace in the lives of their teachers.

NOTE:
Some have been attracted by the Family-Integrated Church ideology. They take parents' job of primary spiritual care-giver for their children and make them the SOLE spiritual care-givers of their children. Local churches are made up of brothers and sisters who work equip each other for the spread of the gospel--to children as well as to everyone else. They commit to encourage one another in whatever God calls them to do. Raising children is one of these very important callings that fellow members can help each other fulfill in a God-honoring way. For more thoughts on this topic please see the article on family-integrated church ideology in Appendix A in the back of this book.

Children: Tomorrow's Church in Your Midst Today

Childhood is at very least an especially responsive time of soaking in biblical truths, and often, even of conversion and fruitful, spiritual growth, Church-shaped Children's Ministry seeks to make the most of these years. In conversations, in classes, in resources, in worship services, church members seek to clearly proclaim the gospel to the children, as well as live out the gospel before them. As they gather together each week to worship God and love one another, the church members seek to paint a picture of the beautiful love of Christ for His Church that not only glorifies God, but that also will remain in these young minds as a winsome testimony. They work to create a legacy of truth in their minds, that the Holy Spirit can ripen in their hearts, and prepare them one day to be well-equipped to commit themselves as followers of Christ and lovers of His Church, as well.

Your Ministry IS Children's Ministry!

- Everyone who attends your church was or is a child. Your current members and leaders WERE children. Your future members and leaders ARE children now.
- The highest concentration of non-Christians attending your church is usually the children in your children's programs.
- The "4-14" age window is the most common age of conversion. It is also when kids are most prone to "make decisions" to please their parents or teachers, without being truly converted.

What Churches Can Do:

- Provide children with a faithful testimony of life with God as they see God's work of grace in the lives of their parents, teachers and others.
- Share the gospel with children that the lost might be saved. Make disciples of those who trust in Christ.
- Make disciples, not baptismal statistics. "Pleasing" can mimic true conversion in the short run. Look for sustained fruit before you baptize. If in doubt, wait, for the sake of the child's true conversion and the purer witness of the Church.
- Pray for families. Include a section in your membership directory listing parents and the names/ages of children. This helps the congregation to easily and regularly pray for them.
- Offer Bible classes for children. These can reinforce what Christian parents teach at home, as well as introduce God's truths to children from non-Christian homes. These can leave a legacy of Bible truth in young hearts that echoes throughout their lives.
- Prepare children to gather together with the members of your local church.
- Mentor non-Christian kids who attend your church, frequently without their parents. Wrap both them and their parents into your families as a display of the goodness and love of God.
- Children are impressionable. They remember how they are treated. They notice how others live, and emulate (or try not to) them. Create a winsome memory of Christ and His church by treating children with love, respect and kindness.
- Provide resources for parents to use at home or at church, through your bookstall, church library, or recommending online resources.

Programs that Support and Are Sustainable

Programs are set by the pastors. They support, not replace, the parents' own spiritual training of their children. Church programs may ebb and flow, depending upon the vision of the pastors; families' needs; and, program sustainability, in terms of church volunteers and other resources required. Care for the WHOLE church--families and volunteers-- is of prime concern to the pastors, and directly affects what programs are offered when.

Your Ministry IS Children's Ministry

- Children's Ministry is sometimes used as the "magic key" that will attract families to church and keep them coming back.
- Sometimes, Children's Ministry programs become so numerous as to crowd out important family time.
- Children's Ministry programs frequently enlist more volunteers than any other ministry in the church.
- Once a Children's Ministry program is offered, the expectation is high to keep it going, sometimes, even at the expense of what is spiritually best for your volunteer teachers.
- Sadly, the most kid-friendly, exciting published curriculums are not always the most biblically sound. The "wow" factor of these curriculums can be very attractive, but can lead to unbiblical, simply moralistic, teaching. Read the curriculum carefully before purchasing!

What Churches Can Do:

- Pastors set teaching priorities and approve curriculum choices for Children's Ministry programs. They decide which programs the church will implement, taking into consideration need, family time, available budget, and number of volunteers needed. Healthy spiritual growth for and healthy sustainability for the whole church, not a program's attractiveness or its potential to swell attendance, drives their decisions.
- Pastors determine when to add, close or modify programs. They teach members to expect some ebb and flow in programs in order to care well for the spiritual needs of all--volunteers and families alike.
- Children's ministry leaders, teachers, parents and others can help the pastors understand their biggest needs in being better equipped to spiritually care for the children. Pastors can regularly seek the wisdom of these people in order to make the best decisions for the whole church.
- Start small. Offer less. Only add more, slowly. When you feel you cannot offer a particular program at church, recommend resources that parents can use to teach these same truths to their children at home.
- In some very small churches, the programs supporting parents might look as bare bones as regularly praying for parents; encouraging them and their children from the pulpit during the worship service; recommending good resources to use with their children in the pew and at home; and, facilitating honest conversations among fellow members.
- As the church expands, the leaders re-visit what might be beneficial to the growing congregation and what is now possible with the increased resources on hand. It very well could expand to a bookstall of resources for family devotions, child care for babies and Sunday School classes for parents and children on all or most Sundays.

From there, it might grow to include many other programs. But always, whatever is done, the pastors take into consideration healthy limits for the spiritual well-being of all.

- Sometimes the volunteer pool or the budget shrinks. Or sometimes, there are so many kids, that the church can no longer provide the same number of programs or for the same group of children. The church shape has changed again, and the leaders respond to these changes, trying to continue to care well for everyone. This might mean only offering classes for K-6th grade, when previously you offered classes for K-12th grade. It might mean putting a cap on the number of children you have in a classroom, rather than over-taxing volunteers beyond what is good for them.

Member Volunteers Who Serve Within Healthy Limits

Member volunteers support and encourage parents by helping to care, teach and mentor their children through the local church. They provide the children with a testimony of God's grace through their lives. They serve within limits set by elders, to meet the needs of Children's Ministry, but not at the expense of their own spiritual nurturing. They may serve in "over-sized" teams that don't require every teacher to teach every session in order to share the teaching load, avoid burn-out, and provide natural substitute teachers for classes. They are a great way to train less-inexperienced teachers by pairing them with more experienced lead teachers.

Church-shaped Children's Ministry strives to care for the spiritual well-being of all church members, not just the families. What programs you offer should be directly influenced by **who you are** and **what resources you have**. You need to live within this "budget" for the spiritual health of all your members. Building size, number of willing and qualified teachers, age and number of children; available finances; maturity of the Christian parents (ability to teach their children truths, themselves), number of services, and many other factors should be taken into consideration.

Your Ministry IS Children's Ministry

- There are often more teachers, teaching more souls, in Children's Ministry than in any venue in your church, outside of the pulpit.
- Most Sunday School teachers are not trained teachers or preachers. Curriculum doesn't just teach children. It often is teaching your teachers, too.
- Typically, more members miss the worship services and adult classes because of Children's Ministry obligations than any other ministry of the church.
- Over-volunteering and under-training are usually the two, biggest reasons why volunteers do not come back.
- Children's Ministry programs can be vulnerable places for child abuse to occur in the local church.

What Churches Can Do:

- Provide pastor-approved curriculum that is biblically solid, developmentally-appropriate, and teacher-friendly.
- Provide teachers with mentors who can teach them how to manage a classroom, as well as engage children in ways that are understandable, memorable and enjoyable.
- Enlist "over-sized" teaching teams for each program (not everyone teaches every week). This helps avoid teacher burn-out; builds in vacation time and good, substitute teacher choices; and, it allows for teachers to regularly attend adult classes and worship services.
- Enforce a child protection policy to keep volunteers and children safe. Know your teachers before they teach. Pair more-experienced, better-known teachers, with newer, lesser-known teachers. Require a waiting period before brand-new members can work directly with kids.
- Set up healthy volunteering limits to make sure all volunteers are being spiritually well-fed themselves.

Children's Ministry Leaders: Preventing Burnout

Children's Ministry leaders work under the leadership of the pastors. They bring the pastoral vision to life through the curriculum they implement, the volunteers they help train and enlist, and by generally encouraging families. They provide regular updates to keep the pastors informed, so they can care well for families and volunteers.

Your Ministry IS Children's Ministry

- Children's Ministry leaders are often the "stop gap" for last minute substitutes and other classroom issues. If there's a need, they are called to meet it.
- They can become so busy filling urgent needs, that their own spiritual needs are neglected.
- They carry most of the huge burden of enlisting, training and managing teachers; finding (or creating) good curriculum; and, caring well for the needs of many, different families.
- They have to be willing to be the "on-call, bad cop" who enforces difficult but necessary policies for everyone's good.

What Churches Can Do:

- Have a designated pastor who oversees and encourages the whole Children's Ministry team. He schedules regular meetings with the team to keep informed and to know how he and the other pastors can best care for the leaders, teachers, and families involved. He initiates any needed pastoral conversations with Children Ministry workers, teachers, or parents. He shares the job of enforcing difficult policies. He reviews and approves any curriculum choices. He reports back to the other pastors for their prayers, input, and further oversight.
- Recognize Children's Ministry deacons who work alongside the Children's MInistry Administrator/team (CMA) to welcome families, support teachers, and otherwise keep Children's Ministry programs running smoothly on Sundays or other program days. They are a great help to families, teachers, and the CMA.
- Designate Children's Ministry team leaders to take over much of the CMA's burden of finding substitutes and other last-minute program issues.
- Shepherd your CMA and deacons well by ensuring they regularly attend worship services. CMA's need regular vacation breaks, too. Well-trained assistants and program team leaders can help your programs run smoothly, even in their absence.

Church-shaped means creating a path towards everyone gathering together as the body of Christ

"After this I looked, and behold, a great multitude that no one could number, from every nation, from all tribes and peoples and languages, standing before the throne and before the Lamb, clothed in white robes, with palm branches in their hands, and crying out with a loud voice, "Salvation belongs to our God who sits on the throne, and to the Lamb!" Revelation 7:9-10, ESV

This is the great Day that God's people yearn for. This is the great Day for which we share the gospel and urge all to accept. And this is the Day which we have a little dress rehearsal of each Lord's Day we gather together to worship God and love one another. Once a week, we are all together-- our own, little version of every nation, tribe, people and languages praising God. So very different, in so many ways, yet unified by our Head and beloved Savior, Christ. This a dress rehearsal that we want to our children to watch and take part in. There is a special reflection of Christ that can be seen in these gatherings of God's people. We don't want our children to miss it.

But in this day when custom, same-age learning is so highly esteemed, sometimes the importance of including children in the church's weekly gathering together is down-played, if not left out almost completely. Unfortunately, the well-intentioned customization can create a diversion from exposure to the whole church body gatherings that starts with children's church, continues with youth church, then ends with college ministry. It may not be until they are adults that they have much opportunity to seeing the beauty of gathering together with others different from us and learn how to be a part of that, themselves. They miss the chance to gradually become familiar, and hopefully come to love these gatherings.

Church-shaped Children's Ministry also sees the great benefit of customized, same-age teaching times. It may include--even often include-- nursery child care as well as classes for younger kids, not only during a separate Sunday School hour, but even during all or part of the worship services. BUT, the eye is always on the goal: everyone gathering together to worship God and hear the preaching of the Word. It sets a path that gradually leads all to this point, and offers parents resources to help their kids along the way.

Your Ministry IS Children's Ministry

- Most congregations include a high percentage of families who are parenting their kids in the pew.
- Children vary a lot in their ability to sit still, listen and understand. Different approaches will be needed to help these different children gather well with the congregation.
- Families can have very different, strongly held opinions on how and when to include their children in the worship services. These strong opinions can sometimes cause friction with others who do not hold to their opinion. This can cause divisiveness.
- Different elements of the worship service are more quickly understood and accessible to younger children.
- Children can be noisy and wiggly, making it difficult not only for parents to focus on the worship service, but those around them, too.
- Volunteers who serve in child-care and Bible classes that take part during the worship services miss the opportunity to gather together with the congregation.
- Many times children's church and youth church strives to provide a very different, "more exciting" experience than the whole congregation worship service. They do not prepare the children well to take part in the church life that will be offered to them their adult life.
- Many times children/youth "church" enlists kids who are not necessarily believers as part the "worship team" or to take other up-front roles that are meant only for mature, Christian leaders. This is not a healthy or a good model of what it means to gather as a church.

What Churches Can Do:

- Provide resources and even hold a panel on parenting in the pew. Make sure to include not just "successful parents" of "well-behaved" children, if you do the panel. Those even-tempered children are the not nearly as common as we might like to think. It will be the parents with the wiggly, inattentive, strong-willed kids who are attempting this that will be most encouraging to those who attend. Victorious overcomer parents are a thing of beauty, but the ones who remain in the war zone despite all odds are the ones who may have the best advice.

- Create an atmosphere that allows for "different strokes for different folks". Help your parents appreciate each other and encourage each other, even when they are choosing a different approach for preparing their children to gather together.

- Provide worship service aids for use during the services. Children Desiring God has some great, little, spiral-bound books that can be used with any worship service. They can be used at home to hold a "service" review discussion on truths learned.

- Provide a "cry" room with audio/video feed for parents with children who are noisy while "in-training." This allows for the training to continue without the worry of distracting others.

- Choose curriculum or adapt your curriculum to include "ramp-up" to worship service elements in the children's classes. This can be easily done by including hymns or other worship songs into the schedule and taking time to explain the meaning of the words. You also can introduce them to the leaders who they will see up front leading the congregation by inviting them to come to the class and talking with the kids. Familiarity with the leaders can really help kids be more interested in what is going on. We (Capitol Hill Baptist Church) have added a "VIPP" (Very Important Prayer Person) activity into our classes for elementary school aged children. They learn about what different leaders in the church do (learn words like deacon, elder, pastor, etc), what they do, how to pray for them. But they also learn fun things like what each person likes to do in their free time and what's their favorite animal.

- Pastors set healthy volunteering limits to make sure all child-care volunteers get to gather together with the congregation on a regular basis.

- Pastors with the helpful input of Children's Ministry leaders and others, look at how they can set age limits on any child-care/Bible classes that takes place during any worship service. They will want to weigh length of service (especially preaching time) as well as understandibility of the service elements as they consider what (if any) child-care/classes to offer children during all/part of the service. The idea is to create an up-ramp that eventually includes the children for the entire congregational gathering. They will also want to think about what parents might most benefit from child care offered during the worship service. Frequently, this may look like care for babies (child-care, no teaching) during the whole service, as well as classes for preschoolers and/or younger elementary school children during the sermon portion of the service. Teachers and parents also look for signs of readiness for children to stay in the whole service. Parents may choose to have their children stay in for the sermon some weeks, but go out for their sermon-time class others.

- Pastors address the children in the application portions of their sermons, reminding children that this message is for them, too.

- At home, family worship time can include songs sung at church. They also can take home a service bulletin and use it in their worship time.

- If you do have a special worship time for children/youth, make sure it echoes the gathering together of the church. Include prayers and songs that they will also sing with the whole congregation. Make sure godly, mature leaders, not the children, lead the worship times.

- Help support and/or welcome Campus Outreach within your church. It is college outreach organization that is church-based. Not only do they work on campus with college students, but they encourage them to become an active member of a local church. This sets these students up well to be members of a local church after they graduate.

Your Ministry IS Children's Ministry

Do you see how Children's Ministry takes on a significant role in your church? It's impact on the congregation can be felt far outside of the Sunday School classroom walls. That's why we say that your ministry IS children's ministry. Because in one way, shape or form, everyone in your church… really is affected.

And that's why, Children's Ministry, which can seem like such a sideline ministry, needs pastoral leadership. And if you give it the leadership it needs, it can bear much good fruit in your church now and in the future.

The rest of this book is dedicated to looking at what Capitol Hill Baptist Church, under the leadership of our elders, has done to try to create a church-shaped Children's Ministry. Every church is shaped differently, so that means what you might do at your church will probably look different than what we have done here. But we hope that there will be enough elements that will be helpful to you as you seek out your own shape.

We will look at the three main ways our church support parents in their role as primary spiritual care-givers of their children: by providing them with safe child-care at church; by providing them resources to use at home with their children; and, by teaching their children biblical truth at church. But we will start by introducing you to our church and the four fundamentals that stand behind all that we do in Children's Ministry here at CHBC.

A Little about Us
and
Our Path to
Gathering Together

A Little about Us and Our Path to Gathering Together

Life in Washington, DC

Capitol Hill Baptist Church is located in Washington, DC, just a few blocks behind the Capitol. It is a vibrant city, that takes much of its life from the people who come here to take part in our nation's government, as well as many stationed here in military positions. It has an unusally high number of young adults in their 20's. DC is a very transient city, with both politicians and their staff coming and going, as well as military postings that usually last no more than three years. It is also a city of many internationals, coming either for college or for work.

Housing prices are very high. Public schools are not the best (though they are getting better), and the price of private school would astound you. While our church as an unusual number of families who somehow find a way to live close to the church in the Capitol Hill neighborhood, many families wind up moving out to the suburbs for the better, public school and somewhat cheaper housing prices by the time their children reach school age.

Capitol Hill Baptist Church: Where We Live Affects Who We Are

The personality of the city is reflected in our church. We have a high percentage of young, unmarried/newly-married members. Chances are they will move out of the area within three years. We turn over a third of our 900+ membership every few years. Those that do stay, are enthusiastic about their families. Many of them three or more children. We average about 100 babies born each year. These babies have about 100 preschool siblings, 100 elementary school siblings, and about 50 siblings in middle school and high school. Campus Outreach is based out of our church. Largely through them, around 100 college students attend/become members during their time in college.

We may be heavy in young singles, married, with or without children, but we are "light" in older adults of the empty-nest and older variety. This number is growing as our congregation ages, but we still only have about members, ages forty and older.

Our Leadership

We are an elder-led (not elder-ruled) congregational church. We have 30 elders, as well as 30 deacons who care for the congregation. We have one senior pastor, five associate pastors, two assistant pastors, plus a number of pastoral assistants. We have a full-time, paid Children's Ministry Adminstrator, a part-time Curriculum Developer/Teacher Trainer, as well as four deacons who support these paid workers and help the member volunteerteachers on Sundays. I (Constance Dever) spend much of my days developing curriculum, but am unpaid.

Our Membership

You must be a member to join in most of the activities of the church. This is not trying to be exclusive, but it is because we are serious about the covenant we make together. We commit our lives to each other. We live under the loving care of our pastors. We try to actively live out the promises to disciple each other and to encourage each other in whatever calllings God has given us, including the raising of our children.

Our Services and Other Programs

We gather together as one body, each Sunday morning for about an hour of music, prayers and Bible reading, followed by an hour long, expositional sermon. We meet together again on Sunday evenings for more worship, an extended time of prayer and sharing, and a shorter message (15 minutes) from the opposite testament of the Bible from the morning service, but on a related passage/theme. These evening services are attended by a majority of our membership and provide a wonderful way to bind our lives together and encourage us in the faith in a more intimate fashion than the morning services.

We also have Core Seminar (Sunday School classes) for adults before the Sunday morning worship service; as well as a Wednesday night inductive Bible study. Many members are also involved in small groups (only men or women) or community groups (men and women). The elders have chosen for the church schedule to remain light from other programs. They want the members to have time to care for their families and build relationships with others, especially non-Christians. Members also meet up less formally to enjoy, disciple and encourage one another.

Capitol Hill Baptist Church: Children's Mininstry

Elders Set Goals
Our Children's MInistry reflect the elders' goals to provide:
- the most child-care help for those parents who will be least likely to hear because of their children's ages/abilities.
- teaching that will support, but not usurp the parents' biblical training of their children.
- what will be taught in those classes (Bible, Theology, Discipleship, etc) and what curriculum will be used to teach it.
- separate teaching for younger children who might be less likely to understand the sermon.
- programs that by their content, and by the age-limitations to whom they are offered, will create an up-ramp to gathering together with the whole congregation.

Reflects the Needs and Opportunities of Our Own Community
They also reflect the realities of our community. For instance, we hold a one-day, Saturday VBS instead of the traditional full-week version because that's what works best for outreach here on Capitol Hill. And, we do not offer child-care of any kind during our Wednesday evening service because most families typically stay at home on Wednesday nights, either because of school schedules or because they live so far away.

Respect for Differences
Many of our families homeschool, though an increasing number have their children in public (usually Charter) schools or Christian (especially hybrid) schools. At church, we have many parents who include their children in classes/child-care and many who do not. We encourage parents to not set up strongholds of opinions about either of these issues, acting like their school or worship-participation choice is the only right way. We agree on the essentials of the gospel. We allow for Christian freedom everywhere else.

Quick to Share Gospel, Slow to Baptize Children
We are quick to share the gospel (in every sermon and every Bible class), but slow to baptize children. The elders have found that it is best for children to be encouraged to grow and become known more broadly within the church as a Christian because pleasing adults can easily mimic conversion in children. This is NOT because the elders think that children cannot become Christians. Many became Christians as children, themselves. It is out of care for the children's souls and for the purity of the church that they have made this decision.

Anyone who is baptized becomes a full member of the church. They go through membership classes like everyone else. Because this can be a hot topic with parents, the elders give out their thought-paper on this decision for them to read and understand before they join the church. Better to be up-front about this, then to get what may feel like an unwelcome surprise later. (See the elders' paper on baptism in Appendix B.)

Safe Child Care

We make safe child care a top priority. Only members can be child-care workers/teachers. They must be members at least six months before they can serve with the children. This is for the volunteers' good, giving them time to get settled into the church body. It is also for the good of the children. We want to know our teachers before they spend time in child care with the children. Every child-care candidate is required to fill out a child-care application form, to attend a child-care workshop and to under-go a background screening. In the nursery/classroom, everyone keeps to the child protection policy, include important elements such no teacher will be alone with the children at any time. The child protection policy was created under the supervision of the elders.

Resources at Home

We know that they are the primary spiritual care-givers of their children. We realize that parents have far more time at home with their children than we will ever have with them at church. But there's a lot we can do to support them as they teach at home. We try to support parents by teaching them well in their own classes and by the preaching of God's Word. We offer them book lists and hold book fairs of great books to use with their children. We pray for them by use of our members' directory. We provide take home sheets and online resources that go with the curriculum we teach in the children's classes.

Teaching Them Well at Church

The Children's Ministry team takes the elders' teaching recommendations and puts them into practice. They seek out good curriculum and good teachers to bring these biblical truths to life in ways that are understandable, enjoyable and memorable. One elder in particular oversees Children's Ministry and helps them as they carry out the elders' recommendations. He also is there to help with difficult situations that arise with parents and children. He cares for the Children's Ministry team and ensures they are being spiritually well-fed, themselves. He keeps the other elders abreast of what is going on in Children's Ministry and seeks their advice on any matters as needed.

Supporting Teachers

Teachers teach in over-sized teams which include more teachers than are needed to teach at a time. This allows us to put more experienced and less experienced teachers together. It also allows for someone to serve as a teacher, but not be "chained" every single Sunday to teach. This provides for vacation time, illness and an opportunity to attend classes/worship services. It goes a long way to prevent burn-out. We also provide teachers with opportunities to be mentored, to be observed, to observe someone else teaching their class, and workshops to improve their teaching skills. Hall monitors and deacons are on hand every Sunday to help teachers with any last minute needs that arise or with escorting children to the bathroom.

Caring Well for Our Volunteers

About a third of our church is involved in child care of babies or in teaching children. Since the elders want to make sure teachers are well-fed, they have set limits on how frequently teachers can teach. This is especially true for any teaching for children (as well as child care for babies) that takes place during the worship services. What happens if we have a consistent problem with filling teaching/child care slots with volunteers, given the elders' limits? First, the issue is brought to the attention of the congregation. Then, if the pattern persists, and enough new volunteers cannot be found, the elders choose to shut down particular classes. These will stay unavailable until a time when we have enough volunteers to fill those slots in a sustainable way. The elders give child care/teaching provided during worship services as the top priority to fill. Child-care during the services may make a big difference in helping some parents learn from God's Word, and therefore, giving them better spiritual food to feed their whole family. They are willing to make up for a consistent short-fall in volunteers by closing other child-care offerings. A few years ago, they shut down Sunday School classes for a year when our volunteer numbers were too low as a way to ensure enough teachers/child care workers during the worship service times. When the volunteer numbers came back up to a sustainable level, Sunday School was added back, grade by grade.

The Path to Gathering Together

Why the Elders Care to Create a Path

The elders hope that all children, 4th grade and up will be a part of all the worship services. For children under that age, they have provided options for children to gradually be a part of the worship services. This "ramp-up" approach helps children become familiar with gathering together with the congreagion, but is mindful that developmentally the whole service (especially the hour long sermons) might be too much for some.

Many Roads Lead to the Same Place

While the elders have set age limits that are the guiderails along what they think is a good path to gathering together, there are almost as many variations as there are parents in terms of how to get there.

Here's some of the variations the parents of these younger children use:

Sunday Morning:
- Include their children in all available child-care/Bible classes. These families will be fully using the "guide-rails" set by the elders for ramping up to gathering together with the congregation.
- Sunday School classes, then join for full worship service.
- Sunday School, then join for the entire, 45 minutes of singing, prayers, Bible readings, then go to their class during the sermon.
- Sunday School, then join for the first 15 minutes of preparation music (just singing), then go to their class.
- Parents will pick up a children's worship bulletin that we provide, or bring along their own version of one, to help the children engage in the service.

Sunday Evening:
- Include their children in child-care/Bible classes through the whole service.
- Join for the first 15 minutes of singing, then go to child care/class.
- Stay in for the whole service.

Preparing to Gather Together through Elements of Classroom Time

There are a number of ways we prepare our younger children in their classroom time to gather together with the whole congregation:
- Introduce hymns and songs that will be used in our worship services. Not only do we teach the music, but we also explain the meaning of the lyrics.
- Pray prayers using the ACTS (Adoration, Confession, Thanksgiving, Supplication) model to introduce the children about the types of prayers that will be used in the worship service.
- Use Bible story sermons, which are much shorter than the expositional preaching they will hear in the main worship service, yet still echoes the teaching model.
- Take time to go through the worship service bulletin, either before or after a service, and help them understand the aspects of the service.

Preparing to Gather Together by What Families Do at Home
- Our church has a sermon card that lets the congregation know what passage will be preached on. Some families read the passage together ahead of time, preparing their hearts for the pastor's sermon on Sunday.
- Many take home and use the worship buletins (especially the songs) to sing together at home.

The elders have chosen to stagger class offerings to create the up-ramp for gathering together:

Sunday School Hour:

- **ages 0-2** childcare (no teaching)
- **ages 2-3:** HIde 'n' Seek Kids (Praise Factory 1 "Theology" Bible truths)
- **ages 4-preschool 5:** Deep Down Detectives (Praise Factory 2 "Theology" Bible truths)
- **K5-4th grade (5-10 year olds):** Treasuring Christ (Old Testament/New Testament Overview)
- **5th-6th grade (11-12 year olds):** Seeking Wisdom (Inductive BIble Study)
- **7th-12th grade (13-18 year olds):** Youth Core Seminars (Variety of topics for growing as a Christian.)

"Ramp-up" Notes for Sunday School:

- Child care/Bible teaching does not interfere with worship service, so it is offered for all ages.
- In Praise Factory classes, the children learn songs and prayers that will help them better gather together with the whole church. The stories used are more like story sermons, helping them prepare for more in-depth preaching in the worship service.

Sunday Morning: One, Main Preaching Worship Service:

- **ages 0-2** childcare (no teaching)
- **ages 2** childcare (no teaching)
- **ages 3:** HIde 'n' Seek Kids, pt. 2 (Praise Factory 1 "theology" Bible truths)
- **ages 4-preschool 5:** Deep Down Detectives, pt. 2 (Praise Factory 2 "theology" Bible truths)
- **K5-3rd grade (5-9 year olds):** participate in worship serivce and dismissed before sermon for a separate teaching time. Praise Factory Investigators (Praise Factory 3 "theology" Bible truths)
- **ages 4th grade and up (10+ year olds):** in the service the entire time

"Ramp-up" Notes for Sunday Morning Worship Service:

- Two year olds have just play time because one teaching time is a good limit for them.
- Three year olds, four and five years olds continue with Praise Factory curriculum that we have stretched over the Sunday School/Worship Hour and stuck play times in between so both Sunday School kids and those who only come to church will get teaching.
- Worship bulletins provided to help the K5-7th graders learn more during this service.
- Younger elementary school comes in for the the first part of the worship service (first 35 minutes) to gather together with congregation.
- In Praise Factory classes, the children learn songs and prayers that will help them better gather together with the whole church. The stories used are more like story sermons, helping them prepare for more in-depth preaching in the worship service.

Sunday Evening Church-wide Prayer/Share Meeting:

- **ages 0-preschool 5:** child care/Bible classes for the ENTIRE SERVICE
- **ages K5-8:** participate in singing time of the worship serivce and are dismissed for a separate teaching time. Great Commission Club (Missions)
- **ages 4th grade and up (10+ year olds):** in the service the entire time

NOTE:

- Younger elementary school comes in for the the first part of the worship service (first 15 minutes) to gather together with congregation.
- Because this service has a shorter preaching time; and, the sharing/praying content is more easily assessible to younger children, we lower the age limit on Bible classes by another year down to 3rd grade.

See this information in a diagram on the next page

The Path to Gathering Together

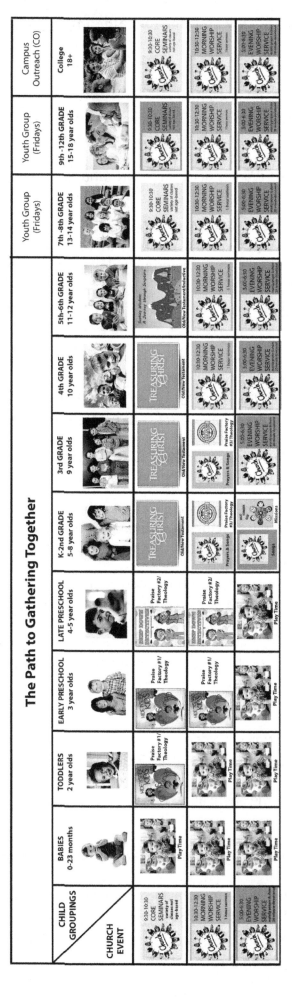

CHILD GROUPINGS → CHURCH EVENT ↓	BABIES 0-23 months	TODDLERS 2 year olds	EARLY PRESCHOOL 3 year olds	LATE PRESCHOOL 4-5 year olds	K-2nd GRADE 5-8 year olds	3rd GRADE 9 year olds	4th GRADE 10 year olds	5th-6th GRADE 11-12 year olds	Youth Group (Fridays) 7th-8th GRADE 13-14 year olds	Youth Group (Fridays) 9th-12th GRADE 15-18 year olds	Campus Outreach (CO) College 18+
CORE SEMINARS 9:30-10:30 variety of classes not age-based	Play Time	Praise Factory #1/ Theology	Praise Factory #1/ Theology	Praise Factory #2/ Theology	TREASURING CHRIST — Old/New Testament	TREASURING CHRIST — Old/New Testament	TREASURING CHRIST — Old/New Testament	Seeking Wisdom — Old/New Testament/Inductive	CORE SEMINARS 9:30-10:30	CORE SEMINARS 9:30-10:30	CORE SEMINARS 9:30-10:30
MORNING WORSHIP SERVICE 10:30-12:30 1 hour sermon	Play Time	Praise Factory #1/ Theology	Praise Factory #1/ Theology	Praise Factory #2/ Theology	Praise Factory #3/ Theology — Prayers & Songs — Songs / Missions	Praise Factory #3/ Theology — Prayers & Songs	MORNING WORSHIP SERVICE	MORNING WORSHIP SERVICE	MORNING WORSHIP SERVICE	MORNING WORSHIP SERVICE	MORNING WORSHIP SERVICE
EVENING WORSHIP SERVICE 5:00-6:30	Play Time	Play Time	Play Time	Play Time	EVENING WORSHIP SERVICE	EVENING WORSHIP SERVICE	EVENING WORSHIP SERVICE	EVENING WORSHIP SERVICE	EVENING WORSHIP SERVICE	EVENING WORSHIP SERVICE	EVENING WORSHIP SERVICE

Our goal is for all to gather together as one body, while being sensitive to developmental needs and special, teaching opportunities.

CHURCH EVENTS

CORE SEMINARS 9:30-10:30 variety of classes not age-based
Sunday School

MORNING WORSHIP SERVICE 10:30-12:30 1 hour sermon
One, Main-Preaching Worship Service

EVENING WORSHIP SERVICE 5:00-6:30
Church-wide Prayer Meeting

FOR THE CHILDREN

Play Time
Caregives take care of basic needs as children play

Hide 'n' Seek Kids
Deep Down Detectives
Praise Factory Investigators
3 curriculums of the Praise Factory family
Theology based around 16 "Big Questions"
Created here at CHBC
Available through Amazon and online at praisefactory.org (free)

Treasuring Christ
Old Testament and New Testament curriculum that always points to Christ.
Everyone learns the same truth each week.
Available through treasuringchristonline annual subscription, pricing varies by church size.
Greatly reduced pricing for missions and church plants

Seeking Wisdom
Highlights of redemptive history & what it has to do with us.
Inductive studies written by Ryan Townsend here at CHBC

Core Seminars
Junior High/High School
Special versions of the adult Core Seminars and other special topics targeted for this age group

Children's Ministry at Capitol Hill Baptist Church

Children's Ministry at Capitol Hill Baptist Church

We believe that Scripture clearly teaches that parents have the primary responsibility to raise their children in the nurture and admonition of the Lord.

This includes parents teaching their children about God, disciplining them, and striving to honor God before them by the example of their lives. The Children's Ministry team here at CHBC sees itself as a support team to parents. It seeks to aid and encourage parents in the nurturing of their children, in accordance with Scripture and the vision of our God-given elders.

Before we get to what our support of parents looks like, it is helpful to first tell you a bit about our parents and our philosophy of children's ministry.

Our CHBC Parents
The vast majority of the parents here at CHBC take this charge to raise their children very, very seriously. They read to their children, they memorize Scripture with them, they pray with them and for them. They discipline them, and strive to live godly lives that glorify God before them.

This is a great blessing to the children, to their families and to those here at church who work with their children. And how wonderful it is to work with children who are so well taught!

The Caution
But with all this diligence, there is an important word of warning we give to both the parents and the teachers of these children:

Doing all these things educates the children and fertilizes their souls with the great things of God, but they neither guarantee nor bring about conversion!

Conversion is a work of the Holy Spirit alone! There is no "to-do list" which, when completed, guarantees that their children will come to a saving knowledge of God. Nor are there any certain three behaviors, if cultivated, guarantee that they will live godly lives. And unfortunately, sometimes knowledge of more facts--even Bible facts and Bible verses-- can breed arrogance, just as much as lack of facts can lead to ignorance. And good behavior--even good, Christian behavior--can breed legalism, just as lack of discipline can breed selfishness and foolishness.

So what do we do? Do we hold back on how much we teach the children about God? Do we stop trying to build good, godly character in their lives? Of course not! And yet, how can we best help our parents and teachers fill young minds with the great things of God, while trying to avoid arrogance? How do we train them in selflessness and godliness, while trying to avoid legalism? And, as those who so deeply desire the conversion of these children, how do we eagerly hold out the gospel to them, yet rest in our good God who alone can change their hearts.

Psalm 66 has become our Children's Ministry Team's favorite scriptural reminder on these things. It points to four fundamentals that lie behind what we do and how we do it.

Four Fundamentals from Psalm 66

#1 Live joyful lives.

"Shout for joy to God, all the earth."   Psalm 66:1, ESV

We can live joyful lives in light of what God has done. True joy is a gift of the Spirit. It is remarkable. It cannot be reproduced by any other religion. It reflects the Spirit of God working within us, giving life where there was death. It is living in faith, despite trials and despite having to let go of what the world holds to be true and dear. And so, as we teach and parent, we ask God to make our joy in Him evident. It is a very potent witness of the truth and power of the gospel to the children watching us.

#2 Live to glorify God in all things...regardless of the outcome!

"Sing the glory of his name; give to him glorious praise! Say to God, "How awesome are your deeds! ... All the earth worships you and sings praises to you; they sing praises to your name."   Psalm 66:2,3,4, ESV

We live to glorify God in all that we do. We do not have control over the conversion of the children who we love, parent and teach. Their conversion is a work of God's Holy Spirit that we pray for and yearn for, but we cannot use it as the measure of success. On the other hand, seeking to glorify God in how we teach, raise and live among the children is a "success" we can strive for. This is freeing! We can strive to please God as we declare the greatness of His name to these children. We can strive to please God as we do, to the best of our ability, all He calls us to do, including raising these children. It makes teaching and parenting yet another venue for glorifying God, regardless of who is converted. And, it makes conversion a matter of trust in God…just where it should be.

#3 Teach the children God's awesome works, as revealed in the Bible.

"Come and see what God has done: he is awesome in his deeds toward the children of man."
Psalm 66:5, ESV

From before the creation of the world, God has had one, big plan to redeem His people as a magnificent display of His glory. We read of it in the Bible—the record of "His awesome works on man's behalf." And so, the Bible is our primary "textbook" for teaching our children about God, and for how we parent. The Bible is central to all we do and long to teach the children.

#4 Tell the children the gospel that has saved us and can save them.

"Bless our God, O peoples; let the sound of his praise be heard, who has kept our soul among the living and has not let our feet slip... Come and hear, all you who fear God, and I will tell what he has done for my soul. I cried to him with my mouth, and high praise was on my tongue. If I had cherished iniquity in my heart, the Lord would not have listened. But truly God has listened; he has attended to the voice of my prayer. Blessed be God, because he has not rejected my prayer or removed his steadfast love from me!"
Psalm 66:8-9,16-20, ESV

As Christians, God has given us grace to hear and believe the gospel. We have repented of our sins and trusted in Him as our Savior. We have the testimony of His good work in our lives…and so, as we teach and parent, we want to testify to the children of God's work in our own lives. This is not a God only of history and past acts. This is the living God who is at work today…and in us! What a story we have to tell to these children every day, of the God whose mercies to us are new every morning!

Summary

So these four things:

1. Taking joy in God
2. Glorifying God
3. Studying His Word
4. Testifying to His Gospel Work in Our Own Lives

are the four fundamentals of how we try to teach the children and how we encourage our parents in their spiritual nurturing of their children.

Supporting Parents in Their Task of Spiritually Raising Their Children

#1
Supporting Them by Providing Safe Child Care at Church

Supporting Parents in Their Task of Spiritually Raising Their Children

We support parents in their task of raising their children in the nurture and admonition of the LORD by seeking to do three key things:

#1 Supporting Them by Providing Safe Child Care at Church

At our church, some parents of younger children choose to have their children in the worship service with them from their birth on up. Others have decided that the opportunity for them to have an undistracted worship and teaching time in God's Word at church helps them to better spiritually care for their family. As they are better equipped themselves, they have more to pour into their children.

So, our first goal is to provide safe, caring childcare for these parents, so that they are not worried about their children, but can focus on learning and worshipping God,themselves. This had led to the development of our child protection policy.

Some key points of this policy:

- Keeping to safe and effective teacher/student ratios, enlisting extra teachers or closing classes when the ratios are in danger of being exceeded.
- Enlisting team leaders for each group of children to help train less experienced workers.
- Assigning family numbers to each family which flash up on small display boards in the worship hall when a parent is needed during the service.
- Oversight of all childcare by our Pastor of Families, our Children's Ministry Administrator, and the Deacon of Children's Ministry.
- An interview process and background checks for all potential caregivers.
- Requiring child training classes and posting safety/evacuation procedures in all classrooms.
- Using numbered wrist bands and other sign-in/sign-out systems which identify both child and parent/s and make sure the children go home with the right adults.
- Enlisting volunteer hall monitors who are on alert for suspicious strangers and are available for emergency help within the classroom during Sunday School and church services.
- Requiring all teachers/caregivers to be a member at least six months before serving in direct contact ministry with the children. This gives us a chance to know them; and, gives them uninterrupted time getting to know people/the church before serving.
- Usually starting out new volunteers with basic nursery duty, then watching for signs of teaching ability (unless someone is already known to be a teacher, etc).
- Mentoring new teachers under the tutelage of experienced teachers who are teaching, whenever possible.

We consider ourselves successful if we have achieved just this goal!

Child Protection Policy and Training Resources

Children's Ministry Child Care Training Notes

This document are the notes used by Capitol Hill Baptist Church Children's Ministry team to introduce prospective workers in Children's Ministry to our philosophy, our policies and opportunities to serve during our regular Child Care Training Classes, held every few weeks.

Vision

Children's Ministry is a subset of CHBC's ministry to families and children.

Children's Ministry is not the same as day care. While we hope the children's time with us will be enjoyable and memorable, entertainment is not a goal.

Our 3-Point Vision Statement:
1. Our first goal is to always keep the children safe and secure.
2. Our second goal is to encourage and assist parents in their role as the primary disciplers of their children.
3. Our third goal is to teach God's Word to the children.

Children's Ministry is Our Chance to Exemplify the Gospel

In Deuteronomy 6:5-7, Moses instructs the people of God saying, "And you must love the Lord your God with all your heart, all your soul, and all your strength. And you must commit yourselves wholeheartedly to these commands that I am giving you today. Repeat them again and again to your children." *NIV 1984*

Later in Deuteronomy 31, he goes on to say, "Do this so that your children who have not known these instructions will hear them and will learn to fear the Lord your God."

So, consider children's ministry your very own and very real mission field. This is evangelism. This is a group of little people who have not yet understood the gospel and we have the very great privilege of working with their parents to share the good news of Jesus Christ with them.

Introduction of Children's Ministry Leadership Team

Introduce the Pastor of Families, the children's ministry administrator, the children's ministry curriculum and teacher support leaders, and the five deacons/deaconesses of Child Care and Children's Ministry.

Protection against Abusers

- Children's Ministry is a privilege and joy, but also a tremendous responsibility.

- As a caregiver or teacher, parents are entrusting you with their children.

- Be wary of abusers and abuse. We need to take this problem seriously. Two of our staff elders recently read a book about the problem of sexual offenders and were surprised by some of the things they learned:

  1. Some sexual offenders will deliberately target churches because they assume Christians are naïve and that they (i.e., the sexual offenders) can get easy access to children.

  2. While single males are the typical profile for a sexual offender, sexual offenders come in all types: single and married, blue and white collar, educated and uneducated. Examples that we read about included a college professor, a Catholic priest, a doctor, a lawyer, the athletic director for a private boys' school, and many other professionals. So don't assume there is just one type of sexual offender!

  3. While it is much less likely for a female to a sexual offender, it does occur, and when it does occur it is much worse than having a male because they tend to be sadistic.

  4. There are two types of sexual offenders: The Bear – who takes by shear force and by using his power to overtake his victim. You can think in terms of a bear when you hear about children being abducted on their way home from school or while playing in a park. The offender we are typically dealing with is not the bear, but the shark. The Shark circles around his prey until it is just the right time to strike, and then he "attacks" when he gets that opportunity.

  5. Sexual offenders work to cultivate a double-life. They work very hard to be respectable members of a community in order to engender trust in that community and then, once they are trusted, gain access to children. That means they are going to work hard to put on a persona of someone who can be trusted.

  6. One myth that most people assume is that they could pick out a "monster" (that is, a sexual offender) if they see one. And, as you can see from the things I've already said that is false. If there is not just one set profile (but instead there are all types of offenders… male, female, blue collar, white collar, etc.) and they work hard to cultivate a double-life, then it is going to be really hard for you to pick one out.

  7. What does that mean for you? Practically speaking, it means 2 things: (1) you need to have a healthy level of skepticism when it comes to protecting our kids; and (2) our polices are designed to protect the children, so take the policies seriously. For example, we deliberately don't allow adults to be alone with children. That is for their protection, and for your protection (to help you from being accused of any wrongdoing).

- It is essential that you conduct yourself in a way that is always entirely above reproach.

- This is a serious issue that we all need to be aware of as we serve in children's ministry. We cannot be too careful to protect not only the children who participate in the ministry but the witness of this church in our community. We want to be known as a church that proclaims the gospel. We don't want our reputation in the community to be associated with a church where sexual abuse occurred. Most of the policies I share with you today are for the purpose of that dual goal—protection of our children and protection of CHBC's witness.

(On Guard: Preventing and Responding to Child Abuse by Deepak Reju offers much more information on this topic)

Child Protection Policy

- In light of the seriousness of the trust we are given, and to help you know what is appropriate, we have implemented a child protection policy.

- Highlights of Child Protection Policy
    1. Importance of children's safety and security above all
    2. 2 caregivers in the rooms at all times, one of which needs to be a woman. (Ask question: Why does one of the child-care workers need to be a woman? Answer: Because the profile of a sexual offender is more often a male.)
    3. Ratios; being aware of them and knowing why they are important. There should be a ratio sign on the bulletin board on the wall of each room. Use common sense to maintain the ratios in a room. If you are under ratio (example, two adults with 25 two year-olds) then you should contact the team leader and ask for help. (Now you can tell them what "100" means…it's not a family who is called all of the time because of difficult children…it is our way of notifying the congregation that we need help and that we are under-ratio in one of our rooms.)
    4. Signing in/ Signing out
        - Only a parent can sign child out, unless it is indicated on the log.
        - If you don't know the parent then you need to ask to see the wrist band. Tell the story of Deepak waiting to pick up his son and noticing Brent Maravilla, who was working as a volunteer in the 4's room…when a parent came to pick up the child and Brent didn't know who she was, he asked to see the wrist band. Brent checked the number and made sure it matched the wrist band on the child. And then, as an added measure of protection, Brent asked the child to look up at the door and tell him who that was (and the child exclaimed, "Mommy!"). While Brent didn't need to take that extra step, it helped him doubly ensure that the child belonged to that particular mother.
        - Wrist bands should be removed when they leave a classroom.
        - **Families should not be in the classroom.** If a kid is having a problem then the family can take them out of child-care until the child is ready to transition back into the classroom setting.
    5. Restroom policy
        - Up through kindergarten, only female workers can take children to the bathroom.
        - After kindergarten, two children can go the bathroom together and they should be accompanied by the women only.

- Two men should never be alone with children at the same time, but exception to this is when a hall monitor fills in for a female who is taking young kids to the bathroom.

6. Allergies/Food – NOTE the red wrist bands.
7. The snacks that we do provide (Kix and water).
8. Wristbands (show them the book; explain what parents do).
9. Reporting Abuse—contact deacon or staff immediately. Required by law to report it. We have a protocol list.
10. Accident Reports – Please be sure to fill them out if something happens to one of the kids (usually the kid gets hurt). This allows us to ensure that the parent was notified and it also helps the staff respond to questions if the parent calls during the week. If you don't write out the accident report then the staff doesn't know about it and they can't respond to questions from parents.
11. Team Leaders—4 child-care teams. They "oversee" the teams and usually are one of the two friendly faces you see when you check in your children on the second floor.
12. Hall Monitors—at least one is assigned to every service. Their main jobs: security and assisting child-care workers in whatever they need.
13. Paging System – it is there for you to get a hold of parents if something is wrong with their children.
14. Be aware of checking and changing diapers for the smaller children (out of care for the parents)

- When in doubt, let this rule be your guide: Decrease Isolation, Increase Accountability

Areas of Service

- Child Care
  1. Expectations
     - Please try to be 15 minutes early (9:15 am for 9:30 am Sunday School; 10:15 am for the 10:30 am Sunday morning service; 5:45 p.m. for the 6 p.m. Sunday evening service; 6:45 p.m. for the 7 p.m. Wednesday night service)—this is especially helpful in transitioning children from Core Seminars (aka Sunday School) to the Sunday morning service.

  2. Schedule
     - We try to schedule you only once a month. If you are serving as a hall monitor, you will not be schedule in the nursery as well.
     - If you are scheduled and cannot serve for some reason, please find your own subs and let us know about it. Give us a call if you cannot come at the last minute.

- Hall Monitoring

- Sunday School teacher

- Praise Factory for preschool and elementary age children during morning service (additional training/ mentoring provided)

- Other non-child related help: Welcome Desk, help prep crafts, etc. This can be done prior to six months in membership which is required for all direct child-related ministry.

Caring for Children

- A few points about spending time with kids:

  1. Don't be passive. Engage the kids, and especially for the younger ones—get down on the floor with them.
  2. Don't leave them to occupy themselves. Provide structure. Children who are bored can quickly find mischief.
  3. Kids who have a hard transition (i.e. separation anxiety) will take some more effort. Take the kid out of the parent's hands at the door, and try to comfort them and get them interested in something right away.
  4. Note: if a child is so upset he cannot be comforted, then get them to page the parents.
  5. For those in diapers, try to change each child at least once in the service. We don't want to hand off children who have messy diapers. It makes parents wonder how long their kids have sat in the mess.
  6. Be aware of kids who are potty training (especially 2's, 3's, 4's). By threes we are usually done with diapers.
  7. Pray for the children. Pray especially for their salvation.

- Our expectations for children

  1. We expect children to respect authority.
  2. We expect children to share.
  3. We expect children to listen during story time.
  4. We expect children to take turns and to treat each other with respect.
  5. Granted, they are sinful children, so you've also got to expect that many of the children will not want to do these things.
  6. Don't act as if they can't do these things, or else they will follow your low expectations.

- Correction

  1. How do we correct children in a way that points them to God?
  2. You must never, ever hit a child.
  3. Remove the child from the situation and speak to them privately.
  4. Point out the problem and ask them to stop. When appropriate, ask them to apologize.
  5. Pray briefly with them; direct them to a new activity.
  6. Be consistent.
  7. Don't be afraid to be the authority. They may not understand everything you say, but they will respect you for noticing and stopping them from bad behavior. This especially points them to God.

- Persisting with kids so that parents can stay in the service

    1. Remember, we are here to help facilitate the parents being in the service and being able to worship with the congregation.
    2. If kids are hurt, sick or inconsolable (i.e., they cry for 45 minutes and won't respond to any type of comfort) then you should obviously call the parent out of the service. Contact the team leader or deacon and they can page the family by posting the family number.
    3. Otherwise, we ask you to do your best to persist with the kids, even when they are being whiney, difficult, or complaining. Story: We had a mother whose husband had been sent to Iraq for three tours of duty. On the most recent tour, she said to the child-care worker as she dropped off her child, "I know that she will be very difficult this morning, but if there is any way you can persist with her, I'd really love a break and the opportunity to actually stay in the service." So, as you might expect, we did everything we could to care for the child and facilitate the mother being able to stay in the service.

How to Get Involved

- You are right now attending training

- In a minute you will fill out application
    1. References—if you don't have them, write down the name, fill out the rest of application, and e-mail us the reference.
    2. Confidential Questions (only Deepak--Pastor for Families--will see the answers and talk to you about them, as needed)

- Explain 6 month waiting period for working with children (for the purposes of getting to know you… and letting us serve you as fellow church members before we ask you to volunteer with the children.)

- But there are things to do ever before the 6 months waiting period is up!
    (Help with administrative tasks in children's ministry, such as cleaning toys, prepping classroom and crafts, etc.)

Time for Questions and Answers
End with a tour of the facilities and then filling out the application

Children's Ministry Safety Resources

WRISTBANDS *(Google search for more companies—very numerous)* *NOTE: Choose duplicate wristbands so parent and child each get same number*	**Wristband Resources** http://www.wristband.com/ 21365 Gateway Court Suite 100 Brookfield, WI 53045
BACKGROUND CHECK AGENCIES	**Protect My Ministry** http://www.protectmyministry.com/ **Screen Now** (pre-employment screening) https://screennow.lexisnexis.com/pub/ **Secure Search** http://www.securesearchfaith.com/ **Department of Justice (DOJ)** http://www.nsopw.gov/Core/Portal.aspx
DIGITAL CHECK-IN SYSTEMS	**Lamb's List** http://www.lambslist.com/ **KidCheck** http://www.kidcheck.com/index.aspx **CCB** http://www.churchcommunitybuilder.com/ **Fellowship One** http://www.fellowshipone.com/

Some Helpful Safety Tips from __The Deacon's Bench__

A publication called The Deacon's Bench has provided us with good, basic guidelines, especially for teacher to child ratios.

The Deacon's Bench recommends:

Child/Caregiver Ratios

Infants *(0-6 months)*   **Two children to one adult**

Crawlers *(6-12 months)*   **Three children to one adult**

Toddlers *(12-18 months)* **Four children to one adult**

Walkers *(18-24 months)*   **Five-six children to one adult**

Other Recommendations

- At bare minimum, least two adults should be present at all time, regardless of the number of children.

- Allow teenagers to only work alongside at least two, properly screened and trained adults, not as a replacement for one.

- Make use of hall monitors who help visitors find their child's classroom and can stand in for short intervals if one teacher must leave the class, preserving the two-teacher- with-children policy.

- Visibility at all time: Make sure every classroom has an interior window, an open door, or some other way for others passing by to see what is going on.
- Supervise restrooms. Do not allow a single teacher to accompany a single child inside a bathroom.

- Ban hot drinks from the care-giving areas.

- Wipe down all surfaces with a disinfectant.

- Avoid stuffed animals and soft dolls.

- Sanitize all toys.

- Require hand washing.

- Use receiving blankets in infant swings and activity saucers over the fabric seats and replace with a fresh one with each child.

Source: The Deacon's Bench Volume 16, Issue 3 www.brotherhoodmutual.com

Application for Ministry to "CHURCH NAME HERE"

Thank you for your interest in serving the children and families of (CHURCH NAME HERE). Once your application has been approved, the Children's Ministry Administrator will work with you to find a spot on our children's ministry team that will be a good fit for you based on our needs and your interests and experience. Please put your completed application in a sealed envelope and place it in the children's ministry mailbox in the church office.

Personal Information

Name: _____   Date: _____

      LAST   FIRST   MI

Street Address: _____

City: _____   State: _____   ZIP: _____

Daytime Phone: _____   Evening Phone: _____

E-mail Address: _____

I prefer to receive information regarding children's ministry via: ☐ e-mail ☐ phone

Family Information

I am: ☐ Single ☐ Married ☐ Divorced ☐ Widowed

Do you have any children? ☐ Yes   How many: _____ ☐ No

Membership Information

How long have you been a member of [CHURCH NAME]? **DATE JOINED:** _____

What other ministries and activities have you participated in at [CHURCH NAME]?

Prior Experience

Have you taught or cared for children in any church or parachurch ministry before?

☐ Yes

Please describe (including dates and places):

☐ No

Please describe any training, education, or other factors (including musical training) that would apply to your ministry to children.

Training
I attended Child Care Training on _____ (date)

Personal Commitment

In dependence on the Holy Spirit and by God's grace:

I will be faithful and dependable in this ministry.
I will seek to learn more about ministering to children, as information and training are available.
I will faithfully pray for the children who are under my care.
I commit myself to continuing personal spiritual growth.
I commit to knowing when I am scheduled to serve and arriving to serve on time.
I have read, understood, and commit to abide by the policies contained in the Children's Ministry Handbook.

Signature: _____   Date: _____

Personal References

Every applicant for participation in children's ministry must provide two personal references. The Director of Children's Ministry will contact these references.
*Applicant waives the right to view reference statements

If you have been a member of (CHURCH NAME) for *less than one year,* please list

1. A pastor or church leader from the church you most recently attended
2.. A person with whom you have worked/served in the past who knows you well. (If you have served in children's ministry in the past, please list someone who served with you in that context.)

If you have been a member of (CHURCH NAME) for *more than one year,* please list

1. An elder, small group leader, or other church leader who knows you well
2.. Another member of (CHURCH NAME) who knows you well and can attest to your suitability to work with children.

Name: _____   Name: _____

Address: _____   Address: _____

_____   _____

Phone: _____   Phone: _____

E-mail: _____   E-mail: _____

Relation: _____   Relation: _____

Verification of Information

The information contained in this application is true and correct to the best of my knowledge. I authorize (CHURCH NAME) to contact any references or organizations listed in this application. Furthermore, I authorize such references and organizations to provide (CHURCH NAME) with any information they may have regarding my character and fitness for working with children. I release (CHURCH NAME), its agents, and all such references and organizations from any and all liability for any damage that may result from furnishing such evaluations to you, and I waive any right that I may have to inspect references provided on my behalf.

I further state that I have carefully read the foregoing release and know and understand the contents thereof. I sign this release as my own free act. This is a legally binding agreement that I have read and understand.

Signature: _____   Date: _____

Consent for a Criminal History Background Check

[CHURCH NAME HERE] has contracted the services of [SCREENING COMPANY NAME HERE] to perform criminal background checks on all children's ministry applicants. A national criminal records search is performed. The following information is required.

Name: First _____ Last _____ Middle _____

Address: _____

Date of Birth: _____ Social Security Number: _____

Driver's License Number/State:_____

Reports are confidential and viewed only by [CHURCH NAME HERE] elders and filed in the applicant's secured file.

Personal information is protected under Privacy Act. Reports obtained from [SCREENING COMPANY NAME HERE] will be guarded accordingly.

Note: Any reported misdemeanor or felony will be discussed with you and the elders and may be grounds for denial of application to work with children.

Name: _____

Confidential Information

The following questions are designed to help us promote a safe, secure, and loving environment for the children who participate in our programs.

This information will be kept confidential, viewed only by the Pastor for Family Ministry or other elders he deems necessary and appropriate.

If you would like to discuss any of these matters further with the pastor overseeing children's ministry, please simply indicate that below or leave the form blank.

Answering "yes' to any of these questions will not necessarily disqualify you from participating in children's ministry at [CHURCH NAME].

1. Have you ever been a victim of abuse?

(Many people have experienced abuse at the hands of others. Most victims of abuse abhor such behavior and are especially alert and sensitive to the need to provide a safe and caring environment for children. At the same time, residual effects may remain in some people's lives, including a hesitancy to report suspected child abuse, which is why we ask this question.)

☐ Yes
☐ No
☐ I would like to discuss this.
Comments:

2. Have you ever been accused of, participated in, plead guilty to, or been convicted of child abuse, child neglect, or any other crime against a minor?

☐ Yes
☐ No
☐ I would like to discuss this.
Comments:

3. Have you ever been convicted of or plead guilty to a crime (other than minor traffic violations)?

☐ Yes
☐ No
☐ I would like to discuss this.

Comments:

4. Have you deliberately and repeatedly viewed pornography in the past three years?
(This includes reading, watching, listening to, or in any other way using pornographic material, including books, magazines, television shows, movies, the Internet, or telephone services.)

☐ Yes

☐ No

☐ I would like to discuss this.

Comments:

5. Do you have any ongoing sin struggles that you think would keep you from ministry to children?

☐ Yes

☐ No

☐ I would like to discuss this.

Comments:

Comments:

6. Do you have any communicable diseases or infections such as TB, Hepatitis B, HIV/AIDS, MRSA*, etc.?

☐ Yes

☐ No

☐ I would like to discuss this.

Comments:

7. As a child or teenager, did you ever have sexual interaction or contact with a child?

☐ Yes

☐ No

☐ I would like to discuss this.

Comments:

Child Protection Policy

Capitol Hill Baptist Church

Revised August 2014

For the use of Capitol Hill Baptist Church Children's Ministry

Table of Contents

Our Vision: Generations of Godliness

"Hear, O Israel: The Lord our God, the Lord is one. You shall love the Lord your God with all your heart and with all your soul and with all your might. And these words that I command you today shall be on your heart. You shall teach them diligently to your children, and shall talk of them when you sit in your house, and when you walk by the way, and when you lie down, and when you rise. You shall bind them as a sign on your hand, and they shall be as frontlets between your eyes. You shall write them on the doorposts of your house and on your gates. (Deuteronomy 6:4-9, ESV)

"But as for you, continue in what you have learned and have firmly believed, knowing from whom you learned it and how from childhood you have been acquainted with the sacred writings, which are able to make you wise for salvation through faith in Christ Jesus." (2 Timothy 3:14-15, ESV)

Our Mission: To Glorify God

The children's ministry of Capitol Hill Baptist Church ("the church") exists to glorify God by:

- Maintaining a safe and secure environment for our children.
- Supporting and encouraging parents who are primarily responsible for teaching biblical truths to their children. (Ephesians 6:4)
- Making the whole counsel of Scripture known to children with special emphasis on the Gospel. (Deuteronomy 6:6-9; Romans 1:16-17)
- Praying for the children and relying on the Holy Spirit to regenerate their hearts through the faithful teaching of His Word. (Romans 10:17; Ephesians 2:4-10)
- Living faithfully before the children and modeling for them how Christians are called to respond to God, interact with each other, and with the world around us. (Matthew 5:16; 1 Corinthians 11:1)
- Encouraging children to learn to serve and to not just be served. (Mark 10:43-45).
- Maintaining the highest ethical standards such that volunteers and teachers always live and serve above reproach, protecting the reputation of the gospel of Jesus Christ.
- Preparing children to one day walk with God as adults, which means getting them ready to be a part of the public services and Lord willing, one day, a fully participating adult member.

Staff and Volunteer Expectations

All children's ministry staff and volunteers share a particular responsibility for:

- Loving the children as Christ loves them.
- Setting an example of proper Christian conduct in the way we live our lives.
- Ministering to the children.
- Understanding that the care of children is not a right, but a privilege; and this privilege embodies responsibilities to God for ministering to and caring for the children.

Child Protection

Our first concern is that children be safe while they are in our care. To this end we:

- Screen all children's ministry volunteers.
- Perform background checks on all full-time church staff, regardless of whether or not they have direct contact with children.
- Require training for all children's ministry staff and volunteers.
- Use parent authentication identification system.
- Employ scheduling procedures and volunteer/child ratios that optimize safety.
- Employ hall monitors to promote and maintain safety in the building.
- Equip each room with a first aid kit.
- Educate our staff and volunteers to recognize suspected child abuse and to require them to understand and follow any applicable reporting laws and to encourage them to report suspected abuse to church officials.
- Adhere to a healthy child policy for admittance to children's ministry.
- Adhere to a two-volunteer room policy whenever possible.
- Equip our volunteers to know how to evacuate children safely in case of an emergency.

Parameters for the Child Protection Policy

This child protection policy applies to children (from birth to 6th grade) who are voluntarily placed by parents under the responsibility of the church for the church's public worship services or specific children's ministry-related church-sponsored activities (parenting and marriage seminars, bible studies held at the church with accompanying childcare, Vacation Bible School, Backyard Bible Club). Any form of abuse, harm, neglect or other problems related to children at home, school, or in any bible-study, activity, or venue not directly related to children's ministry at CHBC is not covered by this policy, but instead is covered by the document entitled, "Elder Policy Related to Church Activities That Involve Children Who Are Not Under the Responsibility of CHBC's Children's Ministry."

Personnel Summary

Adults are individuals eighteen years or older.

Minors are individuals under eighteen years of age (under DC law and for most state laws).
Staff are the paid employees of the church. All full-time church staff are required to receive a background check regardless of whether or not they have direct contact with children.

Volunteers are adults who work with children and are not in the employment of the church. All volunteers who serve in children's ministry are required to go through both the children's ministry training and screening procedures before they serve. Volunteers include childcare workers, team leaders, hall monitors, teachers, coaches, coordinators, and anyone else who serves the children. The term 'volunteer' will be used throughout this policy manual as an all-encompassing term for anyone who serves the children and is not church staff.

Helpers are minors who are at least one grade older than the children they are assisting and are assisting in some area of children's ministry alongside an adult. Helpers do not count towards the adult-to-child ratios. Helpers must be children of members; may or may not themselves be a member the church; will not go through childcare training, but will be vetted by the children's ministry staff. Helpers will be supervised by the adult volunteers in the same room.

Deacons/Deaconess refer to the church's deacons of children's ministry and childcare. They are elected officers of the church who serve the church by assisting in childcare and children's ministry. Just like the volunteers, all deacons are required to go through both the children's ministry training and screening procedures.

Pastors/elders are elected officers of the church who serve the church by providing teaching and leadership to the congregational as a whole. They must go through both the children's ministry training and screening procedures if they are to serve in children's ministry, just like any other volunteer.

Protecting the Children Before They Arrive

Ensuring a safe environment begins long before Sunday or Wednesday services. Every applicant who wishes to serve in children's ministry is required to go through a screening process and attend childcare training.

Screening Procedure
To ensure safe and quality care, CHBC has established a screening procedure to approve all volunteers to work with our children:

- All volunteers must be members of CHBC in good standing for at least six months.
- All volunteers must be eighteen years of age or older.
- Children or youth who are at least one grade older than the children they are assisting are welcome to help (subject to the approval and direction of the Children's Ministry Administrator), but they are always in addition to the adult volunteers.
- All volunteers must have completed CHBC's childcare training.
- All volunteers must have completed the volunteer application and been recommended by or in consultation with the pastor responsible for children's ministry.
- At least one reference check must be satisfactorily completed prior to beginning of service. Criminal records checks and other appropriate screening checks will be completed.

- All completed records of screening procedures will be kept securely along with the original application.
- Volunteers are to be approved by the Children's Ministry Administrator in consultation with one of the pastors.
- All volunteers must repeat the screening procedures and criminal background checks every five years.

CHBC reserves the right to reject any applicant for volunteer service or dismiss an existing volunteer for any reason, including, but not limited to, refusing or failing to complete screening; failing to provide requested information; providing information that is subsequently determined as false or misleading; sin or suffering issues that compromise the applicant or volunteer's ability to care for children; any criminal report or charge; obtaining information from references or criminal record checks that suggest that the applicant is not suitable to help with children.

Any volunteer, helper, deacon, staff or elder (or any CHBC member) who learns of or has knowledge of misconduct by an applicant must report that knowledge to the Children's Ministry Administrator and/or the pastor who oversees children's ministry. He or she also must be personally responsible for any legal obligation that he or she may have to disclose such information to the authorities.

Training
All children's ministry staff and volunteers must attend CHBC's childcare training before they are allowed to work with the children. Additional training sessions will be scheduled for existing volunteers to update them on policies and procedures. Full-time staff who do not have direct contact with children will receive training on child protection policies. Parents with questions about childcare training are welcome to attend these sessions.

Protecting the Children As They Arrive and Depart

Arrival and Departure Times
Volunteers should be ready to accept children 15 minutes prior to the start of any session, so that parents have enough time to transition their children before the session begins.

Parents are encouraged to pick up their children immediately after the conclusion of the session.
In the event that a child is not picked up within 15 minutes of the end of the session, volunteers will ask the Hall Monitor or Deaconess of Childcare to locate the parents.

Signing a Child in to Children's Ministry
Any parent who would like his/her child to participate in a children's ministry program will sign the child in to the appropriate classroom, nursery, or activity when he/she arrives, granting permission for the child to participate in that CHBC event or program. The parent should also use this opportunity to note any allergies or special needs the child may have. For more details on our procedures for caring for children with allergies, please see the "Snacks and Food" section below. Check-in and check-out of children applies to all children birth through 6th grade.

Deacons, team-leaders, and staff have the right to refuse any child at check-in. Some reasons might include potential illness, behavior that endangers other children, the room being closed because the adult child ratio, or anything else that might impair our ability to maintain a safe and secure environment for the children.

A parent or designated guardian must be in the church building at all times while their children are checked-in.

Parental Authentication Identification System

In order to protect the children in our care, each child must be signed into his/her class by a parent or guardian.

Parent/guardian will receive a parent ID card with a family-specific identification code. Visitors will receive this at their first visitor check-in. Members will receive it after they become a parent.

Upon signing the child in, the child will receive a label with the family-specific identification code. The intent is for the family number to be used to match the parent with child.

At the end of the session when the parent/guardian comes to pick up the child:

1. The children's ministry volunteer will bring the child to the door and remove the child's label before releasing the child to the parent.

   a. For children of visitors, volunteers must check the visitor ID card and the child's label to ensure that the numbers match. If a visitor does not have their ID card, send them to the 2nd floor to get a replacement card. Only after the visitor parent has obtained a replacement card can their child be checked out.

   b. For member parents, if the child or parent is unknown to the volunteer, the volunteer will match the number on the member parent ID card and the child's label. If the parent does not have their ID card, the volunteer will use the parent ID booklet in the classroom to make the match between parent and child.

2. Volunteers will REMOVE & DESTROY child labels before children leave their room. This will prevent strangers from referring to the child by name and potentially luring them away from their parents.

Only the parent/guardian who signed the child into the class is authorized to pick up the child. The exceptions to this are:

1. In the event of an emergency that would result in neither parent/guardian being available to sign out the child at the end of a session, the child will be released to the care of an elder, deacon, or staff member of CHBC.

2. A member can send their spouse to pick up their children.

3. A member parent may make prior arrangements with the Children's Ministry Administrator (or any deacon/deaconess) to allow for someone other than him/herself or his/her spouse to pick up the child at the end of a session.

Protecting the Children While They Are In Our Care

Two Volunteer Rule

For all children's classes and programs, at least two qualified, unrelated adult volunteers must be present in each classroom at all times.

Helpers are always in addition to and supervised by the two adults. Helpers are never to be left alone at any time with children without the presence of the two adult volunteers.

Staff, deacons and volunteers must never leave a child alone in a classroom.

The exception to the two volunteer rule is CHBC's Praise Factory and Great Commission Club programs, where at least one adult volunteer must be present in each classroom at all times, and that adult should be highly visible to other adults at all times. In this situation, doors must be open any time there is only on adult present; and the class should be conducted in a room with a window in the door or wall.

Two male volunteers may not serve together in the same room without a female volunteer also being present. The only exception to this rule is when a male Hall Monitor temporarily substitutes for a female volunteer who is taking children to the rest room.

A staff member, deacon or volunteer may take children out of the nursery or classroom only for a compelling reason, such as to use the bathroom or in cases of illness, emergency, or evacuation.

Staff or volunteers should not have private one-on-one meetings with a children. When a meeting on the church premises is necessary, it should be done with at least one other adult present, and held with the knowledge and consent of the staff and the parents.

Visibility

When children's classes or programs are in session, the interior doors and windows should allow for unobstructed views from the outside of everyone inside the room.

Hall Monitors

The Hall Monitor is a qualified male or female volunteer whose duties are not limited to any one classroom. Hall Monitors generally move about the hallways and buildings during scheduled session times to observe any unusual activity and be of service to volunteers (e.g., locating parents or substituting temporarily for another volunteer.) The Hall Monitor and each classroom are equipped with a walkie-talkie to facilitate communication. A Hall Monitor is on duty during Sunday morning and evening services.

Child-to-Volunteer Ratios
In addition to always having at least two volunteers present, the following ratios are maintained during the three regularly scheduled weekly meetings of the church:

- Children 0-11 months: One adult for every three children
- Children 12 – 35 months: One adult for every four children
- Children ages 3-5: One adult for every eight children
- Children ages 6-12: One adult for every twelve children

Once a ratio is met, additional children should not be accepted into a classroom if doing so would exceed the ratio unless and until additional volunteers are added. If for any reason the ratio is exceeded, deacon(s)/deaconess(es) of Childcare, Children's Ministry Administrator or the Hall Monitor should be notified and asked for more volunteers in order to maintain these ratios. Whenever age-groups are combined, the ratio is determined by the age of the youngest child.

Diaper Changing and Rest Room Procedure

0 Months through 2 Years Old
Parents of children with dirty diapers are asked to change their children prior to signing them into the classroom. Volunteers will change diapers at least once or as need during service. Both men and women are allowed to change diapers. Diapers must be changed in the presence of at least two other volunteers.

2 Years Old through Pre-K
Parents should take their children to the restroom prior to signing them into a class.
At check-in and drop-off, parents should let the volunteers know if their child is potty training.
In the event that a child needs to use the rest room, the volunteers will call the Hall Monitors. One hall monitor will step into the classroom (to maintain appropriate child to volunteer ratios). The other hall monitor accompanies a female volunteer and waits outside the door. The female volunteer takes the child and at least one other child to the rest room (but no more than the adult child ratio allows). The volunteer should wait outside the closed restroom stall door unless the child requires assistance. The child and the volunteer must wash their hands with soap and water (or anti-bacterial hand sanitizer) before returning to the classroom.

K to 4th Grade
For all other classes up to 4th grade, any child needing to use the rest room shall go with another child of the same age and sex. A female volunteer will accompany the pair to the rest room and wait outside the closed bathroom door until the children are finished. The children must wash their hands with soap and water (or anti-bacterial sanitizer) and return with the volunteer to their classroom. The Hall Monitor will be available to step into a classroom temporarily if necessary to maintain appropriate child to volunteer ratios.

5th to 6th Grade
For 5th to 6th grade, any child needing to use the rest room may go on his or her own. Children must wash their hands with soap and water (or anti-bacterial sanitizer) and return immediately to their classroom.

Appropriate Discipline

All children's ministry volunteers are responsible for providing a loving, respectful, and orderly atmosphere in which children can learn, play, and interact with others. This atmosphere should be maintained by preparing beforehand, pro-actively directing children towards acceptable activities, verbally encouraging positive behavior, and, when necessary, correcting or redirecting inappropriate behavior.

Acceptable means of redirecting inappropriate behavior may include correcting the child verbally, withholding a certain privilege or activity for a brief time, or separating a child from the situation or problem for a brief time (particularly if his behavior is endangering or upsetting other children). During correction, a child should never be removed from the classroom. Correction should be discrete; in the classroom (not in the hallway); and never outside of the sight of others.

Steps of correction might include (depending on the age of the child): (1) removing the child from the situation or problem; (2) pointing out the problematic behavior; talking to the child about his/her sin and need for Christ; (3) praying for the child and redirecting to a new activity; (4) helping the child to reconcile with the offended children when appropriate. Volunteers should view misbehavior as an opportunity to introduce children to the gospel.

Children's ministry volunteers and staff members are strictly prohibited from using any form of corporal punishment such as slapping, kicking, punching, spanking, or hitting. They should never speak harsh words, insults, belittling comments, threatening words, or any other verbal humiliation to children.

If a child's behavior is uncontrollable or the child does not respond to the acceptable means of discipline indicated above, volunteer or staff should ask the Hall Monitor to call the parents. If the child assaults, harasses or bullies other children, misbehaves beyond minor correction, or has a pattern of misbehavior, the parents should be immediately called so the child can be removed. Volunteers, staff or deacons are allowed to physically restrain a child if he/she is physically endangering other children. Please report any of these problems (as well as the appropriate response taken to deal with the behavior) to a children's ministry deacon or the Children's Ministry Administrator. Once a child is removed from children's ministry, reinstatement is possible at the determination of the pastor who oversees children's ministry and the Children's Ministry Administrator. A child may be reinstated if the risk of re-offense has been adequately reduced.

For further information regarding discipline, please speak with the Children's Ministry Administrator.

Physical Touch Policy

Two types of relationships are important to consider: volunteer-to-child and child/teen-to-child.

Volunteer-to-Child

While appropriate physical contact with children can be an effective means of aiding in communication, redirecting attention, calming restlessness, or showing godly love and care, it can also be misinterpreted. Particularly in our interaction with children, we want to be blameless and above reproach. The following will help workers to avoid any compromise or concerns in this area.

- Always remain in open sight of other adults.
- Appropriate touch is positive physical contact that nurtures children and develops a sense of emotional security and maturity in their interactions with adults. Appropriate touch is applied to meet the needs of children and not the adults.
- Appropriate physical contact will vary according to the age of the child. What is appropriate for nursery children (holding, rocking, sitting on laps, etc.) will not be appropriate for grade school children.
- Inappropriate touch involves, but is not limited to coercion or other forms of physical contact which exploits the child's lack of knowledge, satisfies adult physical needs at the expense of the child, violates laws against sexual or physical contact between adult and child, and any attempt to modify child behavior with physical force.
- For ages 2 thru 5, only women can take children to the restroom.
- Sitting on laps is only appropriate for ages 0 to 5.
- In general, a man will need to limit physical contact more than a woman in the same situation, especially when working with older children.
- Volunteers should refrain from rough-housing, wrestling, shoulder or piggy-back rides, rubbing, massaging, or any physical activity that might make a child feel unsafe or uncomfortable.
- Only touch children in "safe" areas and for brief time. "Safe" areas generally include hands, arms, shoulders, upper back, or gentle pats on the top of the head. Never touch a child on or near any region that is private or personal, unless when necessary while assisting in a diaper change or restroom visit.
- Never touch a child out of frustration or anger. Physical discipline is not an appropriate means of correcting someone else's child.

Child/Teen-to-Child

- No male or female under eighteen should ever be alone together while in children's ministry.
- No inappropriate touching (as defined above and in the appendix) of any kind will be accepted.
- Fighting will not be tolerated and any child participating in violent action will be dismissed from a class/program and placed into his or her parent's care.

Further guidelines on appropriate and inappropriate touch can be found in Appendix 1.

Parents in the Classroom

If a child would feel more at ease with a parent in the classroom, this is allowed temporarily (for a few minutes), especially for visitors or children who are going through separation anxiety. If this goes beyond a few minutes and the child cannot remain without the parents, the parents should remove the child from the classroom and are encouraged to relocate to the family rooms in the basement. While accompanying their children, a parent should be kindly but firmly dismissed if the parent is causing difficulty or presenting concerns for the welfare of the class.

Food and Drink Policy

The primary mission of Children's Ministry at CHBC is to provide a safe and loving environment for the children entrusted to our care so that their parents may be fed spiritually without undue concern.

One of the ways we protect children is to limit the food and drink allowed in classrooms. Volunteers may not bring food or drink with them when they serve.

In most classrooms, an allergen free cereal and water are supplied for snack time. In Praise Factory, children will receive a snack in accordance with that day's lesson. We get parental consent to provide story-related snacks as part of the Praise Factory curriculum. Outside of these three things (an allergen free cereal, water, or a Praise Factory snack), volunteers will not provide any food to children EVEN with parental consent.

Why do we do this?
The nature of childcare is very hectic and dynamic so we cannot guarantee that:

1. A child's bag will be properly marked at all times.
2. The childcare volunteer will reach into the correct bag.
3. Another child won't grab food/drink and eat it.
4. A child won't share his food/drink with other children.

Also, some children will struggle with allergies or react adversely even to mere exposure to certain foods (like peanuts). So we need to limit the types of foods and drinks used on the children's ministry floors.

Why don't we allow children to bring their own food with them and feed themselves?
For the same reasons: we can't guarantee that volunteers will find/give the right food to the right child or that a child won't grab and eat another child's food or that a child won't share his food with other children.

So what do we do?
If a parent wants to feed their child something other than an allergen free cereal, water, or a Praise Factory snack, that parent may check out their child, feed him outside the room then return him to the childcare room. This is the policy throughout the building.

Ages 0-17 Month-Olds

Deacons/deaconesses, staff and volunteers will not serve food to children while they are in the care of our Infant and Crawler nurseries. If a parent desires to feed their child at a certain time during the services, we ask that the parent to administer the food personally to their individual child. Parents who would like to feed their children while they are in our care should alert the Team Leader that they are temporarily checking their child out of class. Parents are welcome to make use of the Nursing Moms Room or the high chairs in the 2nd floor kitchen to feed their children.

12-17 Month –Olds

Volunteers may offer properly labeled sippy cups containing only water, as provided by the parents upon signing the child in.

18 - 23 Month-Olds to 5 Years-Old

An allergen free cereal and water will be offered to the children 18 Months-Old thru pre-kindergarten (4s/5's classroom).

If a child should not be given a snack of this nature, the parent should do the following:

- Verbally notify the team leader on duty.
- Place a red Allergy Alert wristband on the child's ankle or wrist.
- Note the nature of the allergy and how to respond to an allergic reaction in the appropriate spot in the sign-in book.

Volunteers may offer properly labeled sippy cups containing only water, as provided by the parents upon signing the child in.

Ongoing Care for Children with Allergies

Parents of children with allergies should talk with the Children's Ministry Administrator about how to handle any allergic reactions. Upon parental request, allergy information about children of members may be posted in the child's classroom.

No food except for the church-supplied an allergen free cereal and water will be permitted to be eaten anywhere in the classrooms.

If a parent desires to feed their child anything other than the provided snack at any time during the services, we ask that they administer the food personally to their individual child in designated locations such as the Nursing Moms Room or the 2nd floor kitchenette.

Serving Snacks

Volunteers should always check each child's label for allergy information before serving a snack. If instructions are not clear, no food should be given to the child without clarification from the parent/ guardian. The volunteer may send to clarify with the child's parent or guardian.

Normally no snacks will be offered to the children in Sunday School classes for grades K and above.

Snacks of various kinds WILL regularly be offered as part of Praise Factory and the Sunday evening children's classes. Parents should verbally notify teachers upon check-in about the nature of any allergy or food limitations.

Security and Emergency Response

Emergency Situations
In emergency situations, if appropriate, 911 will be called to secure help and/or the display monitors will be used to summon staff and volunteers to the children's ministry floors to assist with the emergency.

Accidents, First Aid and Medical Emergencies
All classrooms are equipped with basic first aid kits. In the event of life-threatening injury or illness, emergency medical services will be called and parents should be located and informed immediately. Volunteers should complete an Accident Report Form for all injuries, whether major or minor prior to leaving the premises on the day of the accident.

In the case of a medical emergency, a deacon, team leader or staff will post "888" on the digital display monitors to summon medical volunteers to the children's ministry floors. Depending the severity of the situation, someone may also call 911.

Evacuation Procedures
A team of key responders has been recruited by the Children's Ministry Administrator. The team practices evacuation procedures at least once a year.

In the event of a fire, a deacon/deaconess, staff, or volunteer should call 911 and also assist all children in immediately evacuating the building. Deacon/deaconess, team leader or staff will also summon the key responders to the children's floors using "999" on the digital display monitors to assist staff, deacons, volunteers and teachers with evacuation. Staff and key responders will help keep parents away from the children's floors. Parents should not report to the children's floors because they risk creating chaos and blocking the exit stairwells for children. Instead, parents will meet their children in the designated areas outside of the church building. Evacuation information is located on all of the floors. Volunteers and parents should familiarize themselves with this information.

A Live Threat
A live threat includes a shooting or some other type of security hazard.

Step 1: Volunteers and Staff Evacuate Children

- As soon as staff, deacon/deaconess or a volunteer is confronted with a real threat, they respond immediately.
- If it is safe to do so, the first course of action should be to evacuate the building.

Step 2: Volunteers and Staff Communicate the Danger

- When it is safe to do so, whoever sees or hears the live threat should notify the deacon/deaconess, team leader, or staff about the problem. Staff, the team leader or deacon/deaconess will then notify the remaining volunteers about the live threat.
- When it is safe to do so, staff, deacon/deaconess or volunteer should call 911. Give the following information:
  > Location and the nature of the threat.
  > If shots have been fired tell police we have an "active shooter." DC Police are trained specifically to respond to an active shooter.

Step 3: Hide
- If running is not a safe option, hide in as safe a place as possible.
- Close the door, including the top portion of each door and pull the latch down.
- Barricade the doors with heavy furniture.
- Close and lock windows and close blinds.
- Turn off the lights.
- Silence all electronic devices.
- Maintain silence.
- Have children lie or sit on the floor away from the door. If possible, stay out of sight of any interior windows.

Step 4: Staff or Volunteers fight the Live Threat
- If neither running nor hiding is a safe option, as a last resort, when confronted by a shooter or some other danger, adults in immediate danger should consider trying to disrupt or incapacitate the shooter by using aggressive force and items in their environment, such as a fire extinguisher or chairs.
- Under no circumstances will a child be allowed to confront the potential danger.

After the area has been made safe and secure by police, the Children's Ministry Administrator, the pastor who oversees children, or staff will communicate an "all clear" sign to anyone who is in lock-down mode.

Missing Child or Kidnapping
In the case of a missing child, the staff will first do a thorough check of the children's ministry floors to make sure the child is not in another part of the building. If the child is not found after a thorough check of the children's ministry floors then post "777" on the digital monitors to summon the key responders, each of whom will then block their assigned door until otherwise notified by staff or the pastor who oversees children. Hall monitors and other volunteers will continue to search for the child until they are found. If the child is not found, the staff or elders will call police to secure further help.

In the case of a kidnapping, staff, deacon/deaconess or the team leader should call 911 to secure help from the police and post "777" on the digital monitors to summon the key responders, each of whom will then block their assigned door until otherwise notified by staff or an elder.

Parent involvement in Emergency Procedures
The pastor who oversees children and/or the Children's Ministry Administrator will decide how and when to notify parents about security or emergency situations. Involving parents too early might cause unnecessary fears or panic. If an emergency does happen, parents will need guidance, pastoral care and counseling, so we rely on an elder or staff to walk with parents through difficult situations.

Healthy Child Policy

Communicable Disease Policy

In order to prevent the spread of communicable diseases among the children, several guidelines are in place concerning disease.

1. Children with infectious diseases should be kept home until they are no longer contagious. If a child is exhibiting symptoms of illness such as fever, diarrhea, open skin lesions or blisters (as in chicken pox), or persistent nasal discharge, the parent should keep the child home.

2. Volunteers will use disposable latex gloves and proper hygiene procedures to change diapers, wipe noses, and handle blood spills.

3. Hand washing or use of anti-bacterial hand sanitizer must be a regular habit for both children and volunteers.

4. Toys and equipment should be washed and disinfected regularly.

5. CHBC is dedicated to preventing the spread of disease among the children. Team Leaders and the Deacon/Deaconess have the right to refuse a child on the basis of questionable symptoms. To prevent this, parents are asked to comply with the Healthy Child Policy guidelines.

A child should not participate in a class if and when any of the following exist:
Fever, vomiting or diarrhea (Note: Children should be free of a fever, vomiting or diarrhea for 24 hours before coming to children's ministry.)
- Any symptom of scarlet fever, German measles, mumps, chicken pox, or whooping cough
- Common cold – from onset of symptoms and one week thereafter
- Sore throat
- Croup
- Lice
- Any unexplained rash
- Any skin infection such as boils, ringworm, impetigo
- Pink eye or other eye infection
- Thick green, yellow or constant nasal discharge
- Any other communicable disease

Children who appear ill during a class will be kept at the nursery sign-in desk with a volunteer while the Hall Monitor locates the parents.

Please inform the Children's Ministry Administrator if your child appears to have contracted an illness while attending a CHBC event so that other parents may be notified if necessary. If a child contracts an illness and has been in contact with other children while at CHBC, it is the responsibility of parents to notify the Children Ministry Administrator.

Neither volunteers nor church staff may give any medication to any child.

Parents of children with special needs are encouraged to contact the Children's Ministry Administrator before signing the child into class. This allows the staff to assess the needs of the child and assist parents in transitioning their child into a classroom setting.

Universal Precautions

Universal precautions are very effective for protecting both the children and volunteers from illness. These methods are employed such that all human bodily fluids are treated as if they carried infectious diseases. Universal precautions are applicable in any setting and should always be used.

Important Points of Universal Precautions:

- Wash hands before and after any contact with bodily fluids, including wiping noses, changing diapers, cleaning vomit, and treating a blood spill.
- Always wear disposable gloves when dealing with any bodily fluids.
- Treat all soiled linen (i.e. sheets, clothing) as potential infectious agents.
- In rooms with children ages 23 months and below, remove toys that children have mouthed from the general play area. Set them in the container by the sink and wash.
- At the end of the session, disinfect the room with Lysol disinfectant spray.

Neglect & Abuse Prevention, Reporting & Response

Definitions

What is child neglect and abuse? It is important to define our terms.

Child neglect is failure, whether intentional or not, of the person responsible for the child's care to provide for the child's basic needs such as adequate feed, clothing, medical and dental care, supervision, and/or proper education, or the failure to protect the child from harm.

Child abuse is any recent act or failure to act resulting in imminent risk or serious harm, death, serious physical or emotional harm, sexual harm or exploitation of a child by a parent or a caretaker who is responsible for the child's welfare.

> *Sexual abuse* perpetrated by an adult is any contact or activity of a sexual nature that occurs between a child and an adult. This includes activity which is meant to arouse or gratify the sexual desires of the adult or child. Sexual behavior between a child and an adult is always considered to be forced whether or not the child consents to it.
>
> *Sexual abuse* perpetrated by a child is any contact or activity of a sexual nature that occurs between children, with or without the consent of either child, when one child has power or perceived authority over the other child. This includes any activity which is meant to arouse or gratify the sexual desires of any of the children.
>
> *Sexual exploitation* includes forcing a child or soliciting a child for the purposes of prostitution; and using a child to videotape or photograph pornography.

Child sexual abuse is any form of sexual contact with a minor, non-touching offenses, or sexual exploitation of a minor. This is criminal behavior that involves children in sexual behaviors for which they cannot be personally, socially, and developmentally ready.

Child spiritual abuse the use of spiritual authority (the Bible or church authority) to emotionally, physically, and/or sexually abuse a child.

<u>Prevention</u>
CHBC takes protection against and reporting of neglect and abuse very seriously. In an effort to prevent abuse and neglect, we:

- Educate and equip staff, deacons and volunteers about neglect and abuse
- Adhere to the procedures and guidelines as set out in this policy manual. Many of the policies are written to protect children, including the two adult rule, visibility guidelines, and diaper and bathroom policy.
- Train and screen volunteers prior to contact with any children. Screening includes filling out an application, getting feedback from references and requiring a criminal background check.
- Require all full-time staff to submit to a criminal background check within a month of joining staff.
- Repeat screening procedures and criminal background checks for full-time staff and volunteers every five years.
- Require volunteers and staff to be members for at least six months prior to serving in children's ministry.

Any instance of suspected or observed abuse or neglect should be handled with the following guidelines.

Child Protection Committee
The Child Protection Committee (CPC) consists of the pastor overseeing children's ministry, the pastor of administration, the Children's Ministry Administrator, and any CHBC member who has been designated by the chairman of the elders. All members of the CPC stand ready to address all allegations of neglect and abuse in accordance with the CHBC church covenant and the laws of the District of Columbia and surrounding jurisdictions.

Reporting of Neglect & Abuse

Point of Contact for Reporting
Anyone who suspects, witnesses, or has any reason to believe that a child has been or is likely to be neglected and/or harmed or threatened with abuse in any form should contact the Children's Ministry Administrator, the pastor who oversees children's ministry, or any elder at CHBC. This reporting includes questionable behavior (overly flirtatious behavior, shoulder massages or other intimate acts, etc.) and/or possible offenses (volunteers observing actual abuse or possible evidence of abuse, like abrasions, lacerations, etc.).

Any person who serves as the initial point of contact is required to report all allegations and/or eye-witness accounts to the entire Child Protection Committee.

Guidelines for Mandatory and Permissive Reporters
In reporting of neglect or abuse to the authorities, it is important to distinguish between permissive and mandatory reporters. A mandatory reporter may include social workers, teachers and other school personnel, physicians and other health care workers, mental health professionals, childcare providers, law enforcement officers, and domestic violence workers. Permissive reporters include anyone who is not a mandatory reporter, which will be the majority of CHBC's volunteers and staff.

The church has a moral and ethical obligation to report any neglect and abuse, so if the person suspects or witnessed or has knowledge of neglect or abuse, the person must talk to the point of contact for reporting—the Children's Ministry Administrator, or the pastor who oversees children's ministry, or any elder at CHBC.

<u>If the person who suspects or witnessed or has knowledge of neglect or abuse is a mandatory reporter, he or she must follow the guidelines and laws set out for mandatory reporters. He or she must fulfill his/ her obligations to the law, including reporting to Child Protective Services or the police. At no time will the mandatory reporter be prohibited from reporting, even if their consultation with staff or leadership in the church results in a disagreement. If you are a mandatory reporter, it is important that you know whether you must report only in the context of your professional duties or whether the obligation to report also applies when you're away from your professional duties or functioning as a volunteer at our church.</u>

If the person who suspects or witnessed or has knowledge of neglect or abuse is a <u>permissive reporter,</u> they should contact the Children's Ministry Administrator and/or the pastor who oversees children, or any CHBC elder. Because permissive reporters do not have professional training or experience in recognizing abuse, and because many of CHBC's volunteers are single adults with very little or no experience with children, they are required to report first to the Children's Ministry Administrator, the pastor who oversees children, and/or any CHBC elder. If reporting to Child Protective Services or police is deemed as warranted by the Child Protection Committee and the elders of CHBC then that person must report. At all times, this person will be required to fulfill their obligations to the law.

District and federal laws authorize civil or criminal penalties or civil liability for failing to report a reasonable suspicion of child abuse. In addition, obstructing or interfering with an investigation of child abuse can result in criminal charges.

The church will not tolerate any retaliation against a reporter who has a reasonable suspicion of neglect or abuse.

More Guidelines on Reporting
When available, the following information will be documented and reported when helpful:
- The name, age, gender and address of the victim(s).
- The name, age, gender and address of the alleged perpetrator/offender(s).
- The nature, frequency, date(s) and location(s) of the abuse alleged to have occurred.
- The relationship between the victim and the alleged perpetrator/offender.
- Other evidence that supports the allegations (eyewitness, medical exams, confessions, etc.)

What should a volunteer, staff, deacon or elder do when they suspect, hear about or observe what appears to be a sign or symptom of neglect or abuse? Talk immediately with the Children's Ministry Administrator and/or the pastor who oversees children. The volunteer, staff, deacon or elder should document this information on the *Child Abuse Reporting* form, which is available in every classroom. After the Children's Ministry Administrator or the pastor who oversees children serve as an initial point of contact, they are <u>required</u> to report all allegations and/or eye-witness accounts to the entire Child Protection Committee.

What should the Children's Ministry Administrator or the pastor who oversees children say or do with the child who is allegedly neglected or abused? Talk with the child and find out how the injury happened, though be careful of the level of detail you pursue. Asking for too much detail might be harmful for a child as it causes them to relive the abusive experience. If the child is describing what might be abuse, the objective is to obtain very general information that may help substantiate or alleviate the suspicion. Ask the child open-ended questions and get them to relay the event in their own words.

Be careful to not suggest answers to the child and be sensitive to the fact that the child will be scared to tell the story, sometimes out of fear that it will upset adults or will not be believed. Write out a report that should include signs or symptoms observed, notations about bruises or injuries that are visible, a summary of the conversation with the child, and a description of any emotions expressed by the child. Do not ask the child to undress in order to show bruises or injuries that are not visible. Include all of this information on the *Child Abuse Reporting* form, which is available in every classroom.

What should volunteers or staff report when they hear of a story of abuse? Note what the child said happened, who the child was with when it happened, where it happened, and when it happened. All of this should be documented

What should a volunteer or staff do when they observe an incident that may be abusive? Immediately intervene to protect the child; follow-up immediately with Children's Ministry Administrator or the pastor who oversees children; write out a report about the incident; and act in accordance with all reporting laws. The volunteer or staff should keep an on-going log of the suspected person's behavior and anything else that is relevant concerning the person or the child or their relationship.

How Can We Learn About the Different Laws, Regulations, and Guidelines in Maryland, DC or Virginia?
Laws, regulations, and guidelines for reporting child neglect and abuse differ from state to state. For general information on guidelines for mandatory or permissive reporters in Maryland, DC or Virginia, ask the Children's Ministry Administrator for the summary page entitled Child Abuse & Neglect Reporting Guidelines in MD, DC & VA. For specific questions regarding your legal obligation under one or more of these laws, please consult with an attorney.

Response to Neglect & Abuse
CHBC will ensure that a caring response is always provided to any suspicion or witnessing of neglect or abuse. Every allegation of neglect or abuse will be taken seriously. Proper guidelines for handling such complaints will be followed diligently and exhaustively. The victim(s) and victim's family will be cared for by the church in whatever way is available. Situations will be handled forthrightly with due respect for all parties' privacy and confidentiality.

Who Should be Notified?
The church will seek professional assistance when deemed appropriate by the Child Protection Committee and the elder board of CHBC. Notification will be limited to those who need to know about the allegation and to those who can provide assistance in responding to neglect or abuse. The church may:

> Report suspicions or firsthand accounts or any knowledge of abuse to civil authorities. Full cooperation must be given to civil authorities.
> Notify church disciplers, counselors or medical personnel in order to obtain ongoing care for the victim(s) and victim's families.
> Notify an insurance agent, denominational leaders, or any other outside officials.
> Notify and consult with a church attorney.

How Will CHBC Respond to Allegations, Admission or Criminal Conviction?

Allegations of neglect or abuse, admission of child abuse by staff, elder, deacon, volunteer, helper, or any member of CHBC, or criminal conviction of abuse should:

> be reported to CHBC's elder board. This disclosure of abuse is to be done regardless of the source of the information and should be conveyed to the elders board within 48 hours of the allegation being made or the admission of child abuse or criminal conviction.

> immediately result in removal of the alleged perpetrator or criminal offender from any activity or program involving children;

> result in immediate ineligibility of the alleged perpetrator or criminal offender from being granted approval to participate in any activity or program involving children.

The Child Protection Committee and the elders of CHBC will decide on other appropriate responses to allegations, self-admission of guilt, or criminal conviction, some of which may include:

- Contacting police or CPS.
- Notification of staff, deacons and any volunteers.
- Reporting allegations, self-admission or criminal conviction to the congregation during CHBC's public services or members' meeting.
- Barring from any activities or church programs with children or the children's ministry floors at the church building.
- The Child Protection Committee will designate CHBC members or staff, who will accompany the alleged perpetrator or criminal offender at all times while he or she is on CHBC's property or anywhere in CHBC's buildings. The alleged perpetrator will be notified of this requirement immediately after allegations are made known to staff or elders.
- Disciplining (removal from membership) of alleged perpetrator or criminal offender in a public members' meeting by the congregation.
- Barring alleged perpetrator or criminal offender from any and all church property.
- Suspension or termination of a paid staff member or volunteer position.
- Acknowledging to another organization about allegations against or termination of staff, an elder, deacon, volunteer, helper, or any member of CHBC for misconduct or abuse against children.

If staff, CHBC elders, or a member of the Child Protection Committee learns from CPS or police that allegations of neglect or abuse are being investigated or criminal charges have been filed, the CHBC elders should:

- Be careful to not interfere with the investigation by police or CPS;
- Prevent contact between the accused and the accuser if appropriate;
- Remove the accused from activities or programs involving children, pending the outcome of the investigation.
- Appoint a member of the Child Protection Committee or the elder board to be a liaison with CPS and the police.

If an adult alleges an incident of neglect or abuse that happened when he was a child in a CHBC program, then:

- Members of the Child Protection Committee should hire a trained mental health professional (preferably who is not associated with the church) who can provide the Child Protection Committee with an assessment. The victim will have to provide consent for such an interview and to have the assessment released to the Child Protection Committee in confidence.
- If the accused is no longer a part of CHBC then the Child Protection Committee should consult with the elders and legal counsel to determine legal and moral need to report to police or CPS and any other organization that the accused may be a part of since his departure from CHBC.
- Even if government officials are no longer bound to investigate due to a statute of limitations, CHBC should respond to all allegations with the care and diligence traced out in this policy manual.

Confidentiality

The church, as well as permissive or mandatory reporters, will maintain confidentiality to the extent that it deems appropriate for the care of its members and consistent with applicable law. Allegations and suspicion should be reported only to the persons specified in this policy manual.

Response to Media

If appropriate, the CHBC elders will respond to the media. Normally, one elder or member will be designated by the elder board to speak to the media on behalf of the church. A written statement should be distributed at the time of media disclosure. Great care should be taken to disclose only facts and not suspicion. Disclosed facts might include the nature of the abuse allegation and when the alleged abuse happened. Great care should be taken to protect the identity of all parties involved (the alleged abuser and victim). Alerting the media lets the alleged victim know that allegations will be taken seriously and gives other vulnerable members of the community a chance to be protected.

Sexual Offenders in the Church

When An Alleged or Convicted Offender Attends CHBC or a CHBC Related Activity

If CHBC's elders or children's ministry staff learn in advance that an alleged or convicted sexual offender is wanting to attend a CHBC service:

- The Child Protection Committee must decide whether to admit him or her to church services or CHBC related activities. Admission of the offender will be based on factors such as extent of prior convictions, and his or her willingness to follow guidelines set out by this policy. This is not a comprehensive list of admission criteria.
- A member of the Child Protection Committee (or a designated member of CHBC) will contact the offender letting him or her know that he or she must be accompanied at all time while on CHBC's property or anywhere in CHBC's buildings.

If an alleged or convicted sexual offender participates in any CHBC related activity or public service that has the possibility of children being present:

- The pastor overseeing children's ministry, children's ministry staff, children's ministry deacons, the nursery team leader serving on that day, and hall monitors should be notified.
- The Child Protection Committee will designate CHBC members or staff, who will accompany the alleged perpetrator or criminal offender <u>at all times</u> while he or she is on CHBC's property or anywhere in CHBC's buildings.
- He or she will not be allowed beyond the basement and first floor of the church. He or she must stay away from the second, third, and fourth floors, where the nursery and children's classes meet.
- The Child Protection Committee will work with members to come up with guidelines for CHBC related activities that are not on church property, but elsewhere.

When An Alleged or Convicted Offender Attends <u>Regularly</u>

If he/she chooses to attend regularly:

- The elders will be notified.
- The congregation will be notified in a public service of the church, most likely the members' meeting. CHBC reserves the right to forbid someone from coming to the church for worship services, programs or activities. When participating in church activities outside of the church building, the same guidelines apply.
- The sexual offender should provide a member of the Child Protection Committee with the name of his/her probation officer. Someone from the Child Protection Committee will contact the probation officer and find out 1) more about the underlying offense – offenders tend to minimize

their offenses, and 2) the specific terms of the probation in order to make sure the offender stays in compliance while at the church.

When A Sexual Offender Seeks Membership at CHBC

If the offender seeks membership at CHBC, the elders retain a right to refuse membership. If the elders offer membership to an offender, it will be conditional on his or her agreement to:

- Verify the history of offenses, convictions, and adjudication of sexual offenses and disclose them to the CHBC elders and the members of the Child Protection Committee.
- A member of the Child Protection Committee contacting his/her probation officer to find out the underlying offense and the specific terms of probation.
- The Children's Ministry Administrator doing a thorough criminal background check. If the information provided by the offender differs from the information given by the probation officer or gathered by the Children's Ministry Administrator that will be grounds for denying membership.
- Disclosure of information to parents and the congregation. The information released to the church is at the discretion of the elders. A letter detailing this information will be sent directly to all member parents.
- Refrain from any form of communication (including phone, IM, texting, e-mail, social media or any type of technology), social fellowship, physical contact, mentoring, baby-sitting, or coaching with children or youth or participate in any activities or programs related to children or youth both inside and outside of the church.
- The Child Protection Committee will designate CHBC members or staff, who will accompany the alleged perpetrator or criminal offender at all times while he or she is on CHBC's property or anywhere in CHBC's buildings or in attendance at any church related services, activities or gatherings that has the possibility of children being present.
- Any restrictions that elders determine.
- Permission to notify the leadership, congregation, and parents of anything that the elders deem significant for these groups to know.
- A warning that the church will report any suspected activity to civil authorities.
- A warning that any violation of the code of conduct (including allegations or suspicion of abusive behavior) can result in discipline and banning from the church facilities or any church related programs and activities.
- Sign a written document that details all of these items, plus anything else that the elders or the Child Protection Committee deems important to include.

Other Guidelines About Sexual Offenders

If a convicted sexual offender applies for a volunteer or staff position, he or she will be denied by the church. Exceptions may only be made upon the approval of the elders, full-disclosure to the congregation and a congregational vote.

If a sexual offender does not disclose a former allegation, conviction or adjudication, and it is revealed later, the offender will be removed from any paid or volunteer position immediately and may be removed from membership as well.

If a sexual offender is a minor, the church reserves the right to bar that minor from any children or youth activities, and will follow the guidelines set out above for any sexual offender who seeks participation in church-related public services, programs or activities.

If a sexual offender leaves CHBC (as a member or regular attender) and begins attending another church, the elders will disclose allegations or self-admission or criminal conviction of neglect or abuse to the leadership at the next church.

APPENDIX 1:
Inappropriate and Appropriate Touch

Inappropriate Touching

- Shoving, hair pulling, shaking, slapping, pinching, biting, kicking, hitting, or spanking a child for any reasons.
- Squeezing of arm, neck, face, or any parts of the body.
- Tickling children over 5 years old. It is over stimulating and is considered by some professionals to be a deceptive device that could lead to inappropriate touching.
- Children sitting on laps of adults is inappropriate for ages 6 and older.
- Holding or restraining children on the lap. However, holding a child 5 years and younger is appropriate for short time spans when comfort is needed by the child or the child's behavior is out-of-control or endangering other children.
- Touching a child in the genital areas except for younger and developmentally delayed children requiring a diaper change, bathing/washing and assistance with toileting procedures. Otherwise, touch in the genital area is only permitted by medical personnel in case of injury or suspected injury.
- Kissing a child on the lips, neck, or anywhere else. A child should never be allowed to kiss a staff member, volunteer, deacon or another child on the lips, neck, or anywhere else. Children are also not allowed to kiss one another. (Note: A kiss is appropriate on the cheek when it is included in a greeting).
- Slapping a child on the behind, even when playing.
- Fondling children, even in non-private areas.
- Carrying a child on the back unless the child is unable to walk.

Appropriate Touching

- A comforting pat on the shoulder and back, or allowing an emotionally distressed child to lean their head on your shoulder is appropriate.
- Back rub to help comfort, or put an irritable child to sleep is appropriate.
- High-Fives, handshakes, or the touching of two fists are appropriate and recommended touch, especially when interacting with older children.
- Holding hands is permitted with children 10 years and under when initiated by the child, or when helping a child to walk, climb stairs, etc.
- Holding a child firmly with your hands to restrain him/her is appropriate when it is used to prevent a child from an accident, injury, hurting self, others, or you.
-

APPENDIX 2:
Child Abuse Reporting Form

Instructions: _If a volunteer, staff, deacon or elder suspect, hear about or observe signs or symptoms of abuse, please: (1) Talk immediately with the Children's Ministry Administrator or the Pastor who oversees children; and (2) document any relevant information on this form._
This report should include signs or symptoms observed, notations about bruises or injuries that are visible, a summary of what the child said, and a description of any emotions expressed by the child. _Do not go back and interview the child._ _Fill this form out based on whatever information has already been obtained._

Today's Date: _____

Name of Child: _____

Name of Parent/Guardian: _____

Name of Volunteer: _____

Signs or Symptoms of Abuse Observed:

Check all that apply:

☐ Team Leader Notified

☐ Deacon(ess) Notified

☐ CMA Notified

☐ CM Elder Notified

Bruises or Injuries that are Visible:

Emotions expressed by the Child:

Summary of the Conversation with the Child:

Anything Else that is Relevant:

APPENDIX 3:
Child Abuse & Neglect Reporting Guidelines in DC,MD & VA

U.S. Department of Health and Human Services Administration for Children and Families Administration on Children, Youth and Families Children's Bureau
http://www.childwelfare.gov/systemwide/laws_policies/statutes/manda.cfm

Introduction
The laws and regulations of the District of Columbia, Maryland, and Virginia differ on their requirements and definitions of persons required and/or permitted to report child abuse and neglect. Therefore, the following guidelines are only intended to serve general educational purposes, and is not intended as a substitute for competent legal advice from an attorney familiar with the laws and regulations regarding child abuse and neglect in the District, Maryland, and Virginia. Each individual CHBC employee and volunteer is responsible for fulfilling his or her personal obligation to comply with the laws and regulations applicable to him or her with respect to reporting child abuse and neglect, and may need to consult with a legal professional in order to understand and comply with applicable laws and regulations. However, in determining any legal obligations that CHBC may have with respect to reporting child abuse or neglect, it may need the assistance of a staff person or volunteer to determine relevant facts and circumstances.

District of Columbia
Professionals Required to Report
Ann. Code § 4-1321.02
Persons required to report include:
- Child and Family Services Agency employees, agents, and contractors
- Physicians, psychologists, medical examiners, dentists, chiropractors, registered nurses, licensed practical nurses, or persons involved in the care and treatment of patients
- Law enforcement officers or humane officer of any agency charged with the enforcement of animal cruelty laws
- School officials, teachers, or athletic coaches
- Department of Parks and Recreation employees, public housing resident managers, social service workers, or daycare workers
- Domestic violence counselors or mental health professionals
-

Reporting by Other Persons
Ann. Code § 4-1321.02
Any other person who knows or has reason to suspect that a child is being abused or neglected may report.

Standards for Making a Report

Ann. Code § 4-1321.02

A report is required when:

- A mandated reporter knows or has reasonable cause to suspect that a child known to him or her in his or her professional or official capacity has been or is in immediate danger of being a mentally or physically abused or neglected child.
- A health professional, law enforcement officer, or humane officer, except an undercover officer whose identity or investigation might be jeopardized, has reasonable cause to believe that a child is abused as a result of inadequate care, control, or subsistence in the home environment due to exposure to drug-related activity.
- A mandated reporter knows or has reasonable cause to suspect that a child known to him or her in his or her professional or official capacity has been, or is in immediate danger of being, the victim of sexual abuse or attempted sexual abuse; the child was assisted, supported, caused, encouraged, commanded, enabled, induced, facilitated, or permitted to become a prostitute; the child has an injury caused by a bullet; or the child has an injury caused by a knife or other sharp object that was caused by other than accidental means.

Privileged Communications

Ann. Code §§ 4-1321.02(b); 4-1321.05

A mandated reporter is not required to report when employed by a lawyer who is providing representation in a criminal, civil, including family law, or delinquency matter, and the basis for the suspicion arises solely in the course of that representation.

Neither the husband-wife nor the physician-patient privilege is permitted.

Inclusion of Reporter's Name in Report

Ann. Code § 4-1321.03

Mandated reporters are required to provide their names, occupations, and contact information.

Disclosure of Reporter Identity

Ann. Code § 4-1302.03

The Child Protection Register staff shall not release any information that identifies the source of a report or the witnesses to the incident referred to in a report to the alleged perpetrator of the abuse, the child's parent or guardian, or a child-placing agency investigating a foster or adoptive placement, unless said staff first obtains permission from the source of the report or from the witnesses named in the report.

Maryland
Professionals Required to Report
Fam. Law § 5-704
Persons required to report include:
- Health practitioners
- Educators or human service workers
- Police officers

Reporting by Other Persons
Fam. Law § 5-705
Any other person who has reason to believe that a child has been subjected to abuse or neglect must report.

Standards for Making a Report
Fam. Law §§ 5-704; 5-705
A report is required when, acting in a professional capacity, the person has reason to believe that a child has been subjected to abuse or neglect.

Privileged Communications
Fam. Law § 5-705
Only attorney-client and clergy-penitent privileges are permitted.
Inclusion of Reporter's Name in Report
The reporter is not specifically required by statute to provide his or her name in the report.

Disclosure of Reporter Identity
This issue is not addressed in the statutes reviewed.

Virginia
Professionals Required to Report
Ann. Code § 63.2-1509
The following professionals are required to report:
- Persons licensed to practice medicine or any of the healing arts
- Hospital residents, interns, or nurses
- Social workers or probation officers
- Teachers or other persons employed in a public or private school, kindergarten, or nursery school
- Persons providing full-time or part-time child care for pay on a regular basis
- Mental health professionals
- Law enforcement officers, animal control officers, or mediators
- All professional staff persons, not previously enumerated, employed by a private or State-operated hospital, institution, or facility to which children have been committed or where children have been placed for care and treatment
- Persons associated with or employed by any private organization responsible for the care, custody, or control of children
- Court-appointed special advocates
- Persons, over age 18, who have received training approved by the Department of Social Services for the purposes of recognizing and reporting child abuse and neglect
- Any person employed by a local department who determines eligibility for public assistance
- Emergency medical services personnel

Reporting by Other Persons
Ann. Code § 63.2-1510

Any person who suspects that a child is abused or neglected may report.

Standards for Making a Report
Ann. Code § 63.2-1509

A report is required when, in his or her professional or official capacity, a reporter has reason to suspect that a child is abused or neglected. For purposes of this section, 'reason to suspect that a child is abused or neglected' shall include:

- A finding made by an attending physician within 7 days of a child's birth that the results of a blood or urine test conducted within 48 hours of the birth of the child indicate the presence of a controlled substance not prescribed for the mother by a physician
- A finding by an attending physician made within 48 hours of a child's birth that the child was born dependent on a controlled substance that was not prescribed by a physician for the mother and has demonstrated withdrawal symptoms
- A diagnosis by an attending physician made within 7 days of a child's birth that the child has an illness, disease, or condition that, to a reasonable degree of medical certainty, is attributable to in utero exposure to a controlled substance that was not prescribed by a physician for the mother or the child
- A diagnosis by an attending physician made within 7 days of a child's birth that the child has fetal alcohol syndrome attributable to in utero exposure to alcohol

Privileged Communications
Ann. Code §§ 63.2-1509; 63.2-1519

The requirement to report shall not apply to any regular minister, priest, rabbi, imam, or duly accredited practitioner of any religious organization or denomination usually referred to as a church as it relates to information required by the doctrine of the religious organization or denomination to be kept in a confidential manner.

The physician-patient or husband-wife privilege is not permitted.

Inclusion of Reporter's Name in Report

The reporter is not specifically required by statute to provide his or her name in the report.

Disclosure of Reporter Identity
Ann. Code § 63.2-1514

Any person who is the subject of an unfounded report who believes that the report was made in bad faith or with malicious intent may petition the court for the release of the records of the investigation or family assessment. If the court determines that there is a reasonable question of fact as to whether the report was made in bad faith or with malicious intent and that disclosure of the identity of the reporter would not be likely to endanger the life or safety of the reporter, it shall provide to the petitioner a copy of the records of the investigation or family assessment.

#2
Supporting Them by Providing Them with Resources to Use at Home with Their Children

But of course, we hope to support parents by doing more than providing them with safe child care for their children at church.

Supporting Parents by Providing Them with Resources to Use at Home with their Children

Who is in the best place to impact the children in the church? Do the math and it becomes quite clear! Most children are in church only a few hours a week, while they spend hours each day with their parents. Our ministry to the children at church is important, but our ministry to give parents good resources to use at home with their children can have a far greater influence.

Here's some of the ways we support our parents here at CHBC:

To name a few....

- Regularly hosting special events: parent lunches, panels/speakers on various topics relevant to parenting.

- Offering Core Seminar classes (Sunday School for adults a la CHBC), both on parenting as well as a wide variety of important topics which aid parents in their own spiritual growth.

- Strongly encourage parents' church attendance and accountability with others to foster spiritual growth through discipleship and the preaching of the Word.

- Planning times for our Pastor for Families and Counseling to be available to speak with them and give advice.

- Encouraging teachers/caregivers to give deliberate, regular feedback about their children.

- Hosting "Daddy" breakfasts and other informal, member-initiated meetings to encourage fathers in godly leadership of their families.

- Offering resources in the bookstall and library.

- Giving out take home resources of what the children are being taught in their church classes so that parents can review and reinforce the concepts at home.

- Offering online curriculum resources and quarterly newsletter of what the children will be learning.

- Giving out booklists of suggested resources for parents to use at home with their children.

- Encouraging members to support each other. Helping them make connections with others going through/gone through similar seasons and issues with their children.

Parent
Support
Resources

Core Seminars at Capitol Hill Baptist Church

One of the best ways we can help the children be well-parented and well-taught, is to teach their parents well. At CHBC, this comes in a number of forms. The main form is expositional preaching and thoughtful worship during the worship services. This is supplemented by small groups and inductive Bible study as well as what we call Core Seminars, the adult education hour at CHBC.

Core Seminars are held for all adults and cover a wide range of topics. While the parenting class may particularly help parents in their parenting, all the classes help teach parents truths that they can pass on to their children.

Below is a listiing of Core Seminars from the CHBC website: capitolhillbaptist.org. They are resources we are happy to share. Visit the website for more information. New courses are regularly added. Please check back for updates. Link: http://www.capitolhillbaptist.org/we-equip/adults/core-seminars/

* The Basics track grounds us in the foundational disciplines of the Christian life.
* The Bible Overview track seeks to improve our understanding of Scripture.
* The History and Theology track exposes us to the history and doctrine both of our church and of Christianity throughout the ages.
* The Christian Life track applies God's wisdom to our relationships.

Membership Matters	Basics	Bible Overview	History & Theology	Christian Roles	Christian Discipleship	Engaging the World
Membership Matters	Two Ways to Live Explaining Christianity Jump Start How to Study the Bible Fear of Man Meeting with God Guidance	Old Testament New Testament	Biblical Theology Systematic Theology Church History	Biblical Manhood and Womanhood Friendship, Courtship & Marriage Parenting	Discipling Suffering Biblical Counseling Living as a Church Spiritual Disciplines	Apologetics & Worldviews Evangelism Missions Christians in the Workplace Money

Styled as lectures, the teachers seek to communicate truth in the Seminars while encouraging more interaction with the material in outside conversations. Ideally, attendees of the Core Seminars begin with the Basics track and follow the rest through to the end, acquiring a comprehensive Christian education in a few years' time.

Download our Core Seminar brochure to learn more.
Please feel free to use this Core Seminar material in your church and reproduce handouts as necessary. External links that are found in some of the classes may direct you to material that is copyrighted by other organizations.

The following articles and booklist are excerpts from <u>Truths to Teach, Stories to Tell</u>, which we give out to parents at our annual Resource Fair for families.

Capitol Hill Baptist Church
Children's Ministry

Truths to Teach, Stories to Tell:

Books and other resources for your family

Connie Dever

Thoughts on Choosing and Using Books with Your Children

When Should I Start Reading to My Child?

Short Answer: As soon as you want!

Reading is simply another form of language, so why not? Most parents begin talking to their children from birth, and children begin absorbing understanding through voice tone even before the words make sense.

But, if you begin reading to your young infant, don't do it with the agenda of getting them to polish off the Bible by the time they are one! (This sounds ridiculous, but it's amazing what ideas we eager parents get into our heads!)

Do it to begin the pattern of enjoying time together, cuddled on your lap, listening to your voice and with an open heart.

Gradually, as your child develops, watch for cues that they are ready for more. You will see them begin to point to pictures or bring you particular books to read (usually over and over again!). Then you know they are engaging with not just the feel of reading, but the content of what you are reading. That's when you can begin to really think about using books to fill their hearts and minds with truth.

Bible Storybooks FAQs

#1: What's the difference between a Bible storybook and a full Bible? Which would you recommend to using?
A Bible storybook is a collection of Bible stories, written by an author, while the Bible is...well....the Bible--a translation of the entire Old Testament and New Testament into a particular language by a group of Bible scholars.

#2: What are some things to consider in using a Bible storybook?
The Advantages: A Bible storybook--like a good sermon-- can add descriptions about people and places that were known and assumed by the original writers and readers of the Bible, but that aren't obvious to us. They can use language that may be much more suitable for younger children to understand. They can give spiritual insights that help both child and parent learn important truths about God and how He wants us to live. These are all wonderful things.

The Tricky Parts: But, Bible storybooks have their down sides, too. In an attempt to bring the story to life and "up-to-date", authors may take quite a bit of creative license with language and emotion--adding things which may or may not be true. People who write Bible stories for children have to walk a very thin tightrope between bringing a story to life and not adding to it what isn't there. Authors also may choose to shift the true main point of the story to something more to their liking--often a more simple, moralistic application. You must be on your guard to edit on the spot.

Tips for Choosing a Bible Storybook *(as well as other Bible-based books)*

#1 Theology: Check for sound theology! The story of Noah is often a good story to look at for this. Is it a story of the animals in the ark, or of the mercy and holiness of God towards sinful people? Praise God there are more and more good Bible storybooks with great theology available! But sometimes these books are so bad that you just can't use them. Other times, there are books with only largely-good theology that are so attractively done, that you may choose to edit as you read them aloud rather than not use them at all.

#2 Pictures: Do they show Jesus' face or not? Christian Focus books and Ella Lindvall do not illustrate Jesus' face, feeling that is breaking the 2nd commandment regarding graven images. Many others disagree. They don't believe it breaks the 2nd commandment to carefully use pictures to help teach young children.

#3 Creative License: Does the storybook add details that bring light to the story, but are in keeping with the original Bible text? How much license does the author take in adding extra details (especially emotional) that are not clearly inferred by the original Bible text? The Jesus Bible Storybook (Sally Lloyd-Jones) is an example of a Bible storybook that takes quite a bit of creative license, both in language and emotion enhancement. The Read-Aloud Stories (Ella Lindvall), The Children's Story Bible (Catherine Vos), The Big Picture Bible (David Helm) and The Beginner's Bible (Zonderkidz) are all examples of ones that do not.

#4 Main Point: Does the author seem to bring his own (often moralistic) main point to the story or does he stick to the main point of the original text? (A favorite example: Is the feeding of the 5000 about a little boy who shared his lunch or is it about Jesus revealing Himself as the Bread of Life, the Manna from Heaven, come to save God's people?)

#5 Child-Appropriateness: Are the stories the right length and right language for your child?

#6 Story Choice in the Collection: Does the book offer enough stories? A good cross-section of stories from every part of the Bible?

#7 Use: Are you looking for one-off stories or for something more like a Bible overview?

#8 Appropriate Applications: Does it offer any resources to help you and your family apply the Bible truths to your life?

Tips for Choosing a Bible for Your Child

#1 What's Your Goal?

Is your goal to begin to familiarize your child with a Bible version he will use the rest of their life, even if it is above his comprehension level (many times by quite a bit)? Realize that you will probably need to do more picking, choosing and explaining of passages for your child to understand what you are reading, if this is your approach.

OR

Is your goal to start your child in the process of understanding/reading with a Bible closer to his own comprehension level? If so, look for an easier translation, written on (or closer to) their level and "promote" them up gradually to Bibles with higher reading level as you go.

#2 Early Readers: They might be reading, but are they understanding?

There is a difference between what your early reader can read and what they are retaining. The technical words for this are "de-coding" (spelling out/pronouncing words) and "comprehension" (understanding and remembering what the words actually mean). Early readers are often working so hard to spell out or pronounce the words (de-coding) that there is little brain space leftover for comprehending at the same time. Check on how much they are comprehending by asking them a few questions about what they read. If they are remembering very little, chances are it's that they are so busy de-coding. You may want to choose a simpler Bible version or largely stick to reading aloud to them as their reading skills improve.

#3 Take Some Translations for a Test Drive

Try out some different translations on your children and see what works best for them, based on your goals.

Bible Translations *(and some notes about our favorite ones)*

READING LEVEL	TRANSLATION
3rd Grade	**New International Reader's Version (NIrV)**
Good NIrV Choices:	**NIrV Adventure Bible for Early Readers** **Kids' Quest Study Bible**
	This is a full, simplified version of the NIV 1984. It is more accessible to both preschoolers and elementary grade children.
7th Grade	**New King James Version (NKJV)**
7th-8th Grade	**Holman Christian Standard Bible (HCSB)**
Good HCSB Choice:	**HCSB Illustrated Study Bible for Kids**
	The "Southern Baptist" Bible is far more than its nickname implies. While it has updated scholarship, like the ESV, it often scores higher than the ESV in terms of readability for younger children especially. If only they could match the quality of notes in the ESV Study Bible!
7th-8th Grade	**New International Version 1984 (NIV 1984)**
Good NIV 1984 Choice:	**NIV Adventure Bible, 1984**
	The version has long been the highly favored translation among evangelicals. It is very readable in both word choice and sentence structure. Most suitable for 5th grade and up. It is, however, being replaced by the NIV 2011, which is headed in a distinctly different direction (read below) NOTE: Soon these will only be available through the used Bible market! Right now you can still get them through www.christainbook.com. Apparently Zondervan sold the end of their inventory to them. Buy now, if you want a new copy!
7th-8th Grade	**New International Version 2011 (NIV 2011)**
	The NIV 2011 has replaced the NIV 1984. It is not simply update of scholarship, but a shift towards gender neutral language. This is because of the NIV's commitment to keep up with cultural changes in language. Furthermore, this same committment means there will be other updates in this version in the future. So, to tie yourself to this Bible version is to tie yourself to futher changes--difficult for curriclum writers and those who hope to memorize a Bible version that will remain available for years to come. For this reason, many conservative evangelicals are holding tightly to their old NIV 1984's or shifting to other translations, frequently the ESV or the HCSB.
10th Grade	**English Standard Version (ESV)**
Good ESV Choice:	**ESV Seek and Find Bible, ESV Grow Bible**
	Definitely the up-and-coming translation among reformed evangelicals, but test drive it with the ears of a child. Sometimes the language and sentence structure is not easily understandable to younger children. The Study Bible versions do have extremely useful notes and very helpful maps.
11th Grade	**New American Standard Bible (NASB)**
12th Grade	**King James Version (KJV)**

Bible Hybrids

A Bible hybrid is a Bible that is a cross between a full translation Bible and a Bible story book. It is like a full translation Bible, because every word in it is from a direct translation of the Bible text. But it is also like a Bible story book, because it only includes selected stories or passages.

#1 The Day by Day Begin-to-Read Bible
A collection of the simplest stories included in the Day by Day Bible, listed below. Lots of pictures.

#2 The Day by Day Bible
This fuller version contains many more passages from every book of the Bible. It is not primarily story-centered, but passage-centered, so it is beginning to feel much/can be used much more like a regular Bible. No pictures.

Other Special Features of The Day by Day Bible
- Chronologically ordered, so that different parts of the Bible that fit together are presented together. So, the Psalms about David are slotted in the stories of his life from 1 Chronicles. The letters of Paul are slotted in with stories from the Book of Acts, etc.
- A checklist for reading through it in 365 days. Nice bite-sized chunks.
- Good bridge for non-readers to confident readers.
- Tons of good lists in the appendix to help you decide what to read to your child, whether with this Bible translation or another version. (lists: Stories by Bible Book; Stories in Chronological Order; 100 Key Teaching Stories; 100 Bedtime Stories; and 100 Stories for Good Family Discussion.)

Should I Do Bible Memory and/or Catechism with My Children?

No one can dispute that young children have an amazing ability to learn and memorize--often the quickest and easiest in their whole lives! Why not harness this skill for the sake of learning Bible truths?

Bible memory verses and catechisms are concise ways of putting a whole library of Bible truth in children's heads. While some people balk at the idea of helping children memorize concepts deeper than they can fully understand, others see the goal not so much as achieving full, immediate understanding in a young child today, but leaving a legacy in his head for the future.

But on the other hand, don't exasperate your child! Yes, they may be little memory sponges, but you can harden their hearts and discourage them with the very truths you want them to love by forcing them to do too much, too soon and in a format that just isn't appropriate or effective for them.

Remember: your point isn't just to check off the list that you taught these truths to your children. It's to try to make them stick in places where they will stay for years. Better to do less but do it well, than to think you've done it all and done it poorly or at the cost of a soft heart.

And one more thing: there is more than one way to skin a rabbit! Bible memory and catechism doesn't always have to take a recitation format. There are many Bible verses and catechism-like questions and answers put to song. There are games you can play to help them learn, too.

If nothing else, check out the resources for Hide 'n' Seek Kids and Deep Down Detectives at www. praisefactory.org. All the Bible verses and catechism-like Big Questions are set to song; and, there are simple movement activities (called Music, Movement and Memory) you can do with them. For elementary-aged kids, all 104 Praise Factory scripture verses are also set to music. And, there is a section of games that can be used as a fun way to memorize any Scripture Verse.

What Books Can and Cannot Do

WHAT BOOKS CAN DO:

#1 Books can help you present truths in an orderly fashion.

#2 Books can be a springboard into important conversations with your children.

#3 Books can help you learn good language to use with your children (or other people's children) on their level as you have those important conversations.

#4 Books can help leave a library of truth in your children that can be used by God their whole life: a kind of time release capsules of wisdom and knowledge.

#5 Books can provide a wonderful time of sharing for you and your child. You can build memories and intimacy as you share thoughts, time, and the warmth of touch with your arm around them.

WHAT BOOKS CAN'T DO

#1 Books can't provide a one-size-fits-all formula for teaching every child. And if the book you read says it can, beware! It can't!

#2 Books can't save your child. No amount of books or information can bring salvation to your child! This is a work of God, by His Holy Spirit, in His perfect timing, according to His perfect will.

#3 Books can't replace the testimony of a godly, faithful life, only enhance it. Books are one thing, but real life is another. How you live is the blank canvas for the truths you teach. Life paints them in vibrant, unforgettable colors. And remember: while God's righteousness and love might be what we would always desire the canvas of our lives to show (and thank God for when it does!), God is just as faithful to use our failings to display Himself. When we do fail and humbly seek His (and others') forgiveness, God is kind to use these times to reflect His mercy and compassion towards sinners--namely us and like our children. Our lives are much more about the business of REDEMPTION, than they are a picture of PERFECTION, as much as we might wish it to be otherwise. And through all of it, the truths about God we tell our children are brought to light.

#4 Books can't replace your common-sense knowledge of your own child. It will take your discernment to know what the right type of book and the right pacing of learning is best for your child. What if your neighbor's child can read already and yours doesn't? Don't push your child to hurry up and read if they aren't ready. Help your child enjoy books as he is able. (FYI: reading is a developmental skill that can fully develop as late as 2nd grade! Be patient!) What if your friend's child has read and memorized the entire book of Leviticus and can recite it backwards in Hebrew...while your child can hardly sit still let alone say their ABC's? Stop comparing! Help your child learn, read and memorize as she is able! The point is making a connection with your child, where they are, not to keep up with the Jones!

Also, just because a book tells you to do something, doesn't mean you should do it...unless it's the Bible, of course! Weigh what you know about your child with what the book is asking them to do or understand. Is he ready for it, or would he be better off with a slower, simpler pace; or, a faster, more complex pace?

#5 Books can't replace the wisdom of parents with children older than yours. It is easy to read a book and latch onto a particular system or ideal, only to find that you and/or your child is frustrated. This is especially true if you are an eager first-time parent. Seek out older, seasoned parents or even teachers who you know! They are invaluable resources! Parents with older children often have wrestled with similar issues and are able to give you good advice about how to use books to teach biblical truths to children and pitfalls to avoid. It can be especially helpful to particularly seek out parents who have a similar type of child as yours. Perhaps you have a wiggly Wade or a studious Susan. Talking to parents with older children of the same type can help you learn more about how to reach and teach your particular type of child, given their strengths and weaknesses.

Where Can I Get These Books?

#1 The CHBC Main Library: Downstairs (to borrow)
Some of these books will be on loan through the main CHBC Library located in the basement of the church. We are hoping to add quite a few more of the titles you see here to that
collection, as space allows.

#2 The CHBC Children's Resource Library: 3rd Floor (to borrow)
Books that we cannot fit downstairs in the Main CHBC Library, we will add to the Children's Resource Library upstairs on the 3rd floor. Why not just put all the books up there? Because this library has a lot of other materials that are used only by the teachers and there is a lot to weed through.

#3 The CHBC Bookstall (to purchase)
Some of these books are available in the CHBC bookstall. If you find them there, they will be at about the best price you can find pretty much anywhere.

#4 Online Booksellers (to purchase)

amazon.com	All books, except Good Book Company and Matthias Media. They are carrying an increasing number of Christian Focus books.
wtsbooks.com	Westminster Theological Seminary Bookstore. Many of our favorite books, at great prices, including some Christian Focus publications.
cvbbs.com	Cumberland Valley Bible Book Service. Many of our favorite books, at great prices. The whole line of Christian Focus publications. Only US source I know of to purchase the Jim Cromarty books (He's Australian.)
matthiasmedia.com (usa)	US source for Australian-based Matthias Media. Books like Who Will Be King? and Gumtree Gully (children's versions of Two Ways to Live)
christianfocus.com (usa)	US source for Christian Focus Books. However, wtsbooks.com and cvbbs.com seem to have better prices, (though more limited quantities).
the goodbook.com	Only US source for books by this publisher.
christianbook.com	Largest, single dealer in Christian Books in the US. They will tend to have only the most "mainstream" books, such as those published by Crossway and Zondervan.

Booklist of Helpful Resources

About This Booklist

This is an excerpt from Connie Dever's book: Capitol Hill Baptist Church Children's Ministry. It lists books by category. Within each category, **books are ordered loosely by age-appropriateness.** Loosely, because children's abilities and interests vary widely. Your best bet is to try out books with your children and see what is a good fit. Borrow it from the church library or a friend. You may also want to read online reviews and see what age child tends to be reading the book.

The Age Ratings: Wherever possible, I have listed the suggested age levels the publisher gives for each book. Again, these are simply guidelines! Look for a good fit for your child, not the publisher's average child! It's a good connection with your child---not with some publisher's opinion that matters.

Where to Find These Books:
Most of these books can be ordered through amazon.com, christianfocus.com, cvbbs.com or wtsbooks.com. If there is an exclusive, unusual source of a particular book, I will list it. Otherwise, assume you can get it in through these four, major websites listed above.

This book list is constantly being updated since great, new books keep coming out! The task is endless!

I am leaving this one in place because of the comments about various books that I've woven into the booklist.

See the Other Children's Ministry Resources section at the back of this book for our most recent booklist.

Parenting Books

First Time parents (especially) beware of using these or any parenting books as a textbook for your child. Each book has its own bent and is most helpful when read in combination with other ones. Input from other parents--particularly those with older children--can be invaluable in learning to apply ideas to real live kids.

Parenting Books: The First Year of Parenting

On Becoming Baby Wise
Garry Ezzo, Robert Bucknam
We recommend only using this "secular" version of the Ezzo book. We do not condone Ezzo's use of Scripture to prove scheduling and other concepts found in the other "Christian" version of this book (This is called Let the Children Come Along the Infant Way). Sleep scheduling, as he presents it, comes across as a strict necessity, rather rigidity put in place, instead of as a matter of helpfulness, nuance and understanding of your particular child. While there is a lot of very good material in this book, we strongly caution you, sometimes desperate first-time parents, who might be grasping for a fail-safe formula for raising children. Ezzo's language can lead you to feel like you must do things his way, all-the-way in order for your children to come out well. Take his advice with a grain of salt and if in doubt, talk to other parents with older children to gain perspective in how to apply ideas to real live kids. Ezzo's best ideas are helpfully balanced with Secrets of the Baby Whisperer, listed next.

Secrets of the Baby Whisperer
Tracy Hogg
This book conveys many of the same helpful ideas as the Ezzo book listed above, but without many of the legalistic trappings.

A Mother's Heart
Jean Fleming

New First Three Years of Life: Completely Revised and Updated
Burton L. White
This secular book is based on Dr. White's 37 years of actual observation and research of the developmental stages children 0 to 3 years go through. He gives very commonsense tips everything from best toys to buy to dealing with many common issues parents face with their child. Interestingly, Dr. White's observations about what works best with children echoes much of biblical wisdom. Use it in combination with other Christian books on parenting.

Parenting Books: Toddlers and Up

The Shaping of the Christian Family: How My Parents Nurtured My Faith
Elizabeth Elliot

Give Them Grace: Dazzling Your Kids with the Love of Jesus
Elyse Fitzpatrick, Tullian Tchividjian
This is a good book to balance out other parenting books that have a very distinct "formula" to raising children. It can help parents remember not just the "method" but the grace that is so needful in winsome, godly parenting.

Don't Make Me Count to Three
Ginger Plowman

Shepherding a Child's Heart
Tedd Tripp
Some very good ideas, but very much influenced by a paedo-baptist covenant view of children in a Christian family.

Hints on Child Training
H. Clay Trumball
This is Elizabeth Elliot's grandfather! While I would not use this book exclusively, he does bring a fresh, different perspective on parenting children that provides a very good balance to other general parenting books.

Raising Real Men: Surviving, Teaching and Appreciating Boys
Hal and Melanie Young

Raising a Christian Daughter in an MTV World
Mary Ruth Murdoch

A Mother's Heart
Jean Fleming

A Manual for the Young: Bridges' Practical Exposition of Proverbs 1-9
Proverbs
Charles Bridge
Two good resource for parents. Easy to reference. Good to read with teenagers.

Feminine Appeal
Carolyn Mahaney
Great resource for parents. Good to read with teenage girls.

Girl Talk
Carolyn Mahaney & Nicole Mahaney Whitacre
Great resource for parents. Good to read with teenage girls.

Childhood Conversion (pamphlet)
How Children Come to Faith in Christ (CD available from Family Life Today)
Jim Eliff

Praying for the Next Generation
Sally Michael   only at *childrendesiringgod.org*

Your Child's Profession of Faith
Dennis Gundersen
Calvary Press

The Heart of Anger
Louis Paul Priolio
Shepherd's Press

Thoughts for Young Men
J.C. Ryle
Great resource for parents. Good to read with teenage boys. *amazon.com,*

Parenting: 14 Gospel Principles That Can Radically Change Your Family
Paul Tripp
Perhaps my all-time favorite parenting book because of the timelessness of the truths.

Age of Opportunity
Paul Tripp
A book on parenting adolescents.

Parenting Adolescents
Making Peace with Your Teenager
Kevin Huggins
Two books that help you think about your hungry parent-heart for your child to be a certain way and points you and them to Christ instead.

Treasuring God in Our Traditions
Noel Piper

CCEF Booklet Series: Help for Stepfamilies; Angry Children; Helping Your Adopted Child; How Do I Stop Losing It with My Kids? Recovering from Child Abuse; ADD: Wandering Minds and Wired Bodies; Teens & Sex: How Should We Teach Them?
Wonderful booklets by various authors
only through ccef.org

Bible Story Books

The Beginner's Bible (and The Beginner's Toddler Bible) (ages 2 and up)
Zonderkidz

The Bible in Pictures for Toddlers (ages 2 and up)
Ella K. Lindvall
Moody Press

God Is Great: A Toddler's Bible Storybook (ages 2 and up)
Carolyn Larsen

A Child's First Bible (ages 2 and up)
New Bible in Pictures for Little Eyes (ages 2 and up)
Kenneth Taylor

The Candle Bible for Toddlers (ages 2 and up)
Juliet David
Candle

Little Hands Story Bible (ages 2 and up)
Carine MacKenzie
Christian Focus

The First Step Bible (ages 1 and up)
Mack Thomas
Gold n' Honey

Marians's Big Book of Bible Stories (ages 3 and up)
Marian M. Schoolland
Out of print but readily available through used book websites, including amazon.com

Read with Me Bible: An NIrV Story Bible for Children (ages 2/4 and up)
Read with Me Bible for Toddlers
Doris Rikkers
Zonderkidz
We use with our preschoolers

Read Aloud Bible Stories, multiple volumes (ages 2 and up)
Parables Jesus Told: the Tell Me Stories
Ella Lindvall
Moody Press
Wonderful illustrations. Great with even very, very young children. *amazon.com*

The Christian Focus Story Bible (ages 4 and up)
Catherine Mackenzie
Christian Focus Publishers

365 Bible Stories for Young Hearts (ages 4 and up)
Leon Hudson
Crossway

365 Great Bible Stories: The Good News of Jesus from Genesis to Revelation (ages 4 and up)
Carine Mackenzie
Christian Focus

My First Study Bible (ages 6 and up)
Paul J. Loth

The Gospel Story Bible: Discovering Jesus in the Old and New Testaments (ages 4 and up)
Marty Machowski
New Growth Press

The New Children's Bible (ages 4 and up)
Anne de Vries

Big Picture Story Bible (ages 2 and up)
David R. Helm & Gail Schoonmaker
Crossway Books
All of redemptive history from before the beginning to after the end! Wonderfully done.

The Mighty Acts of God: A Family Bible Story Book (ages 8 and up)
Starr Meade

The Child's Story Bible (ages 4 and up)
Catherine Vos
Eerdmans

The Children's Bible in 365 Stories (ages 3 and up)
Mary Batchelor
Lion Publishing
Does a wonderful job of tying in Bible stories chronologically so that you get a feel for how the psalms of David fit in with the history of David, the epistles of Paul fit in with Acts, etc.

The Bible History As Told to Our Children, 3 volumes (elementary school age and up)
John Vreugdenhil
Available almost exclusively through Reformation Heritage Books. A bit "old school" but the stories are wonderfully told, as by a grandfather talking to his grandkids.

only at heritagebooks.org

Individual Bible Story Books: Board Books (ages 0-3)

Stories Jesus Told: The Missing Sheep. The Runaway Son, The Selfish Servant, The Lost Coin, The Proud Prayer, The Foolish Farmer
Carine Mackenzie
Christian Focus

Jesus Saves His People, Jesus Helps His People, Jesus Rescues His People
Catherine Mackenzie
Christian Focus

Famous Bible Stories Series:
Noah's Ark, Baby Moses, Joseph's Coat, Samuel's Surprise, Naaman the Soldier, Jonah and the Big Fish, Ruth's Journey
Carine Mackenzie
Christian Focus

The Special Baby-Jesus, Big Crash, Safe at Sea, Safe with the Lions, the Little Rich Man, the Man on the Mat, The Singing Shepherd-David, Amazing Jar of Oil, The Kind Man, The Big Picnic, The Man Who Couldn't Pay; There's a Hole in My Roof
Hazel Scrimshire
Christian Focus

Born to Be King series: Mary and Joseph Love Jesus (1), The Shepherds Find Jesus (2), Simeon and Anna See Jesus (3), The Wise Men Help Jesus (4)
Catherine Mackenzie
Christian Focus

Individual Bible Story Books

The Lord's Prayer for Little Ones (ages 3 and up)
Allia Zobel Nolan

God Creates Series: God Creates Light; God Creates Fish and Birds; God Creates Animals and People; God Creates a Day of Rest; God Creates New Life in Me; God Creates the Land, Seas and Plants; God Creates the Sun, Moon and Stars; God Creates the Water and the Sky
Catherine Mackenzie

Bible Wise Series (ages 2-7)
Daniel: the Praying Prince; Samuel: the Boy Who Listened; Barnabas: the Encourager; David: The Fearless Fighter; Sarah & Abraham: The Wonderful Promise; Elijah: God's Miracle Man; Jonathan: The Faithful Friend; Jesus Is Live: The Amazing Story; Miriam: The Big Sister's Secret; Joseph: God's Dreamer; Saul: The Miracle on the Road; Jesus: The Promised Child; Paul: Journeys of Adventure; Noah: Rescue Plan
Carine MacKenzie
Christian Focus

Life of Jesus for the Very Young (ages 4 and up)
Isobel Tallach

The Special Baby-Jesus, Big Crash, Safe at Sea, Safe with the Lions, the Little Rich Man, the Man on the Mat, The Singing Shepherd-David, Amazing Jar of Oil, The Kind Man, The Big Picnic, The Man Who Couldn't Pay; There's a Hole in My Roof
paperback version of the board books
Hazel Scrimshire
Christian Focus

God's Little Guidebooks: Creation (ages 3 and up)
Catherine Mackenzie
Christian Focus

God's Little Guidebooks: 10 Commandments Box Set (ages 3 and up)
Hazel Scrimshire
Christian Focus

Little Hands Life of Jesus (ages 3 and up)
Carine MacKenzie
Christian Focus

Bible Alive Series: (ages 4-7)
David the Shepherd: A Man of Courage; Jesus the Storyteller; David the Soldier: A man of patience; David the King: True repentance; Moses the Traveller: Guided by God; David the Fugitive: True Friendship; Jesus the Child; Jesus the Healer; Moses the Child: Kept by God; Jesus the Savior; Moses the Leader: Used by God; Moses the Shepherd: Chosen by God; Jesus the Miracle Worker; Jesus the Teacher
Carine MacKenzie
Christian Focus

Caring Creator (ages 3 and up)
Carine MacKenzie
Christian Focus

The Plan: How God Got the World Ready for Jesus (ages 4-7)
Sinclair B. Ferguson
Christian Focus

Bible Time Series: (ages 4-7)
Esther the Brave Queen; Peter--the Apostle; Mary: Mother of Jesus; Hannah: The Mother Who Prayed; Simon Peter: Disciple; Joshua: Brave Leader; Ruth: the Harvest Girl; Martha & Mary: Friends of Jesus; Jonah: the Runaway Preacher; Peter: Fisherman; John: the Baptist; Rebekah: Mother of Twins; Gideon: Soldier of God; Moses: Man of God; Paul: The Wise Preacher; Nehemiah: Builder for God
Carine MacKenzie
Christian Focus

Creation Series (ages 4 to 7)
Carol Leah
Christian Focus

Children of the Bible (ages 4 to 7)
Carine Mackenzie
Christian Focus

Hall of Fame: Old Testament; New Testament (ages 4 to 7)
Catherine Mackenzie
Christian Focus

Jesus Teaches Us Series: How To Be Happy; How to Be Good; How to Be Wise (ages 4-7)
Sinclair Ferguson

Magnificent Amazing Time Machine: A Journey Back to the Cross (ages 4 and up)
Sinclair Ferguson

God, the 10 Commandments and Jesus (ages 4- and up)
Carine Mackenzie
Christian Focus

Wise Words to Obey: Words of Wisdom from the Book of Proverbs
Carine Mackenzie
Christian Focus

How to Be a Bible Princess (ages 8 to 12)
Catherine Mackenzie
Christian Focus
Stories about Bible princesses and what we can learn from them about being daughters of the King of Kings.

Meditations on Individual Scriptures

Sammy and His Shepherd: Show Me Jesus in Psalm 23 (ages 4 and up)
Susan Hunt

David and I Talk to God Series and God's Word in My Heart Series: (ages 4 and up)
Make Way for the King Psalms 145 and 24 for Children
What Can I Say to You, God? Verses from the Psalms on Prayer
God Cares When I'm Thankful
Sometimes I Think "What If?" Psalm 46 for Children
God Cares When I Don't Know What to Do
And many other titles
These are out of print, but obtainable. They are wonderful!
All by Elspeth Campbell Murphy
David C. Cook

available through used book stores only, but can type in title in search engine for amazon.com and find where copies can be located

Bible Story Activity Books and Resources

Colour the Bible Series: (ages 4-7)
Book 1: Genesis - 2 Chronicles
Book 2: Ezra-Daniel
Book 3: Hosea-Malachi
Book 4: Matthew - Mark
Book 5: Romans - Thessalonians
Book 5: 1 Timothy - Revelation
Carine MacKenzie
Christian Focus
Coloring pictures and a fill-in-the-blank verse. New King James Version.

Bible Story Coloring Book Series: (ages 4-7)
Story of Abraham, David, Joseph, Mary, Moses, Jacob, Nehemiah, Peter, Ruth, Paul, Miracles of Jesus
Catherine MacKenzie
Christian Focus

Puzzle Book Series (ages 4-7)
Birth of Jesus
Jesus and the Resurrection
Christian Focus

Bible Numbers, A Bible Alphabet, The Work of His Fingers (ages 4-7)
Alison Brown

Books of the Bible Coloring Books: (ages 4-7)
Book of Genesis
Hebrews-Men of Faith
Colour the Gospel: Matthew
Colour the Gospel: Mark
Colour the Gospel: Luke
Colour the Gopsle: John
My Bible ABC Activity Book
Catherine Mackenzie
Christian Focus
Coloring pictures and a fill-in-the-blank verse. New King James Version.

Go to the Ant Coloring Book (ages 4-7)
Judy Rogers (companion book to her audio CD, listed in Music section)

Coloring Book Series:
Animals of the Bible
Bible Discover and Color
Philip Snow
Christian Focus

Bible People Coloring Book Series: (ages 4-7)
Apostles
Baby Moses
David and the Giant
Bible Work
Bible Miracles
Carine Mackenzie
Christian Focus

Puzzle Book Series
The Greatest Rescue: Jesus and the Resurrection
The Queen's Feast: Esther
The Greatest Gift: Birth of Jesus
Bible Detectives Acts: Fun Bible Studies using Puzzles and Stories
Journey to Jericho: Moses, Joshua and Amazing Journey
God's Builder: Nehemiah
The Big Contest: Elijah
The Brave Ruler: Daniel
Ros Woodman
Christian Focus

God's Little Giants Boys and Girls in the Bible (ages 4-7)
Hazel Scrimshire
Christian Focus

Busy People (Bible People) (ages 4-7)
Connect the dots
Carine MacKenzie
Christian Focus

Big Fish Activity Book (ages 4-7)
Ros Woodman
Christian Focus

Bible Detective Series:
Genesis (ages 4-7)
Exodus (ages 4-7)
1 Samuel (ages 8-12)
Matthew (ages 8-12)
Mark (ages 4-7)
Luke (ages 4-7)
John (ages 4-7)
Acts (ages 8-12)
The Quiz Book (ages 4-7)
Ros Woodman and Marianne Ross
Christian Focus

Flannelgraph Pictures
Yes, I know it seems "old school," but nothing charms preschoolers like flannelgraph. They are a great way to have the children interact with a story you are telling or to re-tell it back to you after you have read it to them.

Proper flannelgraph can be purchased through Betty Lukens
https://www.bettylukens.com

Pictures that you print out on paper and laminate can be downloaded through Praise Factory with the Hide 'n' Seek Kids and Deep Down Detectives. These go with each of the 85 preschool stories. The curriculums also include review games to play with these pictures. You can also purchase these on amazon.com.
only on The Praise Factory website

Children's Bible Story Sermons

These are stories of a slightly longer format which tell the story as well as draw out particular applications.

Ninety Story Sermons for Children's Church
120 Dramatic Story Sermons for Children's Church
New Testament Story Sermons for Children
Marianne Radius
Her materials are excellent. One who inspired me to do the writing I'm doing. Daughter of Catherine Vos. Good reformed stock! Sometimes this is only available through used book stores. Well worth finding and keeping.

available through used book stores only, but can type in title in search engine for amazon.com and find where copies can be located

Bible Hybrids

Day by Day Kid's Bible (ages 7 and up)
Day by Day Begin-to-Read Bible (ages 4 and up)
Karyn Henley
Tyndale Kids
Never seen anything quite like it! Chronological, great lists in back, a quasi-translation rather than just a story Bible. Even includes the prophets and the epistles. A number of great lists at end of book that are very, very helpful for curriculum planners, teachers, and parents.

Bibles

NIrV Adventure Bible (full version)
Reading Level: 3rd Grade

NIV 1984 Adventure Bible
Reading Level: 7th-8th Grade

HCSB Illustrated Study Bible for Kids
Reading Level: 7th-8th Grade

ESV Seek and Find Bible, ESV Grow Bible
Reading Level: 10th Grade

Bible Memory

Fighter Verses: Bethlehem Baptist
(now also have musical versions of these verses available) Very well done. ESV and NIV1984 versions.

Bible Memory Program for the Children of CHBC and Parent Resource Book

Sing & Say along the Way Memory Verse Cards
Sets of memory verses related to each concept taught in the three Praise Factory curriculums. Includes track numbers for related scripture songs. All cards and songs downloadable on the Praise Factory website.

First Book of Memory Verses
Carine Mackenzie
Christian Focus

Also see Truth and Grace Memory Books in Catechism Resources

Bible Memory Activity Books

God Loves Me (ages 4-7)
Sarah Womersley
Christian Focus

God Cares (ages 4-7)
God Is Good
God Loves You
Hazel Scrimshire
Christian Focus

Verses: Bible Pictures to Color (ages 4-7)
God Is Faithful
God Is Everywhere
Carine MacKenzie
Christian Focus

Bible Verses Set to Music

Also see the What God Says Theology Coloring Book Series: (ages 4-7)
Bubble-letter style Bible verses related to each of these topics. New King James Version.

Also see the Colour the Bible and Colour the Gospel Series listed under Bible Story Activity Books
Coloring pictures and a fill-in-the-blank verse. New King James Version.

Hide 'em in Your Heart: Volumes 1 & 2
Steven Green

Sovereign Grace Kids Music:
Awesome God, To Be Like Jesus, Walking with the Wise
Wonderful music!
only sovereigngracemusic.org

Hide 'n' Seek Kids, Deep Down Detectives, and Praise Factory Investigators Songs
These are all the hymns, Bible Verses and Big Questions used in these three curriculums, all set to music.
only on The Praise Factory website

christianbook.com
The children's music section of this website lists quite a few audio CDs of Bible verses.

The Gospel

The Gospel for Children: A Simple, Yet Complete Guide to Help Parents Teach Their Children the Gospel of Jesus Christ (ages 5 and up)
John B. Leuzarder
Very God-centered version of the gospel. Nice little illustrations, too.

Who Will Be King? (ages 4 and up)
Matthias Media
Excellent and very simple for children to remember.

matthisamedia.com

GumTree Gully (ages 5 and up)
Kel Richards
Matthias Media
A tale of the Australian bush that does a fantastic job of illustrating the gospel for kids. We turned it into a puppet show that our grade school kids put on for preschoolers. High schoolers at a local Christian school did the puppet show for their mission trips to some overseas orphanages.

matthisamedia.com

The Gospel Story Bible (ages 4 and up)
Marty Machowski

How Do I Get to Heaven? (ages 4 and up)
Christian Focus

This Is No Fairy Tale (ages 4 and up)
Dale Tolmasoff

Your Child's Profession of Faith
Dennis Gundersen
Calvary Press

Stewardship

In God We Trust: A Christian Kid's Guide to Saving, Spending and Giving
Larry Burkett
Standard Publishing
A board book format that teaches kids about stewardship of their money and can be used as a bank. Sounds crazy, but it is a great resource! A very hands-on and understandable presentation of what can be a confusing, abstract concept.

Theology

Theology: Board Books (ages 0-3)

I Can Say to God, I Love You; I Can Say to God, Please;
Catherine MacKenzie
Christian Focus

God Made Series: God Made Water; God Made Weather; God Made Colors; God Made Food; God Made Me; God Made the World; God Made Time
Catherine MacKenzie
Christian Focus

God Gave Me Series: God Gave Me Hearing; God Gave Me Sight; God Gave Me Smell; God Gave Me Taste; God Gave Me Touch; God Gave Me Feelings
Catherine MacKenzie
Christian Focus

Atrributes of God Series: God Has Power; God Is Everywhere; God Is Faithful; God Is Kind; God Knows Everything; God Never Changes
Carine MacKenzie
Christian Focus

Theology: Paperback and Hardback

Learn about God series   (ages 0-3)
Catherine Mackenzie
Christian Focus Publishers
Board books for very young children. Great.

My 1st Book of Questions and Answers   (ages 0-3)
Carine Mackenzie
Christian Focus

Leading Little Ones to God: A Child's Book of Bible Teachings   (ages 4 and up)
By Marian M. Schoolland
Eerdmans

What God Has Always Wanted: The Bible's Big Idea from Genesis Through Revelation
 (ages 4 and up)
Charles F Boyd

Jesus Is Coming Back! (ages 2 and up)
I Can Talk with God
Jesus Loves Me
Jesus Loves the Little Children
I Love My Bible!
God Knows My Name
Every Child, Everywhere!
Most of All, Jesus Loves You! (with Noel Piper)
Jesus Is With Me
Let's Explore God's World
Debby Anderson
Some of these are available as board books, too.

God Made Something Series: (ages 2 and up)
God Made Something Amazing, Beautiful, Clever, Enormous, Funny, Quick, Strong, Tall
Penny Reeve

Atrributes of God Series: (ages 2 and up)
God Knows Everything
God is Kind
God is Faithful
God Is Everywhere
God Has Power
God Never Changes
Carine MacKenzie
Christian Focus

Stop and Look At Yourself, Stop and Look at God's World, Stop and Look at God's Word
 (ages 3 and up)
Donna Drion
Day One Publications

That's When I Talk to God (ages 4 and up)
Dan Morrow

Big Thoughts for Little Thinkers: The Scripture, The Trinity, The Gospel (ages 4 and up)
Joey Allen
New Leaf Press

Big Book of Questions and Answers (ages 4 and up)
Big Book of Questions & Answers about Jesus
Big Book of Bible Truths
Ferguson Sinclair
Christian Focus

Living With God (ages 4 and up)
Beginning with God
Meeting with God
Nancy Gorrell

How Do I Get to Heaven? (ages 4 and up)
Nancy Gorrell

All Things Bright and Beautiful (ages 3 and up)
Cecil Frances Alexander

The Caring Creator (ages 4 and up)
Carine Mackenzie
Christian Focus

Songs of Creation (ages 4 and up)
Paul Goble
Eerdmans

The Names of God (ages 4 and up)
Sally Michael

Children's Bible Basics Series: (ages 4 and up)
Who is God?
Who is Jesus?
What is a Christian?
What is a Church?
What is Prayer?
What Happens When We Die?
Why Do I Do Things Wrong?
The Holy Spirit in Me
Growing Jesus' Way
Angels
When Jesus Comes Back
And other titles
By Carolyn Nystrom
Moody Press
One caution: the child in these stories is definitely converted. You want to make sure that whoever you read this to understands the decision that must be made in order to become a Christian.

Caleb's Lamb (ages 6 and up)
Helen Santos

A Faith to Grow On: Important Things You Should Know Now that You Believe (ages 7 and up)
John MacArthur
Tommy Nelson

Grandpa's Box: Retelling the Biblical Story of Redemption (ages 7 and up)
Starr Meade

A Young Person's Guide to Knowing God (ages 7 and up)
Patricia St. John

Of Pandas and People: The Central Question of Biological Origins
Percival Davis and Dean Kenyon
High School Level book that looks at the origins of humanity. More of a science book than a theology book, but useful with teenagers grappling with the truth of the biblical theology of creation.

Theology Activity Books

What God Says Theology Coloring Book Series: (ages 4-7)
Bubble-letter style Bible verses related to each of these topics. New King James Version.
God Does It Right
God is Always Fair series
God Does a Swap
Holiness
Salvation
Creation
Redemption
Repenting
Catherine MacKenzie
Christian Focus

Atrributes of God Coloring Book Series: (ages 4-7)
God Knows Everything
God is Kind
God is Faithful
God Is Everywhere
God Has Power
God Never Changes
God Is Forever
Carine MacKenzie
Christian Focus

Why Series: (ages 7-14)
Why Did Jesus Come?
Why Did Jesus Die?
How Do I Know I'm a Christian?
The Best Present
Alison Mitchell
thegoodbook.com

Theology: Catechisms and Catechism-Like Resources

ABC Bible Verses (ages 3 and up)
Big Truths for Little Kids
Susan Hunt
Advocates of believer-baptism only be aware: Hunt's Presbyterian-based covenant theology and infant baptism does show up in how she writes.

My 1st Book of Questions and Answers   (ages 4 and up)
My 1st Book about Jesus
My 1st Book Of Bible Promises
My 1st Book Of Bible Prayers
My 1st Book Of Christian Values
My 1st Book of Memory Verses
Carine Mackenzie
Christian Focus

Bible Questions and Answers--a First Catechism (ages 4 and up)
Carine MacKenzie
Christian Focus

Big Book of Questions and Answers (ages 4 and up)
Big Book of Questions & Answers about Jesus
Big Book of Bible Truths
Sinclair Ferguson
Christian Focus

Catechism: Bible Questions and Answers: Teacher's Manual (ages 4 and up)
Diana Kleyn
Christian Focus
Companion volume to Sinclair Ferguson's book

The Family Worship Book (ages 4 and up)
Terry L. Johnson

Catechism for Young Children, Original Edition (ages 4 and up)
Presbyterian Church of America
wtsbook.com

First Catechism (ages 4 and up)
Presbyterian Church of America
wtsbook.com

Children's "Prove It" Catechism Truth for Eternity Ministries (ages 4 and up)
Reformed Baptist Church Grand Rapids, MI
Catechism for Young Children G.I. Williamson
Makes slight, baptistic changes from the Westminster Shorter Catechism
only through http://www.vor.org/rbdisk/html/proveit/fulltext.htm

Hide 'n' Seek Kids, Deep Down Detectives, Praise Factory Investigators curriculum (ages 2 -grade 5)

These three curriculums are all based on a Question/Answer format and can be used as a catechism resource. Include games, songs, action rhymes as well as a bible story that focuses on each concept/question. The take home sheets, available in the parent resources section for each curriculum, have helpful summaries of all key concepts and include concept-related questions.
on The Praise Factory website

Praise Factory Investigators
The 16 Big Questions and Answers and what they mean set to music. A sing along storybook is also available which provides a story line that includes the lyrics to all the songs and a lot more truth.
Available through amazon.com

The Praise Factory Curriculum Tour (Basic and Extended Versions)
A helpful and colorful overview of Praise Factory family of curriculum, philosophy, FAQ's and Scope & Sequences.
Available through amazon.com

The Westminster Shorter Catechism Songs, Volume 1, Q&A 1-28 (Audio CD) (ages 4 and up)
The Westminster Shorter Catechism Songs, Volume 2, Q&A 29-56 (Audio CD)
The Westminster Shorter Catechism Songs, Volume 3, Q&A 57-85 (Audio CD)
The Westminster Shorter Catechism Songs, Volume 4, Q&A 86-107 (Audio CD)
only through wtsbook.com

The Shorter Catechism Activity Book: Learning The Truth Through Puzzles (ages 6 and up)
Marianne Ross
Christian Focus

Training Hearts Teaching Minds: (ages 7 and up)
Family Devotions Based on the Shorter Catechism
Starr Meade
Puritan & Reformed
Six days of devotions per each catechism question. Great for elementary ages.

Shorter Catechism Activity Book: Learning the Truth through Puzzles (ages 7 and up)
Marianne Ross
Christian Focus

Truth and Grace Memory Books
Tom Ascol
These are a Reformed Baptist set of books which sets catechism questions from the Baptist Catechism as well as memory verses to be learned from 2 years old through 4th (Book 1) and 5th through 8th grade (Book 2). Great words of advice in the foreword about how to approach use of these books. I would caution you to both encourage your child to learn these, yet always put your commonsense hat when looking at what someone else sets as an appropriate agenda for your child's grade/age. Better to learn less with a soft heart than to force through everything listed for your child's age group and actually embitter them.
Available through used book stores. Can find them through amazon.com.

Devotions

Long Story Short: Ten-Minute Devotions to Draw Your Family to God (ages 4 and up)
Marty Machowski

The Building on the Rock Series (ages 4 and up)
By Joel Beeke & Diana Kleyn
Christian Focus Publishers
How God Sent a Dog to Save a Family and other Devotional Stories
How God Stopped the Pirates and other Devotional Stories
How God Used a Thunderstorm
How God Used a Snowdrift
How God Used a Drought and an Umbrella
Christian Focus

A Book for Family Reading Series (ages 4 and up)
Jim Cromarty
Evangelical Press
Multiple volumes in this series: Book 1, Book 2, Book 3, etc.

Training Hearts Teaching Minds: Family Devotions Based on the Shorter Catechism
(ages 6 and up)
Starr Meade
Puritan & Reformed
Six days of devotions per each catechism question. Great for elementary ages.

Wait till you see the butterfly and other short stories for boys and girls (ages 5 and up)
Dorreen Tamminga
Banner of Truth

God's Mighty Acts in Salvation (ages 4 and up)
God's Mighty Acts in Creation (ages 4 and up)
Starr Meade
Crossway

A Year with Your Children in the Bible: A Family Devotional Resource (ages 4 and up)
Jim Cromarty

Lord of Glory (ages 4 and up)
Jim Cromarty
A year with your children in the Bible, Jim Cromarty has here provided another ideal tool to help parents to do just that! Each day's reading covers two full pages and takes the reader through the person and life of our Savior.

Queen Victoria's Request (ages 6 and up)
Charles Spurgeon
Christian Focus

XTB Series: (for your children to use) (ages 4-7)
The Book of Beginnings
Miracles & Dreams
Comings & Goings
Travels Unraveled
Easter Unscrambled
Summer Signposts
Christmas Unpacked
Alison Mitchell
Each book includes three months worth of Bible readings and activities

Table Talk Series (family devotions that tie directly into the XTB Series) (ages 4-7)
The Book of Beginnings
Miracles & Dreams
Comings & Goings
Travels Unraveled
Easter Unscrambled
Summer Signposts
Christmas Unpacked
Alison Mitchell
Each book includes three months worth of Bible readings and activities

God's Alphabet For Life: Devotions for Young Children (ages 4 and up)
Joel Beeke

Why Easter? A Children's Devotional (ages 4 and up)
Barbara Reaoch

Get Wisdom!: 23 Lessons for Children about Living for Jesus (ages 4 and up)
Ruth Younts

A Book for Family Reading Series: (ages 4 and up)
You Sank My Boat
How to Cook a Crow
A Sad Little Dog
The Cat's Birthday
One That Didn't Get Away , Vol. 3
Take Care In The Bath, Vol. 4
Jim Cromarty

Signposts from Proverbs (ages 9 and up)
Rhiannon Weber

Young Peacemaker Set (Paperback Manual and Activity Books on CD-ROM)
(best for older elementary and up, but can be adapted to use with younger children)
Ken Sande

Church History

Polycarp of Smyrna: The Man Whose Faith Lasted (ages 5 and up)
Ignatius of Antioch: The Man Who Faced Lions
Irenaeus of Lyons: The Man Who Wrote Books
Sinclair Ferguson

Trailblazer Series: (ages 7 and up)
Charles Spurgeon: Prince of Preachers
Corrie ten Boom: Watchmaker's Daughter
George Muller: Children's Champion
Isobel Kuhn: Lights in Lisuland
Martyn Lloyd-Jones: From Wales to Westminster
George Whitefield: Voice that Woke the World
Paul Brand: The Shoes that Love Made
Joni Eareckson Tada: Swimming Against the Tide
John Stott: The Humble Leader
Patricia St. John: The Story Behind the Stories
Richard Wurmbrand: A Voice in the Dark
John Newton: A Slave Set Free
Billy Bray: Saved from the Deepest Pit
Robert Murray McCheyne: Life Is an Adventure
John Bunyan: Journey of a Pilgrim
William Wilberforce: The Freedom Fighter
John Welch: The Man Who Couldn't Be Stopped
John Calvin: After Darkness Light
C.S. Lewis: The Story Teller
Mary of Orange: At the Mercy of the Kings
Jonathan Edwards: America's Genius
Various authors
Christian Focus

Footsteps of the Past Series: (ages 6 and up)
John Bunyan
William Booth
William Wilberforce
Andrew Edwards & Fleur Thornton
Day One Publications *only through christianbook.com*

The Church History ABCs: Augustine and twenty-five other heroes of the Faith (ages 6 and up) Stephen J. Nichols and Ned Bustard
Crossway
Artistic, fun, and very information book that will intrigue children younger than you think!

God's Care and Continuance of His Church, 3 volumes (ages 6 and up)
John Vreugdenhil
only at heritagebooks.org

Christian Biographies for Young Readers Series: Athanasius, John Calvin, Augustine of Hippo
(Older elementary and up)
Simonetta Carr

Chronicles of the Church Series (ages 8-12)
Brandon and Mindy Withrow
Christian Focus Publications
A wonderful 5 volume series of church history from beginnings in Acts to modern day.

Other History (some Christian, some not)

Lightkeepers Series: (ages 8-12)
Ten Boys Series:
Ten Boys Who Made History
Ten Boys Who Made a Difference
Ten Boys Who Changed the World
Ten Boys Who Didn't Give In
Ten Boys Who Used Their Talents

Ten Girls Series: (ages 8-12)
Ten Girls Who Made History
Ten Girls Who Made a Difference
Ten Girls Who Changed the World
Ten Girls Who Didn't Give In
Ten Girls Who Used Their Talents
Irene Howat
Christian Focus

Guarding the Treasure: How God's People Preserve God's Word (older elementary and up)
Linda Finlayson

A Mighty Fortress Is Our God: Martin Luther (older elementary and up)
Jim Cromarty

Words to Die For: Verses that Shaped the Lives of 30 People Who Changed the World (ages 7+)
Lawrence Kimbrough
Broadman and Holman

Missions

Granny Han's Breakfast (age 4 and up)
Sheila Groves and Faith Mantzke

Ian and the Gigantic Leafy Obstacle (age 4 and up)
Sheila Miller

Christian Publications Series of Missionary Stories(Christian Missionary Alliance): (age 5+)
The Potato Story and Other Missionary Stories
Beautiful Feet and Other Missionary Stories
 Elynne Chudnovsky
Wonderful little stories that your children will not have heard before!
Out of print, but available.

Window on the World: When We Pray, God Works (ages 6 and up)
Daphne Spraggett with Jill Johnstone
Paternoster Press
Children's version of Operation World. Wonderful! Looks at fifty-two peoples to be reached with the gospel.

From Arapesh to Zuni: A Book of Bibleless Peoples (ages 6 and up)
Karen Lewis

Heroes of the Cross series (ages 6 and up)
Include stories about three missionaries in each volume
Out of print, but obtainable.

Stories of Faith: Inspirational Episodes from the Lives of Christians (ages 6 and up)
Ruth A. Tucker
365 little devotions, many about missionaries. Well documented sources in the back. I have used some of these and the bibliographies to write some of my Praise Factory stories. Some of the stories, however, I would choose to skip over due to theological differences.

Missionary Series: (ages 6 and up)
George Muller: Does Money Grow On Trees?
Helen Roseveare: What's In The Parcel?
John Calvin: What is the Truth?
Martin Luther: What Should I Do?
Catherine Mackenzie
Christian Focus

David Brainerd: A Love for the Lost (ages 7 and up)
Brian Cosby

Trailblazer Series: (ages 7 and up)
George Muller: Children's Champion
Isobel Kuhn: Lights in Lisuland
Hudson Taylor: An Adventure Begins
Helen Roseveare: On His Majesty's Service
Adoniram Judson: Danger on the Streets of Gold
Eric Liddell: Finish the Race
Gladys Aylward: No Mountain Too High
Paul Brand: The Shoes that Love made
Richard Wurmbrand: A Voice in the Dark
John Newton: A Slave Set Free
Isobel Kuhn: Lights in Lisuland
John G. Paton: South Sea Island Rescue
Amy Carmichael: Rescuer By Night
Mary Slessor: Servant to the Slave
Various authors
Christian Focus

Missionary Biography Series: (older elementary and up)
For the Love of India: Henry Martyn
King of the Cannibals: John Paton
The Pigtail and Chopsticks Man: Hudson Taylor
Food for Cannibals: John Paton
Jim Cromarty

Sexuality

The Wonderful Way Babies Are Made
Larry Christenson

God's Design for Sex Series:
Book 1 The Story of Me; Book 2 Before I Was Born; Book 3 What's the Big Deal? Book 4 Facing the Facts; How and When to Tell Your Kids about Sex: A Lifelong Approach to Shaping Your Child's Sexual Character
Carolyn Nystrom, Stanton L. Jones, Brenna B. Jones
Each book is designed for use with a particular age group, introducing the children to more information as they get older and develop themselves.

Why Gender Matters: What Parents and Teachers Need to Know about the Emerging Science of Sex Differences
Sax Leonard

Teens & Sex: How Should We Teach Them?
Paul David Tripp
only through ccef.org

Music and Stories behind Hymns

The Toddler's Songbook (ages 2 and up)
Ellen Banks Elwell
Crossway
Various Children's traditional, Bible and praise songs. Colorful pictures, suggested actions and a music CD.

All Things Bright and Beautiful (ages 2 and up)
Cecil Frances Alexander

Mr. Pipes Series (ages 8 and up)
Mr. Pipes and the British Hymn Makers
Mr. Pipes Comes to America
Accidental Voyage
Douglas Bond
Children love this series of books on hymns through the ages.

Teach Them the Faith (Audio CD)
Vitco, Dan & Karen Vitco

A very very very BIG GOD (Audio CD)

J is for Jesus (Audio CD)

Why Can't I See God? Go to the Ant; Guard Your Heart; Teach Me While My Heart Is Tender (Audio CDs)
Judy Rogers *judyrogers.com*

Hymns for a Kid's Heart Series: (ages 5 and up)
Volume 1, Volume 2 (various hymns) with CDs (Audio)
Christmas Carols for a Kid's Heart, Book with CD (Audio)
Passion Hymns for a Kid's Heart with CD (Audio)
Sergio Martinez, Joni Eareckson Tada and Bobbie Wolgemuth

Hide 'n' Seek Kids, Deep Down Detectives, Praise Factory Investigators Songs (Audio),
These are all the hymns, Bible verses and Big Questions used in these three curriculums, all set to music. (music downloadable from website)
amazon.com, The Praise Factory website

Sovereign Grace Kids Music: (Audio CDs)
Awesome God, To Be Like Jesus, Walking with the Wise
Wonderful music!
only sovereigngracemusic.org

Seeds Family Worship

Christianbook.com has more CDs of Bible songs than you can fit in your mini-van, even when it's cleaned out! Look there for many more titles that your family might enjoy.

Fiction and Fiction-Based History

Board Books: (ages 0-3)
All About God's Animals Series: Around the Water; Color
Janyre Tromp

Paperback and Hardback:
Fool Moon Rising (ages 3 and up)
Kristi and T. Lively Fluharty
Crossway
Wonderful allegory of biblical truth of 1 Corinthians 4:7

Adam, Adam, What Do You See? (ages 2-6)
Bill Martin, Jr. and Michael Sampson

A Children's Version of Pilgrim's Progress: Dangerous Journey (age 9 and up)
Oliver Hunkin
Excellent. Some of the pictures are a little scary, especially of Apollyon. There is a video of this book, too.

Little Pilgrim's Progress (ages 6 and up)
Helen Taylor

The Pilgrim's Progress: From This World to That Which Is to Come (elementary age and up)
C.J.Lovik

The Pilgrim's Progress in Modern English (elementary age and up)
John Bunyan, James Thomas

Treasures of the Snow, Star of Light, A Home For Virginia,Twice Freed, The Safe Place and others (elementary age and up)
Patricia St. John

The Barber Who Wanted to Pray (ages 8 and up)
King Without a Shadow
The Priest with Dirty Clothes
The Prince's Poison Cup
The Lightlings
The Donkey Who Carried a King
R.C. Sproul

Beep (ages 4-7)
Peter Jeffery

Risktakers Series: Adventure and Faith: Volume 1; Strength and Devotion: Volume 2
(ages 8 and up)
Linda Finlayson

Adventures Series: (ages 8 and up)
Great Barrier Reef Adventures
New York City Adventures
Pacific Adventures
Rainforest Adventures
Outback Adventures
African Adventures
Scottish Highland Adventures
Himalayan Adventures
Kiwi Adventures
Wild West Adventures
Rocky Mountain Adventures
Cambodian Adventures
various authors
Christian Focus

Jungle Doctor Series: (ages 8 and up)
To the Rescue
And the Whirlwind
Spots a Leopard
Stings a Scorpion
Operates
Eyes on the Jungle Doctor
Looks for Trouble
Pulls a Let
On the Hop
Meets a Lion
On Safari
Paul White
Christian Focus

Chronicles of Narnia, Boxed Set (ages 5 and up)
C. S. Lewis

Stepping Heavenward (teenage girls)
Elizabeth Prentiss

Bible Study Tools

Commentaries for Children (ages 3 and up)
Herein is Love: Genesis, Exodus, Leviticus, Numbers
Nancy Ganz

Daily Life at the Time of Jesus (ages 5 and up)
Food at the Time of the Bible: From Adam's Apple to the Last Supper
Miriam Feinberg Vamosh

People of the Bible: Life and Customs (preschool and up)
Silvia Gastaldi, Clair Musatti
Wonderful illustrations with information set in a point-at-the-picture format which is very interesting and accessible to even preschoolers. You won't want to put it down either!

Footsteps of the Past Series: (ages 7 and up)
Kings, Pharaohs and Bandits: The World of Abraham to Esther
Romans, Gladiators and Games: The Roman World of the First Christians
Brian Edwards and Clive Anderson
Day One Publications *only through christianbook.com*

International Children's Bible Field Guide: Answering Kids' Questions from Genesis to Revelation (ages 7 and up)
Lawrence O. Richards

International Children's Bible Dictionary: A Fun and Easy-to-Use Guide to the Words, People, and Places in the Bible (ages 7 and up)
Ronald F. Youngblood, F. F. Bruce, and R. K. Harrison

Bible Explorer (ages 7 and up)
Carine MacKenzie
Christian Focus

Jesus Rose From the Dead - the Evidence (ages 7 and up)
Catherine Mackenzie
Christian Focus

The Bible Story Handbook (ages 7 and up)
A Resource for Teaching 175 Stories from the Bible
John H. Walton & Kim E. Walton
Crossway

100 Fascinating Bible Facts (ages 7 and up)
Irene Howat

The Time of Jesus: Crafts to Make that Recreate Everyday Life (ages 7 and up)
Lois Rock

The Victor Journey through the Bible (ages 7 and up)
V. GIlbert Beers
David C. Cook

Children's Education Issues and Aids

A Vision for Ministry to Children and Their Parents
Bethlehem Baptist Church
Desiring God Ministries

Child-Sensitive Teaching: Helping children grow a living faith in a loving God
By Karen Henley
Standard Publishing

Christian's Ministry that Works
Group Publications
While I have GREAT hesitancies about many resources that Group puts out (from both theological and educational standpoints), I do think that they do this basics book quite well. I especially like the age-appropriate lists of different activities to use with children.

Education that Is Christian
Lois LeBar

How Children Come to Faith in Christ
By Jim Elliff
Family Life Audio Series
Tape/DVD Series
Purchase through Family Life: www.familylife-ccc.org

The Wiggle and Giggle Busy Book: 365 Fun, Physical Activities for Toddlers and Preschoolers
The Preschooler's Busy Book: 365 Creative Learning Games & Activities to Keep Your 3-6 Year Old Busy
Trish Kuffner
Fabulous resources!

The Big Book of Bible Games
Gospel Light
Fully Reproducible. Great to slot into any Bible story review or memory verse grouped by age interest

The Praise Factory Website
Lists games for preschoolers and for elementary-age children that can be used with any Bible review game or Scripture memory verse.

My Bible Dress Up Book
Carla Williams
David C. Cook
Great, simple, no-sew Bible times costumes.
out of print, but obtainable through amazon.com marketplace

Big Truths for Young Hearts: Teaching and Learning the Greatness of God
Bruce A. Ware
Crossway

Websites to Purchase Books and Curriculum

www.christianfocus.com
This company offers some curriculum and much of the best Christian children's books. They are extremely prolific, making it almost impossible to keep up with all the quality books they produce each year. Make sure to visit their website and download a catalog! Now most are available through amazon.

www.goodbook.com
Great books for use in family devotions, especially for elementary age children.

www.cvbbs.com
Cumberland Valley Bible Book Service. One of the only US carriers of Christian Focus publications...and everything at GREAT prices! Also carry Banner of Truth, Crossway, and P& R resources, as well as some from Australia that are hard to find elsewhere.

www.wtsbook.com
Westminster Theological Seminary's bookstore. Great prices! Great resources! Great selection!

www. christianbook.com
Largest, single dealer in Christian Books in the US. They will tend to have only the most "mainstream" books, such as those published by Crossway and Zondervan.

www. matthiasmedia.com
US source for Australian-based Matthias Media. Books like Who Will Be King? and Gumtree Gully (children's versions of Two Ways to Live)

www.childrendesiringgod.org
Bethlehem Baptist (John Piper) Extensive offering of curriculum and memory verse resources.

www.treasuringchristonline.com
Treasuring Christ is a new curriculum for preschool through high school that does a great job of pointing to Christ in every Bible story. Everyone has a lesson on the same Bible story at the same time, but at a different level of comprehension. This curriculum is produced by Providence Baptist Church, Raleigh, North Carolina.

www.cartpioneers.org and www.calebproject.org
Some Caleb Project Resources related to T,H,U,M,B. Great resources for telling children about the 10/40 window and the different people groups there. But, be aware that we found that we needed to re-word some of the resources because of theological differences.

www.csionline.org
Christian Schools International has two lines of curriculum, one for use in Christian schools and one more use in homeschools. We have even adapted some of this curriculum for use in our Sunday School. Good content from a reformed perspective. Lots of activities and reproducible sheets.

www.praisefactory.org
The Praise Factory curriculums and music for downloading and ordering hard copies. This resource book in pdf form (or to order hard copy) can be found there, too.

www.newgrowthpress.com
The Gospel Storybook Bible Curriculum can be found here. High quality content and presentation. For preschool through elementary.

www.TenofThose.com
Lotss of great books for kids as well as adults.

#3
Supporting
Them by
Teaching
Their Children
Biblical Truths
at
Church

#3 Supporting Parents by Teaching Their Children Biblical Truths at Church

We may have children at church only a small percentage of their week, but good teaching during this time can still have a great impact! To this end, we provide structured teaching time for 2 year old through 5th grade, with middle school and high school students attending small Bible study groups or sitting in Core Seminars with parents or others (as well as offering teaching and fellowship times in Youth Group on Fridays.)

Now let's look at two key resources in how we teach children at CHBC: our teachers and our curriculum choices.

Key Teaching Resources:

Well-Trained and Well-Supported Teachers

#4 Key Teaching Resources: Well-Trained and Supported Teachers

Teaching is a big responsibility and often a tiring one. Many teachers burn out from frustration or lack of support. We try to train our teachers so they will be well prepared. And, we try not to overtax them by asking for a commitment from them that is greater than is reasonable or spiritually good for them.

We Mentor Our Teachers

We try to mentor all new teachers, so that they see a teaching model before they start teaching themselves. This gives us a chance to observe their teaching before they teach to see if they are suited to teach. And, it allows them to try out teaching before committing to a class. As new teachers watch more experienced teachers, they can become familiarized with the curriculum and with effective teaching skills. This brings both greater continuity to the classroom and greater success among new teachers, which in turn helps our children learn.

We Model Teach for Our Teachers

At least once a year, we model-teach in each classroom. We walk the teachers through lesson preparation before class, then have them watch us teach the lesson. Afterwards, we talk about what went well and what could have gone better. This give-and-take of loving criticism fosters an atmosphere of humility and teachability as well as helps us become better teachers. As teachers (and perhaps even more importantly as fellow believers in community together), we think it is important to model soliciting, giving and receiving this kind of healthy criticism. How will we grow if we are not willing to ask others to help us see not only areas in which we do well, but also those in which we need to grow?

We Observe and Encourage Our Teachers

We try to observe teachers for their encouragement at least once a year, seeking to give helpful feedback that will make for a teaching and learning.

We Teach Classroom Management Skills As Well As Provide Teacher-friendly Curriculum

We try to carefully choose materials that will help our volunteer teachers understand what to teach and how best to teach it. We also give our teachers tips on how to manage children's behavior in ways that help everyone learn and foster respect for the teacher and for the other students.

We Have Our Teachers Teach in Teams

We form teams of teachers that partner together/switch off teaching a particular class of children. A typical team of Sunday School teachers at CHBC commits to one year of teaching. But because they are part of a team of four teachers, with only two teaching any week, they are really teaching twenty-six Sundays rather than all fifty-two Sundays of the year. This allows for teachers to teach a full year without getting burned out and provides built-in substitutes. In our other classroom settings, we have 2 to 6 teachers teaching at a time (depending on class sizes and ages of children). This also allows less experienced teachers to partner and learn from more experienced teachers, making hands-on teacher training a regular part of the classroom experience. It also creates the opportunity for teaching responsibilities within the classroom to rotate from week to week.

We Train Our Teachers

Once a year, we hold training sessions for particular groups of teachers, such as preschool teachers, or elementary school teachers. We also have coordinators who oversee the large number of volunteer teachers who teach in the Praise Factory preschool and elementary school classes. A coordinator helps train new teachers for two, non-consecutive months a year (non-consecutive so that they do not get burned out, themselves!). They also help other teachers prepare and often team teach with them these months. The encouragement, advice and model-teaching of these coordinators often makes the difference in everyone's experience in the classroom. And, often makes the difference in whether a new teacher signs up for other teaching opportunity! Coordinators like these are simply invaluable!

We Give Our Teachers Deacon Support

Each Sunday, our Deacon of Children's Ministry faithfully checks in with our Sunday School teachers and Praise Factory teachers (both preschool and elementary classes). He is on hand to find any needed supplies, extra volunteers or other help a teacher might need. He keeps an eye out for issues that would be important for the rest of the Children's Ministry team to know about, usually communicating these through a weekly e-mail. A deacon volunteers for three years. This long term commitment allows the deacon to gain quite a bit of institutional knowledge as well as becomes a familiar, reliable face to teachers and parents.

We Limit Our Teachers

Out of spiritual care for the teachers, the elders have set limits on how much any one member can spend teaching the children.

Childcare teachers: Volunteer 1 Sunday a month
Sunday School teachers: Volunteer 1 year at a time, on a team of 4 to allow for substitutes
*Praise Factory teachers: Volunteer for 2 nonconsecutive months a year (Sunday a.m. service)
*Great Commission Club: Volunteer for 2 nonconsecutive months a year (Sunday p.m. service)

*Non-consecutive months so that no volunteer will miss a worship service for more than a month.

We Are Willing to Shut Down Programs to Protect Our Teachers

Because we have only one Sunday morning service and one Sunday evening service, the elders are especially careful about how much time members spend away from regular preaching. If we have a consistent, month after month, lack of volunteers, our elders may suggest that we shut down a particular program for a time. They have decided that this action is best for the spiritual welfare of the teachers, who too many times are asked to miss yet another service just to keep a program going--to their own spiritual detriment. We want to support our parents, but not at the expense of over-taxing and under-feeding of the rest of the body. Our elders have developed an order of priority of programs, making child care for infants and toddlers during the two Sunday morning and evening services the top priority.

Children's Ministry roles
- Caregiver
- Hall Monitor
- Sunday School Teacher
- Sunday morning Teacher
- Sunday evening Teacher

We have several categories of teachers and caregivers (caregivers work in the nursery only). Each has different commitments and schedules of service and no one person does more than one thing.

1. **Caregivers** are basically nursery workers **(no curriculum)** for children age 2 and below. They serve on a rotating schedule throughout the year; they are on separate teams (one Sun AM, one Sun PM, one Wed PM) each of which **serve once every four weeks.** (Since some months have 5 Sundays/Wednesdays, we are careful not to say "once a month.") In this way caregivers only miss one service of one type once every 4 weeks.

2. **Hall Monitor:** volunteers who patrol the childcare areas and public spaces in the church to ensure the physical safety of the children. Hall Monitors may be called upon to help with child evacuation and emergency response to unauthorized persons in childcare areas. Serve no more than one Sunday a month.

3. **Sunday School Teacher**s (before the morning service) – these teachers are on a team of 6 per class; they rotate among themselves so that 2-3 of them are teaching on any given Sunday. They commit for an **entire year*** but within that year they are rotating among themselves. The consistency comes in the fact that in one year the kids will get to know 6 people and see them consistently throughout the year.

4. **Sunday morning Teachers** (during the morning service) – these teachers are also on teams; they commit to **2 non-consecutive months in a year.** This has less consistency for the kids (they will see/interact with lots more people throughout a year in these classes) but it reduces the amount of time these teachers miss the morning service. These teachers are also freed up to attend all the evening services and Core Seminar (adult Sunday school). The only classes we have during the AM service are for pre-K (3-5yrs old) and grade school (Praise Factory, K-3rd grade).

5. **Sunday evening Teachers** (during the evening service) – these have the **same team/commitment schedule as the Sunday morning teachers**, except they are teaching in the evening. (K-2nd grade is the only class we have on Sunday nights; everything else is nursery.)

By doing all of this we balance consistency for the kids with spiritual shepherding/feeding of the volunteers.

*We use "school calendar" year, which is September to August.

Key Teaching Resources:

Quality, Biblical Curriculum

Key Teaching Resources: Quality, Biblical Curriculum

Creating or Choosing Curriculum

As we develop or purchase curriculum we ask 3 groups of questions:

The first four key questions we ask:
1. **Is it sound theologically? Is it God-centered?**
2. **Is it developmentally appropriate for the children?**
3. **Does it reinforce key truths about God in different ways?**
4. **If the answer to any of these is not a whole-hearted yes, then we also ask: how hard would it be to make it these things?**

These questions are summarized by "Two Dead Men and a Diamond"

Dead Man #1: Martin Luther
Luther spoke of theology—the study of God—as not just dry, heady stuff, but how you live and how you die. Children want to learn real, solid truths about God because He created them to know Him. They want to know about the world, God and His great plans for the world and their lives. Teaching biblical truth is how they can know these things.

Dead Man #2: John Bunyan
Bunyan spoke of reaching people through the gates to their heart. We want to use every gate we can to reach the children. The eye gate, the ear gate, the hand gate, the feet gate, even the stomach gate. The more gates used, the better the chance for the learning time to be enjoyable, understandable and memorable.

A Diamond
The great Puritan preachers meditated upon a single truth from many different facets, seeking to expand their knowledge of God and the implications and applications of this knowledge to their lives. We strive to lead children in thinking upon God in ways that might expand their own understanding of Him, and help them see implications and applications of this knowledge to their lives. We find that curriculum which reinforces the same biblical truths in different ways and at different levels helps to achieve this goal.

The next question we ask is:
Are the response activities "conduits of truth" or are they "time fillers"?

Conduits of Truth
There are many curriculum on the market which seek to teach Biblical truths to children in a way that is understandable, enjoyable and memorable. However, we have found, especially in the response activity area, that you need to look closely to see if the activities help the children retain the key, biblical truths of the lesson we most want them to remember.

So, when we create or look at a curriculum, we are not only looking for enjoyable, age-appropriate activities, but at whether these activities are filled with truth or whether they just fill the time. Those

the enjoyable-ness of the activity to fill the children with the important truths of your lesson.

For example, if the lesson was on Noah's Ark and the children were asked to pair up and mimic animals entering the ark, the children may have a great time, but only go home making elephant noises. This game would not be a conduit of truth. But, if the children were asked to pair up and mimic animals entering the ark, but asked to freeze each time you blow a whistle, then you ask them a question related to the day's story for them to answer, then you have made the same game into a conduit of truth. You are using the enjoyable-ness of the activity to provide an opportunity to reinforce the biblical truths you want them to understand and remember.

Then we ask:
1. **How well does it fit us?**
2. **Does it include resources for parents to use with their children?**
3. **Is it cost-effective? Re-usable?**

1. How well does it fit us?
    a. the attendance patterns of our children
    b. the staffing and abilities of our teachers

    Particularly:
- It is easy to follow? How much teaching experience is needed to teach this curriculum well?
- How much preparation is involved?
- What kind of preparation is involved? (choosing and shaping activities or creating activties?
- Does the curriculum build upon itself, requiring consistent attendance of same kids and the same teacher/s?
- Or, can the lessons stand alone, being effective with kids who have patchy attendance, with visitors, and/or a rotation of teachers?

2. Does it include resources for parents to use with their children (both those whose children attend a class at church and those whose children don't attend the church class but they want to teach these truths at home)? This is important, since class time with the children is very small compared with the teaching time and opportunities parents have with their children. If parents have a way to reinforce the truths taught in the classroom, there is a much higher chance they will be understood and remembered.

3. Is it cost effective? Re-usable? Does the curriculum rely on single-use materials or can they be reproduced and used again with another group of children without additional expense?

The final question we ask is:
   1. **Does it fit into the teaching emphases set out by our elders?**

Our elders have given Children's Ministry four teaching emphasis:

1. Chronological study of the Bible (OT/NT overviews)
2. Prepare the children to gather together with the church body
3. God's One Big Plan of Redemption/Missions
4. Biblical Theology

It can be amazing curriculum, but if it does not fit with what they want us to teach the children, then we will have to pass on it. We trust our elders' God-given vision for our children!

So, what do we use right now at CHBC to fulfill these four teaching emphases? Let's take a look!

Resources We Have Used, Are Using Or Are Considering Using at CHBC (by teaching emphasis)

#1 Chronological Study of the Bible

Who: K-6th grade
When: Sunday School hour

Resource #1 Treasuring Christ
Developed by Providence Baptist Church, Raleigh, North Carolina, this has become our favorite Sunday School resource.

Pros
- Offered online for easy download. Deep discounts for church plants and overseas churches.
- There is curriculum for preschool through high school that covers the same concept for all ages, each week. This makes review discussion at home easier for the parents.
- There is a teacher devotional for every lesson that our teachers have found to be extremely enriching to their own heart as they prepare to teach the children.
- Great, age-appropriate resources.

Cons
- Only that sometimes the crafts for the kindergarten and first grade assume more writing ability than they have.

Resource #2 CSI: Christian Schools International
A reformed publishing house out of Grand Rapids, MI. These are materials designed for use in Christian schools.

Pros
- They are well-organized, use reproducible masters instead of workbooks, and offer a wide range of teaching suggestions.
- There is curriculum for K through 8th grade that builds upon what was taught in the previous year.
- These materials include textbooks which can be purchased for use with children at home for use in devotionals or in a home school setting.
- Theologically sound, interesting details

Cons
- The activities include spelling lists and other "school-ish" activities which must be weeded through.
- Even some of the more straightforward activities need to be modified to be less school-ish.
- Pricey, if you buy all the textbooks for the kids, but at least you only purchase them once.
- Geared for teachers not for volunteers. Best for teachers who can figure out what to use and what not to use; or for a church with someone who can adapt the curriculum for them.

Resource #3: Children Desiring God
Resources developed by Bethlehem Baptist, Minneapolis, MN. These are materials designed for use in churches with a steady attendance of teachers and students. Based upon 40 week teaching schedule.

Pros
- They are well-organized, God-centered, thoroughly biblical.
- There are a large number of resources available for each age group, preschool through high school. They offer Sunday School, mid-week, and inter-generational curriculum.
- More scripted. Geared for volunteers.
- Great for churches with a steady attendance of teachers and students (because the curriculum builds upon itself each lesson).
- Can order resources and be ready to go. Now most available for download at greatly reduced prices.
- Great memory program (Fighter verses) for the whole church. Have just put their children's fighter verses to music!
- Offer curriculum in ESV and NIV.
- Customer support and annual children's ministry conference that can be very helpful.

Cons
- Curriculum costs can add up quickly, especially if you buy the (one-use) workbooks. Now, though, you can download and print out yourself quite a few resources and save yourself a lot of money.
- Not as effective if you switch teachers or have patchy student attendance since the curriculum builds upon what was previously taught.
- Only 40 weeks of lessons leaves a 12 week gap for those who have a 52 week Sunday School program. (We add a monthly review session to fill in this gap).
- While some of the curriculums provide lots of activities, some do not provide many activities besides the workbooks. Teachers—or someone—may need to supplement the content with more active, hands-on, reinforcement activities. (We have done this using the Praise Factory games which can be used with any Bible story or Bible verse. We simply print them all out and put them in a binder for our teachers to use as needed to supplement the lesson.) **However, we have found that they are updating many of the curriculums, now offering more activities.**

Other Resources We Are Looking at:
God's Story
Developed and used by many Sovereign Grace churches.
from Covenant Fellowship Church
http://www.covfel.org/pages/page.asp?page_id=47115

#2 Preparation to Gather with the Church Body

Who: K-6th grade
When: Sunday School hour

Resources used:

Elementary: Church service, Praise Factory Investigators story, and watch for signs

- K-4th grade are in the service up to the sermon (prayers, singing and Scripture readings). Praise Factory only takes place during the sermon time.

- Help expand attention span in Praise Factory Investigators by longer stories. Don't want to exasperate them or bore them, but do want to slightly challenge their ability to focus.

- In Praise Factory Investigators, we watch for signs of developmental readiness for staying in church and listening to the sermon with their parents. We talk with parents when we see these signs and encourage them to consider keeping their children in the service for the sermon time—even though their child may still be of eligible age for Praise Factory Investigators. Often parents begin this process by alternating keeping their children with them to listen to the sermon and sending them to Praise Factory Investigators.

- Incorporate K-4th in singing time in Sunday evening service. At times, keep the 3rd and 4th graders in for rest of the Sunday evening service.

- Incorporate K-4th in the Adult Wednesday Night Bible Study.

5th-6th grade: Church bulletin and Church service, sermon review

- During Sunday school, they discuss the church bulletin and note key content before attending the service with their parents.

- From 5th grade on, the children are in all of the services. Many of these children take notes during the sermon, with parents' help.

- Parents are encouraged to take time for sermon review at home with their children, after the service, helping them to understand and apply what they've heard at church.

#3 God's One Big Plan of Redemption/Missions

Who: K-2nd (sometimes through 4th, depending upon volunteer numbers)
When: Sunday evening Service after the singing time.

Resources used: Great Commission Club (in-house curriculum)
In-house, quarter-based resources, each with a different focus on a part of God's One Big Plan of Redemption and Missions (The role of God's people in God's One Big Plan)

Quarter 1: Too Small a Thing: (Isaiah 49:6)
"It is too small a thing for you to be my servant to restore the tribes of Jacob and bring back those of Israel I have kept. I will also make you a light for the Gentiles, that you may bring my salvation to the ends of the earth." NIV, 1984

The children learn about different people groups, using Windows on the World and other resources. They learn T,H,U,M,B and people groups around the world and what is being done to reach them with the gospel (T = Tribal, H=Hindu, U=Unreligious, M=Muslim, B=Buddhist. This is an acronym developed by The Caleb Project. We like the acronym, but have hesitancies about elements of the curriculum they offer. So, we have been developing our own instead.)

Quarter 2: Heroes of the Faith:
Centers around different themes, learning about men and women who have gone out to tell others about Jesus through the ages.

*   Blessed are the Persecuted: God's people who have suffered for the gospel
*   Salt and Light (Everyday people)
*   Preachers and Spreaders of the Word (preachers and evangelists)
*   From Every Tribe and Nation

Quarter 3: Those Who Have Gone Out from Us
Focus on one missionary we support for a whole quarter, culminating in a reproduction of that particular place for the children and others in the church to come and experience. This is a very time intensive but incredibly memorable experience for the children. Perhaps the most memorable program we do with the children…and hugely encouraging to the missionary chosen. We've done one couple in Central Asia and one couple in Munich, Germany.
OR,
Have thirteen of our supported workers who are preparing to go, are on the mission field or have come back share with the children.

Quarter 4: Gospel/Mission related Stories, using puppets
Dangerous Journey/Pilgrim's Progress (John Bunyan), The Chronicles of Narnia (C.S. Lewis), Star of Light (Patricia St. John), Gumtree Gully and Who Will Be King? (Matthias Media) and other stories. Perform for the preschoolers.

Unfortunately, these curriculums are not yet available for download.

#4 Biblical Theology

Who: 2 year olds through 4th grade
When: 2 year olds: a portion of the Sunday School hour
**   3- pre K 5 year olds: All of Sunday School and church service**
**   *K-3rd grade: Sermon portion of the church service**

Resources used: The Praise Factory family of curriculum:

2's and 3's: Hide 'n' Seek Kids
4's–pre K 5's: Deep Down Detectives
K-3rd grade: Praise Factory Investigators

The Praise Factory family of curriculum is our own, in-house curriculum and a very important part of what we teach our children here at CHBC. It is available for download at. Since it is both so important to children's ministry here at CHBC and you may find it a useful resource, we will look at them in-depth.

Since these three curriculums are connected together, it is helpful to consider them together as a whole before looking at each one in more depth. A list of Pros and Cons of Praise Factory curriculum follows these sections.

*Praise Factory Investigators is actually appropriate for K-5th grade. We use it with our K-3rd grade, but our 4th and 5th graders are in the church service. This is partly because we do not have enough volunteers or space to offer it to our 4th and 5th graders. We also feel that by 4th and 5th grade, most children are able to sit and glean from the sermon.

Great resources for understanding the Praise Factory family of curriculum:
The Praise Factory Curriculum Tour (Basic and Extended Versions)
A helpful and colorful overview of Praise Factory family of curriculum, philosophy, FAQ's and Scope & Sequences. available through amazon.com.

The Praise Factory Family of Curriculum

Website Resources

www.praisefactory.org

THE PRAISE FACTORY
classic.praisefactory.org

For those who started using Praise Factory years ago and are happy to keep using this NIV-only, "beta" version of the original 12 biblical themes.

THE PRAISE FACTORY
praisefactory.org

The new version of the Praise Factory website. This updated and expanded version of the original curriculum includes NIV and ESV versions of the curriculum, as well as 16 rather than 12 biblical themes. These resources are also available as hard copies through amazon.com.

CURRICULUM DOWNLOADS	PARENTS CORNER	MUSIC	TIPS, TRAINING, +OTHER CHILDREN MINISTRY RESOURCES

Full Curriculum Downloads Just like you will get if you get hard copies on Amazon.	**Bits + Pieces Downloads** The resources split up so you can choose just what you want to use.	**Resources for Parents from Each Curriculum** Stories, music take home sheets	**Music Resources from Each Curriculum** Download or listen online	**Curriculum Start-Up Help + Much More** slideshows and resource downloads

Hard Copy Resources

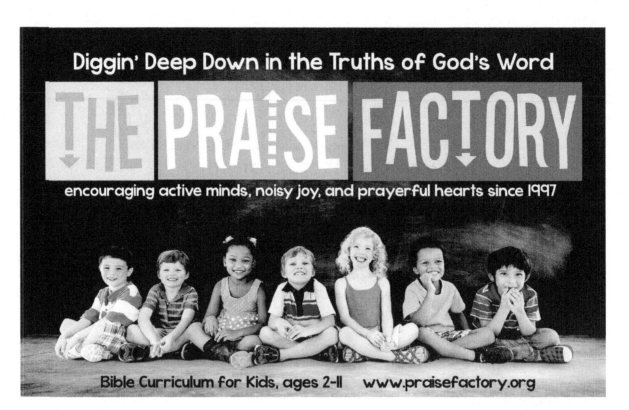

Hide 'n' Seek Kids

Deep Down Detectives

Praise Factory Investigators

3 CURRICULUMS using the same **16** BIBLICAL THEMES to reach EVERY age with the same truths

THEME 1 How God Reveals Himself

THEME 2 God's Word, the Bible

THEME 3 The Gospel, God's Good News

THEME 4 What God Is Like

THEME 5 God, the Good Creator

THEME 6 God, the Just and Merciful (The Fall)

THEME 7 God's Good Laws

THEME 8 God's Love for His People

THEME 9 Jesus, God with Us

THEME 10 God, the Holy Spirit

THEME 11 The God Who Saves

THEME 12 How God's People Live

THEME 13 God's Sustaining Grace

THEME 14 Prayer: Talking to God

THEME 15 The Church: God's People Gather Together

THEME 16 Jesus, The King Returns

The curriculum for each theme forms a unit.
Use the units in any order. Use one; use all. Mix and match.

The Kids DIG DEEPER into the **16** BIBLICAL THEMES with each CURRICULUM

Hide 'n' Seek Kids
16 Themes taught as 16 Bible Truths

for your youngest children

designed for ages 2-3, often used with ages 2-5

Deep Down Detectives
16 Themes taught as 70 Bible Truths

for school starters

designed for ages 4-6, often used with ages 3-7, and even adults!

Praise Factory Investigators
16 Themes taught as 104 Bible Truths

for primary school kids

designed for ages K5-11 year olds, often used with ages pre-K5-12 year olds, and even adults!

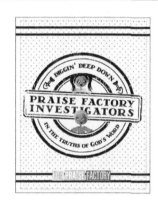

These are ACTIVE curriculums!
Music, crafts, games, and many other activities
are harnessed as "Conduits of Truth"
to help CEMENT biblical truths into hearts and minds.

———

Scripted lesson plans make it easy for teachers to teach.
Take-home sheets make it easy for parents to review at home.

FREE DOWNLOADS   THE PRAISE FACTORY
praisefactory.org   Available at    **HARD COPIES**

THE PRAISE FACTORY
Conduits of Truth

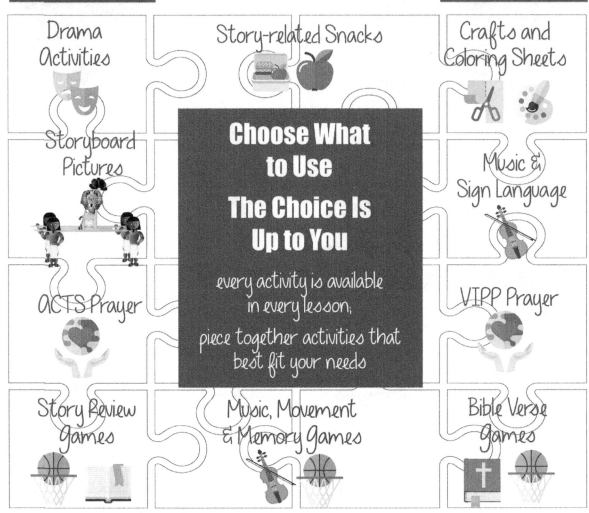

Drama Activities

Story-related Snacks

Crafts and Coloring Sheets

Storyboard Pictures

Music & Sign Language

Choose What to Use

The Choice Is Up to You

every activity is available in every lesson;

piece together activities that best fit your needs

ACTS Prayer

VIPP Prayer

Story Review Games

Music, Movement & Memory Games

Bible Verse Games

Discussion Questions
(and Answers) to make every activity
as truth-rich as it is fun

**Take Home Sheets &
Complete Resources Online**
to keep learning more at home

Ein feste Burg ist Unser Gott

Martin Luther

"theology is not just
dry, heady stuff,
but how you live and die"

2 Dead Man
and a Diamond

"look at truth from many angles" -- the Puritans

JOHN BUNYAN

"use the body
as gates
to the heart"

More about Music

  Each of the 16 Themes & all of the Bible verses are set to music.

 Song games are included that can enhance learning even further.

 Praise Factory Investigators also includes sign language and hymns for each Bible Truth.

More about Prayer Time

A The ACTS prayer not only includes the children's personal prayer requests, but also springboards off of each Bible Truth.

C It broadens their understand of:

A: Who God is (**Adoration**);

C: How we have sinned against Him (**Confession**);

T T: What He has done for us through Jesus (**Thanksgiving**); and,

S: How we need God's help to live (**Supplication**).

S

VIPP stands for "Very Important Prayer Person". The children take time to learn and pray for others in their church or overseas. Coloring sheets and games VIPP are used to introduced the VIPP before praying for them.

More about Games

Each curriculum comes with three sets **3** of simple games that help children review the Bible Truth, the Bible Verse or the Bible Story.

 Assemble each set of games and store them. Use them over and over throughout the curriculum.

Discussion questions (with answers) from the curriculum are used with each game.

The fun of the games makes review of important Bible truths enjoyable and memorable.

More about Crafts and Coloring Sheets

 Every session offers AT LEAST one craft/coloring sheet.

 All crafts include meaningful truth.

 Use the provided discussion questions to add even more learning depth to craft time.

More about Storyboard Pictures

 Available for all Hide' 'n' Seek Kids & Deep Down Detectives Bible stories.

Used to tell story and in playing Bible Story Games.

 Cut out, laminate and go! Ready to re-use as you repeat the curriculum.

Available in **2 SIZES** for smaller or larger storyboards.

More about Drama Activities

Every session of Praise Factory Investigators includes **TWO** drama activities--one for younger children, one for older children. There is a simple script for the teacher to read as the children act out the main elements of the story.

This activity is particularly good for sharing with parents or other classes of children at the end of your session.

More about Story-related Snacks

Every session of Praise Factory Investigators includes a story-related snack that is a great discussion starter after story time.

Hide 'n' Seek Kids

designed for ages 2-3,
often used with ages 2-5

for your youngest children

The Praise Factory **16** BIBLICAL THEMES **presented in** **16** UNITS

THEME 1 How God Reveals Himself

THEME 2 God's Word, the Bible

THEME 3 The Gospel, God's Good News

THEME 4 What God Is Like

THEME 5 God, the Good Creator

THEME 6 God, the Just and Merciful (The Fall)

THEME 7 God's Good Laws

THEME 8 God's Love for His People

THEME 9 Jesus, God with Us

THEME 10 God, the Holy Spirit

THEME 11 The God Who Saves

THEME 12 How God's People Live

THEME 13 God's Sustaining Grace

THEME 14 Prayer: Talking to God

THEME 15 The Church: God's People Gather Together

THEME 16 Jesus, The King Returns

Each **Biblical Theme** *is presented as* **1 Bible Truth** *in a* **5 week unit**

1 Bible Truth per Biblical Theme Unit   *16 Bible Truths/80 weeks of curriculum in all*
one Bible story for each Bible Truth

Scripted lesson plans make it easy for teachers to teach.
Take-home sheets make it easy for parents to review at home.

Music, crafts, games, flannelgraph pictures
and other activities
are harnessed as "conduits of truth"
to help CEMENT biblical truths into hearts and minds.

THE PRAISE FACTORY

praisefactory.org

FREE DOWNLOADS

USE UNITS IN ANY ORDER
Use 1 or Use all
Mix and Match

Available at
amazon

HARD COPIES

Deep Down Detectives
designed for ages 4-6,
often used with ages 3-7... and even adults!

for school starters

The Praise Factory **16** BIBLICAL THEMES presented in **16** UNITS

| THEME 1 How God Reveals Himself | THEME 2 God's Word, the Bible | THEME 3 The Gospel, God's Good News | THEME 4 What God Is Like | THEME 5 God, the Good Creator | THEME 6 God, the Just and Merciful (The Fall) | THEME 7 God's Good Laws | THEME 8 God's Love for His People |
| THEME 9 Jesus, God with Us | THEME 10 God, the Holy Spirit | THEME 11 The God Who Saves | THEME 12 How God's People Live | THEME 13 God's Sustaining Grace | THEME 14 Prayer: Talking to God | THEME 15 The Church: God's People Gather Together | THEME 16 Jesus, The King Returns |

Each **Biblical Theme** is presented as **a series of Bible Truths** with **3 weeks per Bible Truth**

2-8 Bible Truths per Biblical Theme Unit   *70 Bible Truths/210 weeks of curriculum in all*
one Bible story for each Bible Truth

Scripted lesson plans make it easy for teachers to teach.
Take-home sheets make it easy for parents to review at home.

Music, crafts, games, flannelgraph pictures
and other activities
are harnessed as "conduits of truth"
to help CEMENT biblical truths into hearts and minds.

praisefactory.org

FREE DOWNLOADS

USE UNITS IN ANY ORDER
Use 1 or Use all
Mix and Match

Available at
amazon

HARD COPIES

171

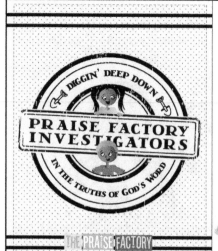

Praise Factory Investigators

designed for ages K5-11 year olds
often used with ages pre K5-12 year olds...
and even adults!

for primary school kids

The Praise Factory **16** BIBLICAL THEMES presented in **16** UNITS

THEME 1 How God Reveals Himself

THEME 2 God's Word, the Bible

THEME 3 The Gospel, God's Good News

THEME 4 What God Is Like

THEME 5 God, the Good Creator

THEME 6 God, the Just and Merciful (The Fall)

THEME 7 God's Good Laws

THEME 8 God's Love for His People

THEME 9 Jesus, God with Us

THEME 10 God, the Holy Spirit

THEME 11 The God Who Saves

THEME 12 How God's People Live

THEME 13 God's Sustaining Grace

THEME 14 Prayer: Talking to God

THEME 15 The Church: God's People Gather Together

THEME 16 Jesus, The King Returns

Each **Biblical Theme** is presented as **a series of Bible Truths** with **3 weeks per Bible Truth**

3-14 Bible Truths per Biblical Theme Unit   *104 Bible Truths/312 weeks of curriculum in all*
Old Testament, New Testament and Church History /Missions story for each Bible Truth

Scripted lesson plans make it easy for teachers to teach.
Take-home sheets make it easy for parents to review at home.

Music, crafts, games, drama, story-related snacks
and other activities
are harnessed as "conduits of truth"
to help CEMENT biblical truths into hearts and minds.

THE PRAISE FACTORY

praisefactory.org

FREE DOWNLOADS

USE UNITS IN ANY ORDER
Use 1 or Use all
Mix and Match

HARD COPIES

Overview of the Praise Factory Curriculum

10 Key Facts about the 3 Praise Factory Curriculums

1. SAME BIBLICAL THEMES	The Praise Factory is a family of three, inter-related curriculums: • Hide 'n' Seek Kids (focus group: ages 2-4; adaptable range: ages 2-pre-K 5's) • Deep Down Detectives (focus group: ages 4--6's; adaptable range: ages 3-2nd grade) • PFI: (focus group: grades K-5th grade; adaptable range: pre-K 5's-6th grade) Each curriculum teaches the same biblical themes, but are presented in greater depth as the children grow and develop. Together, they work like an expanding spiral of truth that returns to reinforce the same truths with each curriculum, yet leading the children to deeper understanding with each step up.
2. SIXTEEN UNITS, SIXTEEN BIG QUESTIONS	All three curriculums have 16 units. The theme of each unit is presented as a Big Question (and Answer) about God and His Truth, as revealed in the Bible.
3. DIFFERENT AMOUNTS OF DEPTH	While all three curriculums use the same units and biblical themes, each offers a different amount of depth to suit the very different developmental needs of preschoolers and elementary school age children. Hide 'n' Seek Kids presents the 16 themes as: • 16 Bible Truths, • each with 1 Bible story Deep Down Detectives provides more depth by presenting the 16 themes as: • 16 units made up of • 70 Bible truths, • each with 1 Bible story PFI provides the most depth by presenting the 16 themes as: • 16 units made up of • 104 Bible truths, • each with 3 stories, an Old Testament, New Testament and Story of the Saints (church history or missions story).

4. SEEKING MASTERY, NOT JUST EXPOSURE TO CONCEPTS	The Praise Factory curriculums seek not just to **INTRODUCE** children to key, biblical concepts, but to present them in such as a way as to help them **REMEMBER** the concepts.
	
	Ideas are reinforced **WITHIN** each lesson by use of activities that reinforce.
	
	Ideas are reinforced **OVER A NUMBER** of lessons by repetition.
	
	In Hide 'n' Seek Kids,
	   • 5 lessons of curriculum are included
	   • for each of the 16 Bible themes,
	   • the same Bible story used for all 5 lessons. (i.e., 16 stories in all)
	
	Yes, that's right... the same truth and Bible story for 5 lessons, but with different reinforcement activities. Instead of getting bored, these little 2 and 3 year olds love the opportunity to hear the same story again. How many times do children this age bring you the same book to read over again? This is applying this same approach to the classroom. You don't have to do all five lessons, but we find that it takes this many for the truth to stick with these little ones.
	
	In Deep Down Detectives,
	
	   • 3 lessons of curriculum are included
	   • for each of the 70 truths
	   • that make up the 16 Bible themes,
	   • the same Bible story used for all 3 lessons. (i.e., 70 stories in all)
	
	That's three lessons on the same truth and using the same Bible story. Again, the curriculum provides different reinforcement activities each lesson to provide variety. These children are older and need less repetition to remember their Bible truths. Here at CHBC, we use two or three of the lessons with our 4 and 5 year olds. This is our target group for this curriculum and we have built it to provide the appropriate amount of repetition for them. If using the curriculum with older, K-5, 6 and 7 year olds, (which have also done sometimes), you would use only one or maybe two of the lessons per Bible truth. Again, the curriculum is written so you can do as few or as many of the three lessons and you want.
	
	In PFI,
	
	   • 3 lessons of curriculum,
	   • each with a different story (an Old Testament, New Testament and Story of the Saints--church history or missions story) are included
	   • for each of the 104 truths,
	   • that make up the 16 Bible themes. (i.e., 312 stories in all)
	
	There are three lessons which all reinforce the same Bible truth, but present a different story each lesson that reflects it. This provides the repetition that elementary age children, but also their readiness for something new with each lesson.

5. CONDUITS OF TRUTH: IMPORTANT REINFORCEMENT THROUGH ENJOYABLE ACTIVITIES	A conduit of truth activity is one that uses the enjoyable-ness of the activity to fill the children with the important truths of your lesson. There are a wide variety of activities included with each lesson, including a craft, multiple games, songs, sheet music and audio, snacks (only PFI) and drama activities (only PFI). All of these are designed to be conduits of truth to make the most of your time with the children. You can use them all or pick just a few. The curriculum is very flexible. The large number of activities available with every lesson makes the Praise Factory curriculums a good choice even for Vacation Bible School.
6. DOWNLOADS OR HARD COPIES	Everything is available for download at the Praise Factory website or you can order hard copies.
7. TONS OF MUSIC	Every Big Question and all the Bible verses are set to music. These songs are also available for download. What makes this music different it that it is directly related to each lesson. Your kids are listening to what you are teaching in class and through the power of music, are far more likely to retain it.
8. NIV 1984 AND ESV VERSIONS	The curriculum is currently available in • NIV 1984 (the Bible version used for the 1st edition of the curriculum) and • a (largely) ESV version • The only difference between the two versions (besides the translation used, of course) is that ALL of the songs for the ESV version were recorded in studio. The older, NIV 1984 Bible verse songs were done in our church worship hall in less professional quality. And in case you're wondering...The reason the ESV version isn't exclusively ESV is that sometimes I felt the translation of particular verses was too confusing for the children. In those cases, I chose the HCSB (Holman Christian Standard Bible) and in a last resort, kept the original NIV 1984 text.
9. A WORK IN PROGRESS	All of Hide 'n' Seek Kids and Deep Down Detectives and about 50% of PFI is available at this point. (PFI units 1,4,5,6,7,8,10,11 and 12. This is three years of curriculum.) More will come available as it is completed.
10. SAMPLES AND DOWNLOADS	For more information, download the samples below or go straight to download the full curriculum.

Some What's and Why's: A Little Philosophy

WHAT: Systematic Theology

All three curriculums teach sixteen, theological themes, introduced as sixteen "Big Questions and Answers"-- one for each theological theme.

WHY: to provide a broad understanding of biblical truth

God created us to know Him. Children, like the rest of us, long to understand about who God is, His plans for this world, our lives, and the wonderful things of the world to come. Systematic theology is simply biblical truth organized into helpful themes that take into consideration the whole counsel of Scripture, not just a verse here or there. It is a great way to help them (and us!) learn what God has revealed about these important topics.

WHAT: Surprising Amounts of Repetition

Most curriculums take the take the one-new-concept-every-lesson approach, but the Praise Factory curriculums repeat truths and even Bible stories for multiple lessons. Hide 'n' Seek Kids--for the youngest children-- provides five lessons on the same Bible truth, Bible verse and Bible story. Deep Down Detectives --for older preschoolers and early elementary--provides three lessons on the same Bible truth, verse and story. PFI--for elementary age children-- provides three lessons on the same Bible truth and verse, though it uses a different story for each of the three lessons.

WHY: to promote understanding and memory of biblical truth

While it might sound boring to revisit the same Bible truth, verse and story, we have found that repetition allows children to actually understand and remember the truths we are teaching them. The extensive number of activities offered with each lesson provides the variety needed to keep the learning fresh over multiple lessons.

WHAT: Rich Reinforcement through Conduit of Truth Activities

A conduit of truth activity is one that uses the enjoyable-ness of the activity to fill the children with the important truths of your lesson.

WHY: to make class time activities as rich in biblical truth as they are fun

There are many ways to help children enjoy their time in class, but not all activities reinforce what we most want the children to understand and remember. Choosing and using activities that are conduits of truth help achieve this very important goal. All the activities used in the Praise Factory curriculums--crafts, games, music, even snacks-- have been designed to be conduits of truth that will reinforce the important concepts of each lesson, not just fill class time.

WHAT: The Same Theological Themes, But Different Depth within Each Curriculum

While all three of the curriculums cover all sixteen Big Questions and Answers Theology Themes, they vary in the amount of time and depth they spend on each one.

- **Hide 'n' Seek Kids** covers the 16 theological themes simply as sixteen, single-concept truths. (16 Bible truths presented, 16 Bible stories presented--1 per Bible truth, 5 reinforcing lessons per Bible truth.)

- **Deep Down Detectives** covers the same 16 theological themes but now as units with multiple Bible truth (sub-concepts), that expand and build upon the Big Question basics the children learned in Hide 'n' Seek Kids. (70 Bible truths, 70 Bible stories presented--1 per Bible truth. 3 reinforcing lessons per Bible truth.)

- **PFI** covers the same 16 theological themes also as units, but now in even greater depth. (104 Bible Truths, with three stories for each: one Old Testament, one New Testament and one Missionary/Church history story for each.

WHY: to take advantage of the increasing capacity children have to grasp biblical truth as they grow

While it certainly would make for easier shop-keeping to have everyone spend the same amount of time on each Big Question, Praise Factory has opted to focus on maximizing what children of different ages can learn, and how much reinforcement they need to master what they are learning. We call this approach a Spiral of Truth, that returns to reinforce the same truths while also expanding ever-more broadly with each circuit.

The next two pages provide an overview of the 16 Big Questions and their theological theme; as well as, a comparison chart of the three curriculums.

	PRAISE FACTORY UNIT	THEOLOGICAL THEME
1	Unit 1: The God Who Reveals Himself Big Question: How Can I Know What God Is Like? He Shows Me What He's Like!	Revelation
2	Unit 2: God's Wonderful Word, the Bible Big Question: What's So Special about the Bible? It Alone Is God's Word!	The Bible
3	Unit 3: The Good News of God, the Gospel Big Question: What Is the Gospel? Salvation through Faith in Christ!	The Gospel
4	Unit 4: The God Like None Other Big Question: Can Anybody Tell Me What the LORD Is Like? He's Not Like Anyone Else!	The Attributes of God
5	Unit 5: God, the Good Creator Big Question: Can You Tell Me What God Made? God Made All Things Good!	Creation
6	Unit 6: God, the Just and Merciful Big Question: How Did Bad Things Come to God's Good World? Bad Things Came through Sin!	The Fall
7	Unit 7: The Law-Giving God Big Question: What Are God's Laws Like? God's Laws Are Perfect!	God's Laws
8	Unit 8: The God Who Loves Big Question: What Is God's Love for His People Like? It's More than They Could Ever Deserve!	God's Enduring Love for His People
9	Unit 9: Jesus Christ, Immanuel, God with Us Big Question: What Did Jesus Come to Do? Jesus Came to Bring Us to God!	Jesus, the Son of God
10	Unit 10: The Holy Spirit: The Indwelling God Big Question: What Does the Holy Spirit Do in God's People? He Changes Their Heart!	The Holy Spirit
11	Unit 11: The God Who Saves Big Question: How Can We Be Saved? It's God's Free Gift!	Salvation
12	Unit 12: God's People Live for Him Big Question: How Should God's People Live? They Should Live Like Jesus!	Discipleship
13	Unit 13: The Sustaining God Big Question: Why Do God's People Keep Believing in Him? It is God's Sustaining Grace!	Perseverance of the Saints
14	Unit 14: The God Who Delights in Our Prayers Big Question: How Does God Want Us to Pray? Every Night and Day!	Prayer
15	Unit 15: God's People Gather Together Big Question: Why Do God's People Go to Church? To Worship God and Love One Another!	The Church
16	Unit 16: Jesus, the Returning King Big Question: What Will Happen When Jesus Comes Back? God Will Make Everything New!	The Return of Christ

HIDE 'N' SEEK KIDS	DEEP DOWN DETECTIVES	PFI
Focus group: 2-3 year olds Adaptable use: 2-pre-K 5's	Focus group: 4-6 year olds Adaptable use: 3's -2nd grade	Focus group: K-5th grade Adaptable use: pre-K 5's to 6th grade
16 Big Questions/16 Bible truths	16 Big Questions/70 Bible truths	16 Big Questions/104 Bible truths
taught as 16 units consisting of a single truth per unit	taught as 16 units, consisting of 2-8 Bible truths per unit	taught as 16 units, consisting of 3-14 Bible truths per unit
1 Bible story per unit	1 Bible story per Bible truth	1 Old Testament story 1 New Testament story 1 Church History/Missions story per Bible truth
1 Bible verse per unit	1 Bible verse per Bible truth	1 Bible verse per Bible truth
5 lessons per unit same story, all 5 lessons can use 1-5 of the lessons	*3 lessons for each Bible truth same story, all 3 lessons can use 1-3 of the lessons	3 lessons for each Bible truth different story each of the 3 lessons can use 1-3 of the lessons (but will lose stories if you do)
16+ months of curriculum	4+ years of curriculum	6 years of curriculum
	*If desired, you can start out each of the 16 units of Deep Down Detectives with one session (or more) from Hide 'n' Seek Kids curriculum. This creates a nice introduction to the over-arching theme for each unit. It would also add 16 or more sessions to the curriculum.	

The following pages are overviews of each of the
three curriculum in the Praise Factory family of curriclum.

Learn a lot more about the Praise Factory family of curriculum in
From the Ground Up:
Getting Started in Children's Ministry
and with the Praise Factory Family of Curriculum.

Found at praisefactory.org and on Amazon.

Hide 'n' Seek Kids Curriculum Overview Flyer

This (and the Praise Factory Tour: Extended Version book) is great to give to church leaders or other prospective teachers who want to know more.

Hide 'n' Seek Kids Session Overview

Session Format: Circle Times, Free Play and Your Choice of Activities

Each session is structured around Circle Time and Free Play Time. Circle Times are used to introduce and review the concept, Bible verse, Bible story, and the ACTS prayer. (A prayer including **A**doration, **C**onfession, **T**hanksgiving, and **S**upplication related to the Bible truth they are learning.) Free play is not only enjoyable, but helps to replenish attention spans and prepare the children for more group listening later in the session. However, every session includes response activities that you may choose to use during free play time to add as much reinforcement as best suits your children. Each Hide 'n Seek Kids session follows the same four-part format, as described here:

PART 1: Getting Started

A time to welcome the children to the class, enjoy free play, music, and/or play a Bible verse game.

PART 2: Opening Circle Time

The children are gathered together for their primary teaching time. The Big Question (and related songs) are introduced. A listtening assignment* is given; the Bible story told; then, the listening assignment answered at the end of story time.

PART 3: Free Play/Activity Time

The children participate in free play and/or response activities.

PART 4: Closing Circle Time

The children gather together for a brief review of what they have learned and a closing prayer. Teachers give out take home sheets as children are dismissed.

*As with the other two Praise Factory curriculums, Hide 'n' Seek Kids has a few detective-ish elements to it. (1) There is the "Big Question Briefcase" that contains the key concept visual aids and the Bible storyboard pictures that the teacher uses as he teaches. And (2), Each story is called "The Case of the ..." and comes with "Detective Dan's Listening Assignements." These are listening assignments to be solved as the children listen to the story. There are 5 different listening assignments--one for each of the 5 sessions of curriculum included with each Hide 'n' Seek Kids unit. These questions are especially good for use with three-year-olds or older preschoolers.

Session Length

The resources for each Hide 'n' Seek Kids session-- as described in the lesson plan--are designed for a 60 to 90 minutes session. However, they can easily be tailored to fit a shorter or longer session.

Hide 'n' SEEK KIDS

designed for ages 2-3, often used with ages 2-5

the first of 3 curriculums in the Praise Factory family

downloads and hard-copies available through praisefactory.org

16 Big Bible Truths to Hide in Little Hearts

Hide 'n' SEEK KIDS... at a glance

- Teaches the 16 Biblical (theological) themes used in all three Praise Factory curriculum in its simplest form.

- Each of the 16 themes are taught as a simple Big Question & Answer, set to the music of a simple nursery rhyme.

- One Bible truth, one Bible story, and one Bible verse are used with each of the 16 themes. All Bible verses are set to music, which can be a great aid in learning and remembering the verses.

- There are five sessions of curriculum per theme. Use as few or as many as you want. Each is jam-packed with activities.

- The multiple sessions for each theme give children the time they need to really learn it. The new activities keep the learning fresh each session.

- The curriculum for each theme comes with a fully-scripted lesson plan, beautiful storyboard pictures, games, crafts, take-home sheets, and lots of music.

- The curriculum is flexible and is easily adaptable to many different teaching settings.

- Both downloads and hard copies are available.

Hide 'n' SEEK KIDS Scope & Sequence

UNIT	BIBLE RESOURCES
Unit 1: The God Who Reveals Himself Q: How Can I Know What God Is Like? A: He Shows Me What He's Like!	Bible Verse: Amos 4:13 Story: The Case of the Old Man Who Looked for God *Luke 2:25-32*
Unit 2: God's Wonderful Word, the Bible Q: What's So Special about the Bible? A: It Alone Is God's Word!	Bible Verse: Psalm 18:30, 46 Story: The Case of the Women's Best Gift *1 Timothy*
Unit 3: The Good News of God, the Gospel Q: What Is the Gospel? A: Salvation through Faith in Jesus Christ!	Bible Verse: John 3:16 Story: The Case of the Stranger's Very Good News *Acts 8:1-8*
Unit 4: The God Like None Other Q: Can Anybody Tell Me What the LORD Is Like? A: He's Not Like Anyone Else!	Bible Verse: 1 Kings 8:23 Story: The Case of the Big Showdown *Exodus 1-12*
Unit 5: God, the Good Creator Q: Can You Tell Me What God Made? A: God Made All Things Good!	Bible Verse: Genesis 1:1, 31 Story: The Case of the Wild and Wonderful Words *Genesis 1-2*
Unit 6: God, the Just and Merciful Q: How Did Bad Things Come into God's Good World? A: Bad Things Came Through Sin!	Bible Verse: Romans 5:12 Story: The Case of the Terrible, Terrible Day *Genesis 3-4*
Unit 7: The Law-Giving God Q: What Are God's Laws Like? A: God's Laws Are Perfect!	Bible Verse: Psalm 19:7, 9,11 Story: The Case of the Big Voice *Exodus 19-20, 24*
Unit 8: The God Who Loves Q: What Is God's Love for His People Like? A: It's More than They Could Ever Deserve!	Bible Verse: 1 Chronicles 16:34 Story: The Case of the Eager Enemy's End *Acts 7-9*

UNIT	BIBLE RESOURCES
Unit 9: Jesus Christ, Immanuel, God with Us Q: What Did Jesus Come to Do? A: Jesus Came to Bring Us to God!	Bible Verse: 1 Peter 3:18 Story: The Case of the The Son Who Came Down *The Gospels*
Unit 10: The Holy Spirit: The Indwelling God Q: What Does the Holy Spirit Do in God's People? A: He Changes Their Hearts!	Bible Verse: Ezekiel 36:26-27 Story: The Case of the Heart Helper *Acts 1-2*
Unit 11: The God Who Saves Q: How Can We Be Saved? A: It Is God's Free Gift!	Bible Verse: Romans 6:23 Story: The Case of the Most Important Question *Acts 16*
Unit 12: God's People Live for Him Q: How Should God's People Live? A: They Should Live Like Jesus!	Bible Verse: Ephesians 5:1-2 Story: The Case of the Runaway Who Came Back *Philemon*
Unit 13: The Sustaining God Q: Why Do God's People Keep Believing in Him? A: It Is God's Sustaining Grace!	Bible Verse: Philippians 4:5,6 (ESV), Luke 18:1 (NIV) Story: The Case of the Man with Big Teeth *Daniel 6*
Unit 14: The God Who Delights in Our Prayers Q: How Does God Want Us to Pray? A: Every Night and Day!	Bible Verse: Psalm 55:22 Story: The Case of the Terrible Trouble *Acts 17, 1 & 2 Thessalonians*
Unit 15: God's People Gather Together Q: Why Do God's People Go to Church? A: To Worship God and Love One Another!	Bible Verse: Hebrews 10:24-25 Story: The Case of the People Who Loved a Lot *Acts 2*
Unit 16: Jesus, the Returning King Q: What Will Happen When Jesus Comes Back? A: God Will Make Everything New!	Bible Verse: Revelation 21:5-7 Story: The Case of the Wonderful Ending *2 Peter 3*

DEEP DOWN DETECTIVES SESSION OVERVIEW

Session Format: Circle Times, Free Play and Your Choice of Activities

Each session is structured around Circle Time and Free Play Time. Circle Times are used to introduce and review the concept, Bible verse, Bible story, and the ACTS prayer. (A prayer including **A**doration, **C**onfession, **T**hanksgiving, and **S**upplication related to the Bible truth they are learning.) Free play is not only enjoyable, but also helps to replenish attention spans and prepare the children for more group listening later in the session. Every session also includes lots of response activities that you may choose to use during free play time to add as much reinforcement as best suits your children. Each Deep Down Detectives session follows the same four-part format, as described here:

PART 1: Getting Started

A time to welcome the children to the class, enjoy free play, music, and/or play a Bible verse game.

PART 2: Opening Circle Time

The children are gathered together for their primary teaching time. The Big Question and Bible Truth (and related songs) are introduced. A listening assignment* is given, the Bible story told, then the listening assignment answered at the end of story time.

PART 3: Free Play/Activity Time

The children participate in free play and/or response activities.

PART 4: Closing Circle Time

The children gather together for a brief review of what they have learned and enjoy a closing prayer. Teachers give out take home sheets as children are dismissed.

*As with the other two Praise Factory curriculums, Deep Down Detectives has a few detective-ish elements to it. (1) There is the "Big Question Briefcase" that contains the key concept visual aids and the Bible storyboard pictures that the teacher uses as he teaches. And (2). Each story is called "The Case of the ..." and comes with "Detective Dan's Listening Assignments." These are listening assignments to be solved as the children listen to the story. There are 3 different listening assignments—one for each of the 3 sessions of curriculum included with each Deep Down Detectives Bible Truth. These questions are especially good for use with three-year-olds or older preschoolers.

Session Length

The resources for each Deep Down Detectives session—as described in the lesson plan—are designed for a 60 to 90 minutes session. However, they can be easily tailored to fit a shorter or longer session.

69 Bible Truths
for
Inquisitive 4-7's   by Constance Dever

DEEP DOWN DETECTIVES

designed for ages 4-6,
often used with ages 3-7

the second of 3 curriculums
in the Praise Factory family

downloads and hard-copies
available through
www.praisefactory.org

DEEP DOWN DETECTIVES... AT A GLANCE

- Teaches the 16 Biblical (theological) themes used in all three Praise Factory curriculums, but in greater depth than in Hide 'n' Seek Kids. Each of these themes is presented as a "Big Question and Answer."

- Each theme is taught as a series of Bible truths that develop the theme. There are 70 Bible truths in all.

- There is one Bible story and one Bible verse for each of the 70 Bible truths. All of the Bible verses are set to music, which can be a great aid in learning and remembering them.

- There are three sessions of curriculum per Bible truth. Use as few or as many as you want. Each is jam-packed with activities.

- The multiple sessions give children the time they need to really learn each truth. The new activities keep the learning fresh each session.

- The curriculum for each Bible truth comes with a fully-scripted lesson plan, beautiful storyboard pictures, games, crafts, take-home sheets, and lots of music.

- The curriculum is flexible and is easily adaptable to many different teaching settings.

- Both downloads and hard copies available.

*Note: *If desired, you can start out each of the 16 units of Deep Down Detectives with one session (or more) from Hide 'n' Seek Kids curriculum. This creates a nice introduction to the over-arching theme for each unit. It would also add 16 or more sessions to the curriculum.*

DEEP DOWN DETECTIVES SCOPE AND SEQUENCE

UNIT	BIBLE TRUTHS TAUGHT	UNIT	BIBLE TRUTHS TAUGHT
Unit 1: The God Who Reveals Himself Q: How Can I Know What God Is Like? A: He Shows Me What He's Like!	1. By the Heart He Gave Me to Know and Love Him 2. In Everything I See All Around Me 3. In the Bible, the Perfect Word of God 4. Through His Very Own Son, Jesus Christ	**Unit 9: Jesus Christ, Immanuel, God with Us** Q: What Did Jesus Come to Do? A: Jesus Came to Bring Us to God!	1. He Left His Home in Heaven to Save Us 2. He Never, Ever Disobeyed God 3. He Taught about God and Did Amazing Things 4. He Died on the Cross for His People's Sins 5. He Rose from the Dead 6. He Went Up to Rule in Heaven
Unit 2: God's Wonderful Word, the Bible Q: What's So Special about the Bible? A: It Alone Is God's Word!	1. God Made Sure It Was Written Down Just Right 2. It Tells Us about God and His Plans 3. God Uses It to Save His People 4. God Uses It to Change His People	**Unit 10: The Holy Spirit: The Indwelling God** Q: What Does the Holy Spirit Do in God's People? A: He Changes Their Hearts!	1. The Holy Spirit Lives in God's People 2. The Holy Spirit Gives God's People Courage 3. The Holy Spirit Gives God's People Wisdom 4. The Holy Spirit Builds God's Church
Unit 3: The Good News of God, the Gospel Q: What Is the Gospel? A: Salvation through Faith in Jesus Christ!	1. God Made Us and We Should Obey Him 2. We Have All Disobeyed God and Deserve His Punishment 3. God Sent Jesus to Pay for God's People's Sins 4. God Saves All Who Repent of Their Sins and Trust in Jesus	**Unit 11: The God Who Saves** Q: How Can We Be Saved? A: It Is God's Free Gift!	1. When We Trust in Jesus as Our Own Savior 2. When We Tell God Our Sins and Turn Away from Them 3. When the Holy Spirit Works in Our Hearts
Unit 4: The God Like None Other Q: Can Anybody Tell Me What the LORD Is Like? A: He's Not Like Anyone Else!	1. He Is a Glorious Spirit 2. He Is the One, True God 3. He Is God the Father, Son and Holy Spirit: One God, but Three Persons 4. He Is Everywhere, All the Time 5. He Knows Everything There Is to Know 6. He Is Perfectly Holy, Purely Good 7. He Can Do Anything He Wants to Do 8. He Is Always Faithful, Through and Through	**Unit 12: God's People Live for Him** Q: How Should God's People Live? A: They Should Live Like Jesus!	1. By Asking God for His Help 2. By Loving Him Most of All 3. By Loving Other People as God Has Loved Them 4. By Trusting God and Being Happy with What He Wants 5. By Learning God's Word and Obeying It 6. By Saying "No" to Disobeying God 7. By Telling the Good News of Jesus 8. By Making Much of God
Unit 5: God, the Good Creator Q: Can You Tell Me What God Made? A: God Made All Things Good!	1. He Made Everything Good in Heaven and Earth 2. He Made People in a Special Way	**Unit 13: The Sustaining God** Q: Why Do God's People Keep Believing in Him? A: It Is God's Sustaining Grace!	1. God Alone Sustains His People 2. God, the Father, Promises to Help His People 3. Jesus Provides God's People with Everything They Need to Live for Him 4. The Holy Spirit Works Inside of God's People 5. The Word of God Feeds God's People 6. God Uses His People to Strengthen and Comfort Each Other
Unit 6: God, the Just and Merciful Q: How Did Bad Things Come into God's Good World? A: Bad Things Came Through Sin!	1. When Adam and Eve Chose to Disobey God 2. When It Spread to the Whole World	**Unit 14: The God Who Delights in Our Prayers** Q: How Does God Want Us to Pray? A: Every Night and Day!	1. He Wants Us to Praise Him 2. He Wants Us to Confess Our Sins to Him 3. He Wants Us to Thank Him 4. He Wants Us to Ask Him to Do Great Things
Unit 7: The God Who Saves Q: How Can We Be Saved? A: It Is God's Free Gift!	1. When We Tell God Our Sins and Turn Away from Them 2. When We Trust in Jesus As Our Own Savior 3. When the Holy Spirit Works in Our Hearts	**Unit 15: God's People Gather Together** Q: Why Do God's People Go to Church? A: To Worship God and Love One Another!	1. By Praising God for Jesus' Win over Death 2. By Learning from God's Word, the Bible 3. By Caring for Each Other's Needs 4. By Telling What God Has Done and Praying 5. By Baptizing People Who Trust in and Live for Jesus 6. By Remembering Jesus Died to Save Them
Unit 8: The God Who Loves Q: What Is God's Love for His People Like? A: It's More than They Could Ever Deserve!	1. He Gave His Son, Jesus to Save Them 2. He Always Takes Care of Them 3. He Uses Their Sadnesses for Good 4. He Will Never Stop Loving His People	**Unit 16: Jesus, the Returning King** Q: What Will Happen When Jesus Comes Back? A: God Will Make Everything New!	1. Jesus Will Judge All People Fairly 2. God's People Will Live Happily with God Forever

PRAISE FACTORY INVESTIGATORS PFI

designed for ages K-11,
often used with pre-K5 -12 year olds

the third of 3 curriculums
in the Praise Factory family

downloads and hard-copies
available through

www.praisefactory.org

PFI... AT A GLANCE

- Teaches the 16 Biblical (theological) themes used in all three Praise Factory curriculums, but in greater depth than in Hide 'n' Seek Kids or Deep Down Detectives. Each of these themes is presented as a "Big Question and Answer" and set to music.

- Each theme is taught as a series of Bible truths that develop the theme. There are 104 Bible truths in all.

- There is one Bible verse and three stories (an Old Testament, New Testament and Church History/Missions story) for each of the 104 Bible truths. All of the Bible verses are set to music, which can be a great aid in learning and remembering them.

- Each of the three sessions for each Bible truth is jam-packed with activities. Use as few or as many as you want.

- The multiple sessions give children the time they need to really learn each truth. The new stories and activities keep the learning fresh each session.

- The curriculum for each Bible truth comes with a fully-scripted lesson plan, games, crafts, take-home sheets, and lots of music (with sign language).

- The curriculum is flexible and is easily adaptable to many different teaching settings.

- Both downloads and hard copies available.

PFI SESSION OVERVIEW

Session Format: Regular Classroom or Large Group/Small Group Format
The PFI curriculum can be used in a regular classroom setting, in which all the children participate in the same activities at the same time; or, in a large group/small group format, in which the children gather together for opening activities and the story, then split up into small groups, each with their own activity, and finally coming back together for each group to make a presentation to the other children (or to the parents) at the end of session. Small groups alternate at the end of session. Small groups alternate a different activity each lesson for variety. Each PFI session follows the same three-part format, as described here:

PART 1: GETTING STARTED
A time to welcome the children to the class, introduce the class rules and the "Big Question and Answer" (and related songs) of the theological theme they are studying.

PART 2: DIGGIN' DEEP DOWN
The Bible truth (and related songs) is introduced. The Case Questions* are revealed. The Case of the ... story told, then the Case Questions answered. The teacher closes with an ACTS prayer (A prayer including Adoration, Confession, Thanksgiving, and Supplication related to the Bible truth they are learning.)

PART 3: TAKING ACTION
The children participate in the response activities chosen for the day and (if desired), presenting what they've learned to each other or to parents at the end of the session. Teachers give out take home sheets as children are dismissed.

*As with the other two Praise Factory curriculums, PFI has a few detective-ish elements to it. Each story is called "The Case of the ..." and comes with "Case Questions": a listening assignment of questions about the story to be solved as they listen.

Session Length
The resources for each PFI session-- as described in the lesson plan--are designed for a 60 to 90 minutes session. However, they can be easily shaped for you to tailor them to fit a shorter or longer session.

PFI SCOPE AND SEQUENCE

UNIT	BIBLE TRUTHS TAUGHT
Unit 1: The God Who Reveals Himself Q: How Can I Know What God Is Like? A: He Shows Me What He's Like!	1. God Made Our Hearts to Know and Love Him 2. God's Creations Tell Us about Him 3. God Spoke to His People through Prophets Long Ago 4. God Speaks through His Word, the Bible 5. God Reveals Himself Most Completely through His Son, Jesus
Unit 2: God's Wonderful Word, the Bible Q: What's So Special about the Bible? A: It Alone Is God's Word!	1. God Inspired Many People to Write Down His Word Perfectly 2. God's Word Tells God's Way and Plans for His People, Past, Present and Future 3. God Uses His Word to Save His People 4. God Uses His Word to Change His People
Unit 3: The Good News of God, the Gospel Q: What Is the Gospel? A: Salvation though Faith in Christ!	1. God Is the Good Creator and King of the World 2. All Have Rejected God and Deserve His Eternal Punishment 3. God Sent Jesus to Bear the Punishment for Sin 4. God Saves Those Who Repent and Trust in Jesus

185

PFI Scope and Sequence, Continued

UNIT	BIBLE TRUTHS TAUGHT
Unit 4: The God Like None Other Q: Can Anybody Tell Me What the LORD Is Like? A: He's Not Like Anyone Else!	1. The LORD is a Glorious Spirit 2. The LORD is the Only True God 3. The LORD is God the Father, Son and Holy Spirit: One God, But Three Persons 4. The LORD is Everywhere, All the Time 5. The LORD Knows Everything There is to Know 6. The LORD is Holy 7. The LORD is Omnipotent 8. The LORD is Faithful 9. The LORD's Names Tell Us About Him
Unit 5: God, the Good Creator Q: Can You Tell Me What God Made? A: God Made All Things Good!	1. God Created All Things Good in the Beginning 2. God Created People Good in the Beginning 3. He Made Everything Good in Heaven and Earth 4. God's Plans For His Creation Are Good and Unfailing
Unit 6: God, the Just and Merciful Q: How Did Bad Things Come into God's Good World? A: Bad Things Came Through Sin!	1. Angels and People Rebelled against God in the Beginning 2. God Treated the First Sinners with Justice and Mercy 3. All People Are Born Sinful, All People Need God's Mercy
Unit 7: The Law-Giving God Q: What Are God's Laws Like? A: God's Laws Are Perfect!	1. God's Laws Are Written in the Bible 2. God Created Us Perfect Law Keepers, But We Are All Lawbreakers 3. God Gave Us His Laws to Convict Us of Our Sin that We Might Be Saved 4. Jesus Kept God's Law Perfectly to Save God's People by His Grace 5. The Heart of God's Law is Love
Unit 8: The God Who Loves Q: What Is God's Love for His People Like? A: It's More than They Could Ever Deserve!	1. God Blesses All People with Many Good Gifts 2. God Loved His People Before They Loved Him 3. God Showed the Depths of His Love by Giving His Son to Save His People 4. God Loves His People by Caring for Their Needs 5. God Uses Everything in His People's Lives for Their Good and His Glory 6. God Will Never Stop Loving His People
Unit 9: Jesus Christ, Immanuel, God with Us Q: What Did Jesus Come to Do? A: Jesus Came to Bring Us to God!	1. Jesus, the Servant King 2. Jesus, the Obedient Son 3. Jesus, the Amazing Teacher 4. Jesus, the Lord over Life and Death 5. Jesus, the Ruler of All Creation 6. Jesus, the Forgiver of Sins 7. Jesus, the Christ, the Son of the Living God 8. Jesus, the Glory of God 9. Jesus, the Ransom for Sinners 10. Jesus, the Conqueror of Death 11. Jesus, the Firstborn of the Resurrection 12. Jesus, the Reigning Son in Heaven
Unit 10: The Holy Spirit: The Indwelling God Q: What Does the Holy Spirit Do in God's People? A: He Changes Their Hearts!	1. The Holy Spirit Lives in God's People 2. The Holy Spirit Gives God's People Courage 3. The Holy Spirit Gives God's People Wisdom 4. The Holy Spirit Builds God's Church

UNIT	BIBLE TRUTHS TAUGHT
Unit 11: The God Who Saves Q: How Can We Be Saved? A: It Is God's Free Gift!	1. God Saves Sinners Who Confess Their Sins 2. Jesus is the Only Way to Be Saved 3. We Must Trust Jesus as Our Savior 4. The Holy Spirit Changes Our Hearts so We Can Be Saved
Unit 12: God's People Live for Him Q: How Should God's People Live? A: They Should Live Like Jesus!	1. God's People Grow to Be More Like Jesus 2. God's People Love Him with All Themselves 3. God's People Love Others 4. God's People Trust Him 5. God's People Are Good Stewards of His Gifts 6. God's People Obey Him 7. God's People Do Good Works God Has Prepared for Them 8. God's People Read His Word, the Bible 9. God's People Think about Him 10. God's People Say "No" to Temptation 11. God's People Tell Others about Him 12. God's People Suffer According to His Plan 13. God's People Know Heaven is Their Home 14. God's People Delight in His Glory
Unit 13: The Sustaining God Q: Why Do God's People Keep Believing in Him? A: It Is God's Sustaining Grace!	1. God the Father Promises to Help His People 2. Jesus Provides God's People with Everything They Need 3. The Holy Spirit Works in His People 4. The Word of God Grows God's People 5. Jesus is Why God Answers His People's Prayers
Unit 14: The God Who Delights in Our Prayers Q: How Does God Want Us to Pray? A: Every Night and Day!	1. God Delights in Our Adoration of Him 2. God Delights in Our Humble Confession of Sin 3. God Delights in Our Thanksgiving to Him 4. God Delights in Our Supplications to Him 5. God Always Answers Prayers 6. Jesus is Why God Answers His People's Prayers
Unit 15: God's People Gather Together Q: Why Do God's People Go to Church? A: To Worship God and Love One Another!	1. God's People Gather Together for a Special, Weekly Worship Day 2. God's People Gather to Hear God's Word 3. God's People Gather to Pray 4. God's People Gather to Give 5. God's People Gather for Fellowship 6. God's People Invite Others to Gather with Them 7. God's People Proclaim Their New Life in Christ through Baptism 8. God's People Celebrate Christ's Redeeming Sacrifice for Them 9. God's People Love One Another with a Covenant Love 10. God's People Are Led by Godly Leaders 11. God's People Are Called the Body of Christ
Unit 16: Jesus, the Returning King Q: What Will Happen When Jesus Comes Back? A: God Will Make Everything New!	1. King Jesus Will Return to End the World 2. King Jesus Will Return When God's Work on Earth is Done 3. When King Jesus Returns, God's People Will Be Made Like Him 4. King Jesus Will Return to Bring the Wicked to Just and Final Punishment 5. King Jesus Will Return to Judge God's People, Too 6. King Jesus Will Be United with His Bride, God's People, Forever 7. King Jesus Will Reign Forever

Bible Truths that Match Up Across the Curriculums

Hide 'n' Seek Kids	Deep Down Detectives	Praise Factory Investigators
Unit 1: The God Who Reveals Himself Q: How Can I Know What God Is Like? A: He Shows Me What He's Like!	1. By the Heart He Gave Me to Know and Love Him	1. God Made Our Hearts to Know and Love Him
	2. In Everything I See All Around Me	2. God's Creations Tell Us about Him
	included in DDD Unit 1 Bible Truth 3, below	(3. God Spoke to His People through Prophets Long Ago)
	3. In the Bible, the Perfect Word of God	4. God Speaks through His Word, the Bible
	4. Through His Very Own Son, Jesus Christ	5. God Reveals Himself Most Completely through His Son, Jesus
Unit 2: God's Wonderful Word, the Bible Q: What's So Special about the Bible? A: It Alone Is God's Word!	1. God Made Sure It Was Written Down Just Right	1. God Inspired Many People to Write Down His Word Perfectly
	2. It Tells Us about God and His Plans	2. God's Word Tells God's Way and Plans for His People, Past, Present and Future
	3. God Uses It to Save His People	3. God Uses His Word to Save His People
	4. God Uses It to Change His People	4. God Uses His Word to Change His People
Unit 3: The Good News of God, the Gospel Q: What Is the Gospel? A: Salvation through Faith in Jesus Christ!	1. God Made Us and We Should Obey Him	1. God Is the Good Creator and King of the World
	2. We Have All Disobeyed God and Deserve His Punishment	2. All Have Rejected God and Deserve His Eternal Punishment
	3. God Sent Jesus to Pay for God's People's Sins	3. God Sent Jesus to Bear the Punishment for Sin
	4. God Saves All Who Repent of Their Sins and Trust in Jesus as Their Savior	4. God Saves Those Who Repent and Trust in Jesus
Unit 4: The God Like None Other Q: Can Anybody Tell Me What the LORD Is Like? A: He's Not Like Anyone Else!	1. He Is a Glorious Spirit	1. The LORD is a Glorious Spirit
	2. He Is the One, True God	2. The LORD is the Only True God
	3. He Is God the Father, Son and Holy Spirit: One God, But Three Persons	3. The LORD Is God the Father, Son and Holy Spirit: One God, But Three Persons
	4. He Is Everywhere, All the Time	4. The LORD Is Everywhere, All the Time
	5. He Knows Everything There Is to Know	5. The LORD Knows Everything There Is to Know
	6. He Is Perfectly Holy, Purely Good	6. The LORD is Holy
	7. He Can Do Anything He Wants to Do	7. The LORD is Omnipotent
	8. He Is Always Faithful, Through and Through	8. The LORD is Faithful
	included in DDD Unit 4 Bible Truth 2, above	9. The LORD's Names Tell Us About Him
Unit 5: God, the Good Creator Q: Can You Tell Me What God Made? A: God Made All Things Good!	1. He Made Everything Good in Heaven and Earth	1. God Created All Things Good in the Beginning
	2. God Made People in a Special Way	2. God Created People Good in the Beginning
	included in DDD Unit 5 Bible Truth 1, above	3. God Created the World to Praise and Glorify Him
	included in DDD Unit 5 Bible Truth 1, above	4. God's Plans For His Creation Are Good and Unfailing
Unit 6: God, the Just and Merciful Q: How Did Bad Things Come into God's Good World? A: Bad Things Came Through Sin!	1. When Adam and Eve Chose to Disobey God	1. Angels and People Rebelled against God in the Beginning
	included in DDD Unit 6 Bible Truth 1, above	2. God Treated the First Sinners with Justice and Mercy
	2. When It Spread to the Whole World	3. All People Are Born Sinful, All People Need God's Mercy
Unit 7: The Law-Giving God Q; What Are God's Laws Like? A: God's Laws Are Perfect!	1. They are Written in the Bible, God's Word	1. God's Laws Are Written in the Bible
	included in DDD Unit 7 Bible Truth 2, below	2. God Created Us Perfect Law Keepers, But We Are All Lawbreakers
	included in DDD Unit 7 Bible Truth 2, below	3. God Gave Us His Laws to Convict Us of Our Sin that We Might Be Saved
	2. They Show Us that We Need God to Save Us	4. Jesus Kept God's Law Perfectly to Save God's People by His Grace
	3. They Tell Us How to Love God and Others	5. The Heart of God's Law is Love

187

Bible Truths that Match Up Across the Curriculums

Hide 'n' Seek Kids	Deep Down Detectives	Praise Factory Investigators
Unit 8: The God Who Loves Q: What Is God's Love for His People Like? A: It's More than They Could Ever Deserve!	*included in DDD Unit 8, Bible Truth 1, below*	1. God Blesses All People with Many Good Gifts
	included in DDD Unit 8, Bible Truth 4, below	2. God Loved His People Before They Loved Him
	1. He Gave His Son, Jesus, to Save Them	3. God Showed the Depths of His Love by Giving His Son to Save His People
	2. He Always Takes Care of Them	4. God Loves His People by Caring for Their Needs
	3. He Uses Their Sadnesses for Good	5. God Uses Everything in His People's Lives for Their Good and His Glory
	4. He Will Never Stop Loving His People	6. God Will Never Stop Loving His People
Unit 9: Jesus Christ, Immanuel, **God with Us** Q: What Did Jesus Come to Do? A: Jesus Came to Bring Us to God!	1. He Left His Home in Heaven to Save Us	1. Jesus, the Servant King
	2. He Never, Ever Disobeyed God	2. Jesus, the Obedient Son
	3. He Taught about God and Did Amazing Things	3. Jesus, the Amazing Teacher
	included in DDD Unit Bible Truth 3, above	4. Jesus, the Ruler of All Creation
	included in DDD Unit 9, Bible Truth 5, above	5. Jesus, the Lord over Life and Death
	included in DDD Unit 9, Bible Truth 4, below	6. Jesus, the Forgiver of Sins
	included in DDD Unit 9, Bible Truth 2, above	7. Jesus, the Christ, the Son of the Living God
	included in DDD Unit 9, Bible Truth 1	8. Jesus, the Glory of God
	4. He Died on the Cross for God's People's Sins	9. Jesus, the Ransom for Sinners
	5. He Rose from the Dead	10. Jesus, the Conqueror of Death
	included in DDD Unit 9, Bible Truth 5, above	11. Jesus, the Firstborn of the Resurrection
	6. He Went Up to Rule in Heaven	12. Jesus, the Reigning Son in Heaven
Unit 10: The Holy Spirit: **The Indwelling God** Q: What Does the Holy Spirit Do in God's People? A: He Changes Their Hearts!	1. The Holy Spirit Lives in God's People	1. The Holy Spirit Lives in God's People
	2. The Holy Spirit Gives God's People Courage	2. The Holy Spirit Gives God's People Courage
	3. The Holy Spirit Gives God's People Wisdom	3. The Holy Spirit Gives God's People Wisdom
	4. The Holy Spirit Builds God's Church	4. The Holy Spirit Builds God's Church
Unit 11: The God Who Saves Q: How Can We Be Saved? A: It Is God's Free Gift!	1. When We Tell God Our Sins and Turn Away from Them	1. God Saves Sinners Who Confess Their Sins
	included in DDD Unit 11, Bible Truth 2, below	2. Jesus Is the Only Way to Be Saved
	2. When We Trust in Jesus As Our Own Savior	3. We Must Trust Jesus as Our Savior
	3. When the Holy Spirit Works in Our Hearts	4. The Holy Spirit Changes Our Hearts so We Can Be Saved
Unit 12: God's People Live for Him Q: How Should God's People Live? A: They Should Live Like Jesus!	1. By Asking God for His Help	1. God's People Grow to Be More Like Jesus
	2. By Loving Him Most of All	2. God's People Love Him with All Themselves
	3. By Loving Other People As God Has Loved Them	3. God's People Love Others
	4. By Trusting God and Being Happy With What He Wants	4. God's People Trust Him
	included in DDD Unit 12 Bible Truth 8, below	5. God's People Are Good Stewards of His Gifts
	included in DDD Unit 12 Bible Truth 5, below	6. God's People Obey Him
	included in DDD Unit 12 Bible Truth 5, below	7. God's People Do Good Works God Has Prepared for Them
	5. By Learning God's Word and Obeying It	8. God's People Read His Word, the Bible
	included in DDD Unit 12 Bible Truth 2, above	9. God's People Think about Him
	6. By Saying "No" to Disobeying God	10. God's People Say "No" to Temptation
	7. By Telling the Good News of Jesus	11. God's People Tell Others about Him
	included in DDD Unit 12 Bible Truth 4, above	12. God's People Suffer According to His Plan
	included in DDD Unit 12 Bible Truth 4, above	13. God's People Know Heaven Is Their Home
	8. By Making Much of God	14. God's People Delight in His Glory

Bible Truths that Match Up Across the Curriculums

Hide 'n' Seek Kids	Deep Down Detectives	Praise Factory Investigators
Unit 13: The Sustaining God Q: Why Do God's People Keep Believing in Him? A: It Is God's Sustaining Grace!	1. God, Alone, Sustains God's People	1. God, Alone, Sustains God's People
	2. God the Father Promises to Help His People	2. God the Father Promises to Help His People
	3. Jesus Provides God's People with Everything They Need	3. Jesus Provides God's People with Everything They Need
	4. The Holy Spirit Works in God's People	4. The Holy Spirit Works in God's People
	5. The Word of God Grows God's People	5. The Word of God Grows God's People
	6. God Uses His People to Strengthen and Comfort Each Other	6. God Uses His People to Strengthen and Comfort Each Other
Unit 14: The God Who Delights in Our Prayers Q: How Does God Want Us to Pray? A: Every Night and Day!	1. God Wants Us to Praise Him	1. God Delights in Our Adoration of Him
	2. God Wants Us to Confess Our Sins	2. God Delights in Our Humble Confession of Sin
	3. God Wants Us to Thank Him	3. God Delights in Our Thanksgiving to Him
	4. God Wants Us to Ask Him to Do Great Things	4. God Delights in Our Supplications to Him
	included in DDD Unit 14 Bible Truth 4, above	5. God Always Answers Prayers
	included in DDD Unit 14 Bible Truth 4, above	6. Jesus Is Why God Answers God's People's Prayers
Unit 15: God's People Gather Together Q: Why Do God's People Go to Church? A: To Worship God and Love One Another!	1. By Praising God for Jesus' Win over Death	1. God's People Gather Together for a Special, Weekly Worship Day
	included in DDD Unit 15 Bible Truth 2, below	2. God's People Are Led by Godly Leaders
	2. By Learning from God's Word, the Bible	3. God's People Gather to Hear God's Word
	included in DDD Unit 15 Bible Truth 3, below	4. God's People Are Called the Body of Christ
	3. By Caring for Each Other's Needs	5. God's People Love One Another with a Covenant Love
	included in DDD Unit 15 Bible Truth 3, above	6. God's People Gather to Give
	4. By Telling What God Has Done and Praying	7. God's People Gather for Fellowship
	included in DDD Unit 15 Bible Truth 4, above	8. God's People Invite Others to Gather with Them
	included in DDD Unit 15 Bible Truth 4, above	9. God's People Gather to Pray
	5. By Baptizing People Who Trust in and Live for Jesus	10. God's People Proclaim Their New Life in Christ through Baptism
	6. By Remembering Jesus Died to Save Them	11. God's People Celebrate Christ's Redeeming Sacrifice for Them
Unit 16: Jesus, the Returning King Q: What Will Happen When Jesus Comes Back? A: God Will Make Everything New!	1. Jesus Will Judge All People Fairly	1. King Jesus Will Return to End the World
	included in DDD Unit 16 Bible Truth 1, above	2. King Jesus Will Return When God's Work on Earth is Done
	included in DDD Unit 16 Bible Truth 1, above	3. When King Jesus Returns, God's People Will Be Made Like Him
	included in DDD Unit 16 Bible Truth 1, above	4. King Jesus Will Return to Bring the Wicked to Just and Final Punishment
	included in DDD Unit 16 Bible Truth 1, above	5. King Jesus Will Return to Judge God's People, Too
	included in DDD Unit 16 Bible Truth 2, below	6. King Jesus Will Be United with His Bride, God's People, Forever
	2. God's People Will Live Happily with God Forever	7. King Jesus Will Reign Forever

VBS, Camps and other Programs

Programs like camps, VBS and short-term missions Children's Ministry usually involve such a wide, age-range of children that it's best to use two or three curriculums, instead of just one, to meet everyone's learning level. This is easy to do with the Praise Factory family of curriculum, since you are using the same, sixteen Big Question Units in all three curriculums.

There are so many ways to do these programs. Here are the most common ones I've heard of:
- One, half day
- One, full day
- One evening
- Friday Night-Saturday
- Five, half days
- Five, full days
- Five evenings in a row
- Five one-day evenings (such as five Wednesday nights in a row)
- Two, five-day weeks in a row

Although these programs take place at many different times, they typically run one of three, standard lengths of time:
- 1 1/2 hour programs
- 2 1/2 hour programs
- 6 hour programs

Here are session suggestions for each of these three lengths of programs:

NOTE: I have put some place holder times in schedules. You change them to your actual times.

1 1/2 Hour Multi- Age Programs

1 1/2 Hour Program (for 2 year olds):
- 9:00   Free Play/Activity Centers
- 9:15   Opening Circle Time (Singing, Big Question, Bible Verse and Bible Story)
- 9:30   Free Play/Activity Centers
- 9:45   Activities: Game, Craft and/or Music
- 10:20 Closing Circle Time
- 10:30 Dismissal

1 1/2 Hour Program (for ages 3-5):
Hide 'n' Seek Kids or Deep Down Detectives Session, as written

1 1/2 Hour Program (for elementary age kids):
Praise Factory Investigators Session, as written

1 1/2 Hour Program (for 2 year olds): (Hide 'n' Seek Kids or Deep Down Detectives)
- (9:15 – Early Arriver Activity – a few puzzles or paper and crayons on a table)
- 9:30 – Activity Centers
- 9:40 – Clean Up Toys
- 9:45 – Opening Circle Time (Add actions to songs to make this time more active)
- 10:05 – Craft Time (Use one of the Extra Crafts)
- 10:15 – Play with Toys /Check Diapers/Potty Break
- 10:25 – Clean Up Toys
- 10:30 – Memory Verse Time: Music, Movement & Memory; Bible Verse Review Game
- 10:40 – Snack Time
- 10:50 – Closing Time/Take Home Sheet/Coloring Time (Ask them the Closing Time questions as they are coloring at the tables)
- 11:00 – Parents come

1 1/2 Hour Program (for 3-preK 5 year olds): (Hide 'n' Seek Kids or Deep Down Detectives)
- (9:15 – Early Arriver Activity – a few puzzles or paper and crayons on a table)
- 9:30 – Activity Centers
- 9:40 – Clean Up Toys
- 9:45 – Opening Circle Time (Add actions to songs to make this time more active)
- 10:05 – Craft Time (Use one of the Extra Crafts)
- 10:15 – Play with Toys /Check Diapers/Potty Break
- 10:25 – Clean Up Toys
- 10:30 – Memory Verse Time: Music, Movement & Memory; Bible Verse Review Game
- 10:40 – Snack Time
- 10:50 – Closing Time/Take Home Sheet/Coloring Time (Ask them the Closing Time questions as they are coloring at the tables)
- 11:00 – Parents come

1 1/2 Hour Program--elementary school (Praise Factory Investigators)
- 9:00   Opening Large Group Time: Welcome, Singing
- 9:15   Opening Large Group Time: Big Question, Bible Truth, Bible Verse and Bible Story
- 9:45   Small Group Activities (Discussion and Games/Music/Craft Activities) If desired, each small group can prepare their activity for Small Group Presentations in Closing Large Group.
- 10:15 Closing Large Group Time: Small Group Presentations and/or Singing
- 10:30 Dismissal

VBS, Camps and other Programs: 2 1/2 Hour Schedule

2 1/2 Hour Program (for 2 year olds): (Hide 'n' Seek Kids or Deep Down Detectives)
- (8:45 Early Arriver Activity – a few puzzles or paper and crayons on a table)
- 9:00 Activity Centers (first set)
- 9:10 Clean Up Toys
- 9:15 Opening Circle Time (Add actions to songs to make this time more active)
- 9:25 Activity Centers (first set)
- 9:35 Craft Time (Use one of the Extra Crafts)
- 9:45 Play with Toys /Check Diapers/Potty Break 2
- 9:55 Clean Up Toys
- 10:00 Snack Time
- 10:10 Memory Verse Time: Music, Movement & Memory; Bible Verse Review Game
- 10:20 Activity Centers (second set)
- 10:30 Clean Up Toys
- 10:45 Craft Time (one of the extra crafts)
- 10:55 Play with Toys /Check Diapers/Potty Break 2
- 11:00 Clean up Toys
- 11:05 Active Indoor/Outdoor Play
- 11:25 Closing Time Circle Time
- 11: 15 Coloring Time/Take Home Sheet
- 11:30 Parents come

2 1/2 Hour Program (for 3-preK 5 year olds): (Hide 'n' Seek Kids or Deep Down Detectives)
- (8:45 Early Arriver Activity – a few puzzles or paper and crayons on a table)
- 9:00 Activity Centers (first set)
- 9:15 Clean Up Toys
- 9:20 Opening Circle Time (Add actions to songs to make this time more active)
- 9:40 Craft Time (Use one of the Extra Crafts)
- 9:55 Activity Centers (first set)
- 10:10 Clean Up Toys
- 10:15 Potty Break/Wash Hands
- 10:25 Snack Time
- 10:35 Active Indoor/Outdoor Play OR Activity Centers (second set)
- 10:50 Clean Up Toys
- 10:55 Memory Verse Time: Music, Movement & Memory; Bible Verse Review Game
- 11:10 Closing Time Circle Time
- 11:20 Coloring Time/Take Home Sheet
- 11:30 Parents come

2 1/2 Hour Program--elementary school (Praise Factory Investigators)
- 9:00   Opening Large Group Time: Welcome, Singing
- 9:15   Opening Large Group Time: Big Question, Bible Truth, Bible Verse and Bible Story
- 9:45   Small Group Activity 1: Discussion and Craft Activity
- 10:15 Active Outdoor/Indoor Play
- 10:30 Snack (Story-related snack) ACTS and Discussion Time (related to activity they are about to do 10:45 Small Group Activity 2: (Prepare this one for presentation to the rest of the children during Closing Large Group Time, if desired)
- 11:15: Closing Large Group Time: Small Group Presentations and/or Singing
- 11:30 Dismissal

6 Hour (Full Day) Program (for 3-preK 5 year olds): (Hide 'n' Seek Kids or Deep Down Detectives)
Use one Bible Truth and Bible story for the whole day's session. Afternoon provides an opportunity for reinforcement.

Morning Schedule
- 8:45 Early Arriver Activity – a few puzzles or paper and crayons on a table)
- 9:00 Activity Centers (first set)
- 9:15 Clean Up Toys
- 9:20 Opening Circle Time (Add actions to songs to make this time more active)
- 9:50 Active Indoor/Outdoor Play (Playground or organized games)
- 10:30 Potty Break/Wash Hands/Snack Time
- 10:45 Music, Movement & Memory Game and Singing
- 11:00 Craft Time (Use one of the Extra Crafts)
- 11:30 Activity Centers (second set)
- 12:00 - 1:00 Lunch and Play Time/Rest Time

Afternoon Schedule
- 1: 00 Bible Story Review & Bible Verse Review (repeat story and storyboard or use games to review)
- 1: 20 Craft Time (Use one of the take home sheet coloring activities of the Extra Crafts)
- 1:40 Activity Centers (second set)
- 2:00 Snack and Potty Break
- 2:30 Closing Circle Time Review/Singing
- 2:40 Free play, games, possibility outdoors
- 3:00 Dismissal

6 Hour (Full Day) Program--elementary school (Praise Factory Investigators)
Use two stories from same Bible Truth: one in the morning, one in the afternoon.
- 8:45 Greet children and parents as they arrive
- 9:00 Small Group Time: Introduce Big Question, Bible Truth, Bible Verse, etc.
- 9:15 Large Group Singing and Bible Story
- 9:45 Small Group Activity 1: Bible Truth Game
- 10:15 Small Group Activity 2: Craft
- 10:45 Snack and ACTS Prayer Time
- 11:00 Outdoor Fun - Active Game 1
- 12:00 Lunch and Free Play Time

Afternoon Schedule
- 1:00 Large Group Singing and Second Story (Other Bible Story or Story of the Saints)
- 1:30 Small Group Activity 1: Presentation Activity (Choose a different activity for each small group to work on during this time. They will present it to the rest of the children at the end of the session, if desired.)
- 2:15 Snack Time
- 2:30 Closing Large Group Time: Small Group Presentations and/or Singing
- 3:00 Dismissal

VBS, Camps and other Programs: Choosing Curriculum

You've figured out how many sessions your program will run and how long each session will last. Next, you need to figure out whichcurriculum you want to use. We suggest using Hide 'n' Seek Kids and/or Deep Down Detectives with your pre-schoolers and Praise Factory Investigators for your elementary school kids.

Find a unit you want to become the theme of your VBS. Choose the Bible Truths you want to teach. The charts of the following pages should help you see how the Bible Truths match up in the three curriculums. You've got tons of resources within each concept to fill up your schedule.

Here's a reminder of what you have in each:

Each Hide 'n' Seek Kids unit has:
- There is just one Bible Story and one Bible verse per unit.
- There are 5 lessons of curriculum in each unit.
- There is tons of music.
- The activities in each of the 5 lessons include:
    1 Bible Story Review Game
    1 Bible Verse Game
    1 Music, Movement & Memory Activity (especially good for Bible Memory)
    1 Coloring Sheet/Take Home Sheet
    There are also 3 extra crafts

Each Deep Down Detective unit has:
- There are multiple Bible truths within each unit.
- There are three lessons of curriculum, per Bible Truth, within each unit.
- There is one Bible story for each Bible Truth.
- There are 3 lessons of curriculum for each Bible Truth.
- There is tons of music
- The activities in each of the 3 lessons include:
    1 Bible Story Review Game
    1 Bible Verse Game
    1 Music, Movement & Memory Activity (especially good for Bible Memory)
    1 Coloring Sheet/Take Home Sheet
    There are also 3 extra crafts

Each Praise Factory Investigators unit has:
- Multiple Bible truths within it.
- There are three lessons of curriculum, per Bible Truth
- There are 3 stories for each Bible Truth: 1 Old Testament, 1 New Testament, and one Church History/missions.
- There are 3 lessons of curriculum for each Bible Truth--one for each of the three stories.
- There is tons of music.
- Each of the 3 lessons includes:
    1 Bible Story Review Game with Discussion Questions
    1 Bible Verse Game with Discussion Questions
    1 Bible Truth Game with Discussion Questions
    1 Craft with Discussion Questions
    1 Bible Verse Game with Discussion Questions
    1 Bible Verse Song with Discussion Questions, Sign Language and Song Game
    1 Hymn with Discussion Questions, Sign Language and Song Game
    1 Story-related Snack
    1 Take home sheet with the key concepts, the story and some discussion questions

Other Children's Ministry Resources

Children's Church and Family-Integrated Worship

Are You an Advocate of Children's Church or the Family-Integrated Model of Worship?

We see parents as the primary spiritual caregivers of their children. They are the ones whom the Lord will judge for the spiritual nurture of their children. We see all of children's ministry as only a humble support to godly parents; and, that any way we can help prepare the children in our church to gather well with our local body of Christ as one of the most important ways we support our parents in this God-ordained task.

We are agreed on the goal of deliberate, parent-led spiritual nurturing, yet within our church we have seen that the way parents choose to best fulfill this task varies from family to family and even from child to child. And, we have seen that this variance is a matter of godly discretion. In other words, we do not prescribe one particular method, when there seem to be a number of godly options that bear good fruit. So, we encourage parents to understand the great importance of spiritual nurturing their children, both at home and at church. We offer various kinds of support to the parents. And, we help them consider what might be the best way to do this for their particular children/their particular family. So as you can see, we agree upon the mandate, but will not divide over enforcing only one particular godly method.

No one can doubt that children have many cognitive and developmental differences from adults: the younger the children, the greater these differences. Nor can it be doubted that there is a wide variety of spiritual maturity among parents. While some parents may be mature saints, many are new converts. They are hungry to be fed and eagerly welcome help in teaching biblical truths to their children. Teachers of children with this kind of parent often help teach the parents how to better spiritual nurture their children as well as teach the children, themselves. There are yet other children coming to our church whose parents who are not Christians and may not even attend church at all. The teachers of these children may provide some of the only spiritual feeding they receive.

For all of these reasons, many parents at our church feel that they are serving their children best by supplementing their own daily spiritual nurturing of their children with special Sunday classes that convey biblical truths on their own level. This is particularly true while the children are young and the cognitive and developmental gap between themselves and the adults is especially large. And of course, for the children of non-Christians, these classes—presented on their level-- may be the best opportunity they have to understand and remember the gospel and other biblical truths.

And so, we endeavor to encourage and support our parents in a number of different, appropriate ways, helping them to raise their children in the nurture and admonition of the Lord.

What exactly does this look like at our church? It takes on a few different forms. We have some parents who feel that it is best and even biblical for their children to be taught only by themselves. Their children do not attend Sunday School or Church hour programs offered at our church. They feel that regardless of age or ability to understand the sermon or other elements of the service, they are best fulfilling their God-given duties by raising their children this way. These parents choose to keep their children with them from birth on up. But even these parents are not partnering without us. The sermons and other teaching they hear informs their own hearts and minds and helps them to better train their own children.

We have another set of parents who choose to partner with other godly church members to teach their children biblical truths during the Sunday School hour, yet choose to keep their children with them during the entire church service. They often use Sunday lunch time to review key points from the sermon and church service with their children.

And we have yet another set of parents who choose to partner with godly church members to teach their preschoolers and early elementary school children not just during Sunday School, but also during all/part of the church service, too. The K-4th graders of these parents are in the church service until the sermon time (we have hour-long sermons), when they leave to participate in The Praise Factory. Some parents of preschoolers follow this same model, while others choose to have their children to participate in their own teaching time during the whole church service. These parents feel that the quality teaching offered at their child's developmental level in our church hour programs provides a helpful supplement with their own teaching of their children. They do not see the teachers as usurpers of their responsibilities, but partners who are helping to lay a theological foundation that will help their children understand and be better prepared to gather with the congregation. Teachers are careful to give feedback to the parents about any behavior issues or spiritual conversations that might be particularly helpful for the parents to know about. We also provide take home sheets and other parents resources so that parents know what their children were taught and can engage with them about these truths at home. Teachers and parents also watch for signs of readiness to join the service for the sermon portion, too. So, even though a child is age-eligible to be in a Church Hour program, sometimes we are encourage the parents to go ahead and begin keeping their child in with them for the sermon and see if indeed they are ready. Gathering **together** is always our ultimate goal.

Because of this, we steer clear of calling any of the programs we offer a "Children's Church." They are really just children's classes that we hold during the Sunday morning service. We want to reserve the name "church" for the gathering of the congregation all together. It is this gathering we are preparing all the children to join for the full duration, as they are ready, and certainly by the time they start 5th grade.

So, you can see that we have a wide variety of parents, all taking seriously their responsibility to be the primary spiritual caretakers of their children, but doing it in a number of different ways. That while we offer programs during the church hour, we are not advocates of children's church. And, that while we are always trying to prepare children to gather with the congregation for the entire service, we provide quality, biblical teaching during all or the sermon portion of the service, for the children of parents who feel it is spiritually beneficial for them to have that, through 4th grade.

The Baptism of Children:

Capitol Hill Baptist Church

The Baptism of Children at CHBC-- CHBC Elders, 2004

We, the elders of the Capitol Hill Baptist Church, after prayerful searching of the Scriptures and discussion conclude that, while Scripture is quite clear that believers only are to be baptized, the age at which a believer is to be baptized is not directly addressed in Scripture. We do not understand the simple imperative command to be baptized to settle the issue, nor do we understand the imperative to be baptized to forbid raising questions about the appropriateness of a baptismal candidate's maturity. We do understand that the consideration of an appropriate age for a believer to be baptized is a matter not of simple obedience on an issue clearly settled by Scripture, but rather is a matter of Christian wisdom and prudence on an issue not directly addressed by Scripture. Though the baptisms in the New Testament seem largely to have occurred soon after the initial conversion, all of the individuals we can read of are both adults and coming from a non-Christian context. Both of these factors would tend to lend credibility to a conversion. The credibility of the conversion is the prime consideration, with the effect upon the individual candidate and the church community being legitimate secondary concerns.

We believe that the normal age of baptism should be when the credibility of one's conversion becomes naturally evident to the church community. This would normally be when the child has matured, and is beginning to live more self-consciously as an individual, making their own choices, having left the God-given, intended child-like dependence on their parents for the God-given, intended mature wisdom which marks one who has felt the tug of the world, the flesh and the devil, but has decided, despite these allurements, to follow Christ. While it is difficult to set a certain number of years which are required for baptism, it is appropriate to consider the candidate's maturity. The kind of maturity that we feel it is wise to expect is the maturity which would allow that son or daughter to deal directly with the church as a whole, and not, fundamentally, to be under their parents' authority. As they assume adult responsibilities (sometime in late high school with driving, employment, non-Christian friends, voting, legality of marriage), then part of this, we would think, would be to declare publicly their allegiance to Christ by baptism.

With the consent and encouragement of Christian parents who are members, we will carefully consider requests for baptism before a child has left the home, but would urge the parents to caution at this point. Of course children can be converted. We pray that none of our children ever know any lengthy period of conscious rebellion against God. The question raised by baptism is the ability of others to be fairly confident of that conversion. The malleable nature of children (which changeableness God especially intends for the time when they are living as dependents in the home, being trained in all the basics of life and faith) is a gift from God and is to be used to bring them to maturity. It should also give us caution in assuming the permanence of desires, dreams, affections and decisions of children. Nevertheless, should the young person desire to pursue baptism and membership in the normal course set out by the church, we will examine them on a case-by-case basis, with the involvement of the parents.

In the event of young persons from non-Christian families coming to the church for an extended period of time, professing faith and giving evidence of the reality thereof, requests for baptism and membership would be considered without the involvement of the parents. While all the previous comments on the nature of immaturity still pertain, the fact that such a young person would be doing so despite indifference, or even opposition from their parents would or could be evidence for the reality of their conversion.

Nothing in this statement should be construed as casting doubt about the legitimacy of the baptism of any among us, regardless of how young they were when they were baptized. Because they have continued in the faith into their adult years we assume the legitimacy of their initial profession made at baptism. The question we are concerned with here is looking forward, not backward. To put it another way, we are raising the question about how many people have been baptized at this church in the past as younger people and children who went on to give no evidence of ever having been savingly converted, and what damage was done to them, and to the witness of the gospel through the church's premature baptism of them. It is our judgment that while there is some danger of discouragement on the part of those children who do give some good evidence of being converted and yet are not baptized and welcomed into communicant membership in the church, through good teaching in the home, and through the loving inclusion of the families in the church as we currently do, that danger is small. There is, however, we believe, a greater danger of deception on the part of many who could be wrongly baptized at an age in which people are more liable to make decisions which are sincere, but ill-founded and too often short-lived.

Two other notes in conclusion. First, we realize that this issue is an issue of great emotion for some, and we in no way are trying to lead anyone to disobey their conscience on this matter; we simply are trying to inform and educate our consciences from the Scriptural necessity of a credible profession of faith for baptism. Second, while it is not generally known among American evangelicals today, the practice of baptizing pre-teenage children is of recent development (largely early 20th century) and of limited geography (largely limited to the United States, and places where American evangelicals have exercised great influence). Baptists in the past were known for waiting to baptize until the believers were adults. Baptistic Christians around the world are still much more cautious than modern American Christians, often waiting in Europe, Africa and Asia to baptize until children are grown and are in their twenties.

25 Lessons I've Learned in Children's Ministry at Capitol Hill Baptist Church

with application questions for

your ministry setting

excerpt from:

From the Ground Up

The Twenty-Five Lessons

GENERAL

#1: Four Fundamentals from Psalm 66

#2: Parents are the primary spiritual care-givers of their children, but Children's Ministry can help equip parents in their role as spiritual care-givers.

#3: Know your "critters."

#4: Children's Ministry works best when guided by the church leaders.

#5: God has given us the job of praying, nurturing, and educating children, but it is He who brings the fruit of saving faith.

SUPPORTING PARENTS AS THEY TRAIN THEIR CHILDREN AT HOME

#6: Shoot for what happens after hours.

#7: Be careful what you catechize.

SUPPORTING PARENTS BY PROVIDING SAFE CHILD CARE AT CHURCH

#8: Be safe before you are sorry. Put a Child Protection Policy in place now!

SUPPORTING THE PARENTS AS WE CARE FOR THEIR CHILDREN AT CHURCH

BASICS:

#9: Practice finiteness. Start with less and do it well.

#10: Twirl with your swirls.

#11: Prepare the children to gather together for worship with the whole congregation.

#12: Pray! Pray! Pray! There are eyes that watch and minds that remember, even when there seems to be no ears to hear.

CURRICULUM AND TEACHING:

#13: Think outside of the boxed curriculum box.

#14: Two Dead Men and a Diamond

#15: The remarkable results of repetition.

#16: Think like a missionary.

#17: "Oh, I know that old story...or do I?" Fight Bible boredom in well-taught children.

#18: Change your activities from time-fillers to conduits of truth.

#19: Pray Bible-based, life-expanding ACTS prayers.

#20: Don't throw out the baby with the bathwater! Go pirating, instead!

#21: Skip the chaos! Plan your transitions between activities.

#22: Skip the chaos! Teach with a predictable schedule.

#23: The Triple-Crown of Teaching

RECRUITING VOLUNTEERS AND SUPPORTING TEACHERS:

#24: A few, good men are hard to come by... but they go a long way!

#25: Care well for your teachers and they will come back.

Lesson #1: Four Fundamentals from Psalm 66

Psalm 66 points to four fundamentals of how we try to teach the children and how we encourage our parents in their spiritual nurturing of their children.

Fundamental One: Live joyful lives

"Shout for joy to God, all the earth."   *Psalm 66:1, ESV*

We can live joyful lives in light of what God has done. True joy is a gift of the Spirit. It is remarkable. It cannot be reproduced by any other religion. It reflects the Spirit of God working within us, giving life where there was death. It is living in faith, despite trials and despite having to let go of what the world holds to be true and dear. And so, as we teach and parent, we ask God to make our joy in Him evident. It is a very potent witness of the truth and power of the gospel to the children watching us.

Fundamental Two: Live to glorify God in all things...regardless of the outcome!

"Sing the glory of his name; give to him glorious praise! Say to God, "How awesome are your deeds! ... All the earth worships you and sings praises to you; they sing praises to your name."   *Psalm 66:2,3,4, ESV*

We live to glorify God in all that we do. We do not have control over the conversion of the children who we love, parent and teach. Their conversion is a work of God's Holy Spirit that we pray for and yearn for, but we cannot use it as the measure of success. On the other hand, seeking to glorify God in how we teach, raise and live among the children is a "success" we can strive for. This is freeing! We can strive to please God as we declare the greatness of His name to these children. We can strive to please God as we do, to the best of our ability, all He calls us to do, including raising these children. It makes teaching and parenting yet another venue for glorifying God, regardless of who is converted. And, it makes conversion a matter of trust in God…just where it should be.

Fundamental Three: Teach the children God's awesome works, as revealed in the Bible

From before the creation of the world, God has had one, big plan to redeem His people as a magnificent display of His glory. We read of it in the Bible—the record of "His awesome works on man's behalf." And so, the Bible is our primary "textbook" for teaching our children about God, and for how we parent. The Bible is central to all we do and long to teach the children.

Fundamental Four: Tell the children the gospel that has saved us and can save them

"Bless our God, O peoples; let the sound of his praise be heard, who has kept our soul among the living and has not let our feet slip... Come and hear, all you who fear God, and I will tell what he has done for my soul. I cried to him with my mouth, and high praise was on my tongue. If I had cherished iniquity in my heart, the Lord would not have listened. But truly God has listened; he has attended to the voice of my prayer. Blessed be God, because he has not rejected my prayer or removed his steadfast love from me!"
Psalm 66:8-9,16-20, ESV

As Christians, God has given us grace to hear and believe the gospel. We have repented of our sins and trusted in Him as our Savior. We have the testimony of His good work in our lives…and so, as we teach and parent, we want to testify to the children of God's work in our own lives. This is not a God only of history and past acts. This is the living God who is at work today…and in us! What a story we have to tell to these children every day, of the God whose mercies to us are new every morning!

Lesson #1: Questions for You in Your Ministry Setting:

1. How can we show the joy we have in the Lord to our children at home or in the classroom? Why is this so important? Why can this be so compelling?

2. How does teaching children to glorify God free us up in the classroom and/or as parents? Does it mean that we no longer care whether the children are converted or not? Why or why not?

3. Why is it so important that the Bible, not simply moralistic, character-building lessons, be central to all we teach? Does the curriculum you use reflect this? How or how not? If not, how could you help it do this?

4. What is the difference between sharing the gospel with the children and sharing the gospel that saved us with them? How would that difference show up in how you teach or share with the children?

Lesson #2: Parents are the primary spiritual care-givers of their children, but children's ministry can help equip parents in their role as spiritual care-givers.

We believe that Scripture clearly teaches that parents have the primary responsibility to raise their children in the nurture and admonition of the Lord.

This includes parents teaching their children about God, disciplining them, and striving to honor God before them by the example of their lives. The children's ministry team here at CHBC sees itself as a support team to parents. It seeks to aid and encourage parents in the nurturing of their children, in accordance with Scripture and the vision of our God-given elders.

It is very important for parents to realize that your church's children's ministry program isn't a way for them to out-source their own responsibility to their children, even when they feel ill-equipped or overwhelmed. The great news is that the God who calls them to this task will also equip them...and He often uses the church leaders, the children's ministry team and other members of the local church to do this.

Pastors can teach parents about their role as primary spiritual care-givers and can equip them for it:
* in their preaching and other teaching times
* in their public prayers
* by providing parenting classes, workshops and resources
* in counseling
* in conversation
* in providing an example as they raise their own children

The children's ministry team can teach parents about their role as primary spiritual care-givers and can equip them for it by:
* providing partner curriculum resources that help the parents discuss with their children at home what they have been learning in their classes at church.
* giving the parents feedback about how their children act and respond in class.
* staying connected with parents, face-to-face, through email, before and after class.
* regularly praying for the families of the church.
* exposing the parents to good resources they can use with their children, through a book stall, lending library, book fair, book reviews, etc.
* providing resources (such as kids' bulletins) and advice to parents as they help their children worship alongside of them in the worship service.
* not filling the regular church schedule so full of programs that there is little time for families to spend time together.
* providing safe child-care for their children that allows parents to learn and grow in their own classes.

Other members can teach parents about their role as primary spiritual care-givers and can equip them for it by:
* discipling each other, helping each other grow in their love and knowledge of God and His ways.
* mentoring and providing examples through older, more experienced parents inviting younger parents (or even singles or couples who do not yet have children) to come to their homes and observe them with their children.
* younger parents asking older, more experienced parents for feedback on how to best parent their children.
* sharing and praying for each other.
* serving in child-care/children's ministry classes and learning how to teach and train children.

Within the children's classes at church: parents can be supported, without being usurped, in their primary role by:
* by the witness, influence, love and prayers of other fellow, godly members for the children who teach in their classes.
* by providing the children with meaty teaching that builds upon what the parents are teaching their children can be very helpful, especially for less-mature Christian parents who need help most of all.

There has been a recent movement called "family-intergrated church" that emphasizes the parents' role as primary spiritual care-givers to such an extent that it seems to exclude the local church's support in this task. I appreciate the seriousness with which people who hold this position take concerning parents' responsibility before God to teach and train their children. But, I think that Scripture clearly calls the members of the local church, under the guidance of the church leaders, to work together to encourage and equip each other in the faith. I believe this naturally includes equipping believers for their role as spiritual care-givers of their children. See the article in Appendix A for more reflections on this topic.

Lesson #2: Questions for You in Your Ministry Setting:

1. What does it mean to be a primary, spiritual care-giver of children?

2. Who do you see as the primary spiritual caregivers of the children in your church?

3. Would parents be surprised to hear that they are the primary spiritual caregivers of their children? Why or why not?

4. Would your children's ministry team be surprised to hear that they are NOT the primary spiritual caregivers of the children of the church? Why or why not?

5. How does your pastoral staff educate parents in this role? Do they do this regularly?

6. How does your children's ministry team educate parents in this role?

7. Who would your children's ministry program say is the primary caregiver of the children in your church? How does your children's ministry team's decisions, prayers and programs reflect this view?

8. Look at your weekly children's ministry program. When do your families have time to spend together?

9. How does your children's ministry program support your parents in their role….at church? at home?

10. How do you regularly connect with parents? How do you communicate with them about resources or learning opportunities for their children or for themselves as parents?

11. What (if anything) would you like to do to improve your support of the parents in your church?

12. How does your church provide or expose parents to resources to use with their children at home? What are some ways you would like to improve in this? How might you do this?

Lesson #3: Know Your "Critters."

A "critter", in case you didn't know, is just a down-home, backwoods, slang word for creature. The point of this lesson is that you first need to know WHO you are supporting and teaching, if you are going to know HOW to best support and teach them.

The two types of "critters" you most want to know are your parents and their children. Here are some types of things it might be helpful to know about them:

Parents:
- Are they type "A" driven or laid back?
- Are they spiritually mature or just baby Christians?
- Do they come from a Christian background or other?
- Do they have very little disposable income or are they able to afford extras (like biblical resources to use with their children)?
- Is English their first or second language?
- Are they single-parents or are they married? Do they both work outside the home?
- Are they very involved in church or sporadic attenders?
- Do they like to communicate by email, phone or in person?
- Do they tend to use the take-home resources you give out or not?
- Do they have a transient occupation (student, military, etc) or one that allows them to settle more permanently in one place?
- Do they have much family support in the area or are they on their own?
- How do they educate their children: home-school, private, public school?

Answers to questions like these can help you better understand how to support parents and their children. For example, parents who are spiritually mature themselves will probably have a naturally easier time in teaching truths to their children. A young Christian or one from a non-Christian background might be hungry for a lot more help. Understanding that a parent appreciates receiving take home sheets and newsletters through email rather than being handed them on Sunday morning will help you better communicate resources and opportunities to him. Or, knowing that a family has very little disposable income might lead you to giving a Bible or other devotional resources (and pointing them to resources in your church library) that they could not otherwise afford.

Children:
- Do they have any special needs?
- Have they/their family been experiencing a particularly difficult situation that the child is trying to understand?
- What kinds of learning activities do they respond best to: movement/music/workbooks/etc.?
- Are they showing signs of spiritual hunger or boredom?
- Are they often a hand-full, behavior-wise?
- How familiar are they with the Bible?
- Can they read and write yet?
- What do they like to do?

Questions like these can help your Children's Ministry team/teachers better understand how to care for the children and reach them with the gospel, when they are under their care in class. It also can help them suggest resources to support the parents in spiritually caring for their children, too.

Lesson #3: Questions for You in Your Ministry Setting:

1. How well could you answer these questions about the parents/children in your church?

2. What other questions would you add to these?

3. How might you find out this information?

4. Do you see trends in any area? Do a lot of your parents seem to fall in the same categories? How could noticing any trends affect how you support the parents and their children?

Lesson #4: Children's Ministry works best when guided by the church leaders.

Here are four, big reasons why your children's ministry should be under the direct and regular guidance of your church leaders:

Reason #1: Because your church leaders are specially gifted and responsible before God for the teaching that takes place in the church—even to the children.

Reason #2: Because children are being raised by the adults under their pastoral care and raising children is an important part of God's calling on their lives.

Reason #3: Because children's ministry often involves a high percentage of your church membership, and your church leaders are responsible to make sure that those members are receiving the care they themselves need, even as they are serving the children.

And Reason #4: if your church leaders don't provide leadership, someone else will, and too many times this leads to pockets of friction, division and sometimes poor teaching.

What does direct and regular guidance look like? Here are some ideas:
- The leaders decide upon (or review and approve suggestions from the children's ministry team) teaching themes and resources used with the children at church.
- The leaders set guidelines for who can volunteer in children's ministry and how frequently they can serve to make sure that no one is over-serving and thereby under-feeding their own souls.
- The leaders approve any major program changes, making sure that the church is not becoming too program-centered and thereby starving families of time together.
- One church leader is given particular oversight of the children's ministry team, having regular meetings with them, praying with them, receiving updates on children, parents, teachers, resources and programs. He is the point person to talk with teachers, parents or the children's ministry team as situations in children's ministry arise. He keeps any other pastors updated with children's ministry issues.
- The leaders decide upon important issues, such as the baptism and church membership for children/youth and putting their decisions in writing and making them available to parents, teachers and the children's ministry team.

At CHBC, we enjoy the guidance of our elders in all of these ways. Here's what it looks like for us:
The elders have given us four teaching emphases:
1. Chronological study of the Bible (OT/NT overviews)
2. Prepare the children to gather together with the church body
3. God's One Big Plan of Redemption/Missions
4. Biblical Theology

They have set guidelines for members wanting to serve in children's ministry that they think will provide enough continuity for the children being taught, while also being sensitive to ensuring that the volunteers, themselves, are in a position of being taken good care of, spiritually. These guidelines are spelled out on pp.150,152.

One elder in particular--the pastor of families--is the overseer of our children's ministry team. He meets regularly with the team, giving them advice and receiving updates on the children, parents, programs, etc. They pray for the families. He reports to the elders at elders' meetings any information of note; or, brings up any issues that they need to discuss and decide upon. He reports back to the children's ministry team and helps them implement the elders' decisions. He also gives a children's ministry report to the congregation at Members' Meetings, held every two months.

Our elders' have written up their wisdom on the baptism of children at CHBC and give it out to all parents who are seeking membership at CHBC. They do this because not everyone has come to the same conclusion as them and they want to be up-front with their conclusions, in case a family would rather go to a church with a different view on this matter.

(Our elders' paper on the baptism of children at CHBC can be found on p.193.)

Lesson #4: Questions for You in Your Ministry Setting:

1. How would you describe the current guidance/oversight your children's ministry team receives from your church leaders? What do you appreciate about this? Is there anything else would you like to see them do?

2. What would be hard about receiving more spiritual oversight from the church leaders? Are there areas of individualism among the children's ministry program that either does not receive enough oversight from the church leaders? How does this show? What changes could be made?

3. What issues, such as baptism of children, would you like to see your church leaders give your team spiritual guidance upon?

4. Who decides upon the teaching emphases, the curriculum and the programs that children's ministry implements?

5. Do you have a statement of faith that provides a foundation for the truths you believe and teach? If not, what are the Biblical truths that under-gird your ministry?

6. Do you have a mission statement for what you hope to do within this ministry? If not, what would it be?

7. Do you have guidelines for who or how often someone can serve in children's ministry? Do you have a few members who over-serve?

8. Who takes care of difficult, pastoral issues that arise with children or with parents?

Lesson #5: God has given us the job of praying, nurturing, and educating children, but it is He who brings the fruit of saving faith.

Oh, how we love our children! Oh, how we desire for them to know the Lord and to be saved from their sins! This leads us to pray for our children, to teach our children, to catechize our children and talk to our children. This is a great blessing to the children, to their families and to those here at church who work with their children. How wonderful it is to work with children who are so well taught!

The Caution
But with all this diligence, there is an important word of warning we give to both the parents and the teachers of these children: **Doing all these things educates the children and fertilizes their souls with the great things of God, but they neither guarantee nor bring about conversion! It is God who brings the fruit of saving knowledge of and faith in Him, in His way and in His timing.**

Sometimes our small, pea-sized minds and anxious, un-trusting hearts are not too happy about this fact. This may be a temptation especially among those whose children get older and older and still show little or no desire for God. But the truth is, God is far wiser and good than we are. We can rest in Him… or at times, fight to rest in Him… even about the salvation of our children. It is certainly very important that we, as parents and as teachers, do the best job we can of training up the children in the nurture and admonition of the Lord. But, it is just as important that we are on our knees, asking for God to work, in His perfect timing, in the hearts of those children. And it is important for God to work in us, right now, a restful, hopeful, trusting, joyful spirit that acknowledges Him as the good, powerful Giver of faith. We should ask Him to show us our heart concerning these matters...and grow them in all of these graces.

Yes, conversion is a work of the Holy Spirit alone! There is no "to-do list" which, when completed, guarantees that their children will come to a saving knowledge of God. Nor are there any certain, three behaviors, if cultivated enough by faithful teachers and parents, will guarantee that the children will become followers of Christ and will godly lives. And unfortunately, sometimes knowledge of more facts--even Bible facts and Bible verses-- can breed arrogance, just as much as lack of facts can lead to ignorance. And good behavior--even good, Christian behavior--can breed legalism, just as lack of discipline can breed selfishness and foolishness.

So what do we do? Do we hold back on how much we teach the children about God because we can't know that it will produce the desired effect? No! Believing comes through hearing and hearing through the word of Christ! We will teach and pray that God works in their hearts through His Word! Do we stop trying to build good, godly character in their lives, because there's no guarantee that we can make it "stick"? Of course not! God calls us to be faithful teachers of His ways and beckon everyone--including children--to turn to Him and live for Him. Let's us fully use the means God typically uses to convert people! But, let us rest in God in our good God who alone can change their hearts!

Another way parents' and teachers' strong desire for salvation assurance comes out in the form of baptism pressure. That is, baptizing children at their early signs of spiritual interest, but before the child is truly converted. At CHBC, we have prospective members share their testimony with the elders before being put forward for membership. Too many times, the testimony includes the story of how they "made a profession of faith as a child and were baptized, but then "fell away from the Lord" for years. And now, just recently, sought the Lord and desire to walk with Him truly now"—or something like that. Was the child truly converted back then, or only now, as an adult who is bearing the fruit of true conversion? Only God knows...and we certainly never question a person's childhood experience. But, it has caused our church leaders to help our teachers and Children's Ministry team learn to both encourage children on towards trusting faith in Christ, while also being patient to wait for fruit of true conversion before baptism takes place. Baptized is a command for the converted, but it does not mean someone is converted. In our eagerness, we may wind up actually creating greater difficulty for our children by baptizing them too soon. If they think they are converted when they are not, then they think that have tasted all there is to a relationship with God, when in truth, they have never tasted it at all.

God made children to want to please their parents. What pleases a Christian parent more than a child's decision for the Lord? "Hallelujah! My child is safe!" I know those feelings all too well. But, we have come to recognize that if we can encourage the child's desire and teach them what it means for them to be a disciple who loves the Lord and lives for Him…but wait until he/she is older and shows signs of true conversion to the congregation at large and in his life as he feels the tug of the world and says "no" to it, that we are far more likely to have less of these false decisions. This is so important for everyone involved. It is important for the church to look like Jesus by, as closely as we can, recognizing, baptizing and including in membership those who truly have repented of their sins and trusted in Jesus as their Savior. And for the children, baptizing them too early, maybe before they truly have become Christians makes them think they know what life with God really is. There are so many people in the world who think they are Christians because they made a decision as a child, often at VBS it seems, were baptized and hardly ever darken the door of a church again or think about living a Christ-honoring life. Jesus spoke of the fruit being the best indication of a type of tree. That's simply what we have chosen to do here at CHBC for our children.

Do we put pressure on ourselves or on our children to do more or say more to help "force" them to make a decision that is not much more than a façade? What the world needs now is not more hypocrites. Be faithful. Be prayerful. Point them to Christ in your words and your life. Encourage them where you see signs of life. Teach them as you sit and as you rise. As you walk, and as you wait in carpool. But watch your heart! Keep watching your heart!

For more information on our elders' decision about the baptism of children, see Appendix C.

Lesson #5: Questions for You in Your Ministry Setting:

1. What are ways you as a parent or as a teacher can raise up your children in the nurture and admonition of the Lord?

2. What have been effective means of doing this? (examples: worship services or Sunday School classes at church, catechisms and other memory work, music, family devotions, etc.)

3. Where do you see symptoms of worry or pressure from parents/teachers for their children to make a profession of faith?

4. How do your church leaders think through the baptism of children?

5. If you are a baptistic church that baptizes young children frequently, do you find these children straying away as they grow up? Or, do you find many wanting to be "re-baptized" when they are young adults because they felt the first baptism (at the younger age) didn't "count"? How does this affect the witness of the church and what true Christians look like? How does this confuse these children concerning their spiritual state? What could you do to help with these issues?

6. What signs of conversion do you look for in children before proceeding with baptism?

7. How can you encourage the children who seem to be seeking the Lord and may have actually been converted, even if you do choose to wait for them to grow up and show fruit across their lives?

8. How do you talk to parents when they want their child baptized? How can you help them to understand what it means for the child to be baptized and why you might choose to have them wait for clear fruit to be borne?

Lesson #6: Shoot for what happens after hours.

Remarkably little children's ministry actually takes place at church, under our care. If you want to support parents in their roles are primary spiritual care-givers, you need to focus on more than the few hours of teaching time you have with their children at church. Focus on the time the children have with their parents!

We like to think of our church as a sit-down, eat-in restaurant that fills our members' spiritual "bellies" with great food while at church, yet also gives so much food that they have plenty to take home in "doggie bags" to keep feeding themselves and their children on the rest of the week.

Here's some of the ways we do this:

- Regularly hosting special events: parent lunches, panels/speakers on various topics relevant to parenting.

- Offering Core Seminar classes (Sunday School for adults a la CHBC), both on parenting as well as a wide variety of important topics which aid parents in their own spiritual growth. (See p.97 for a listing of some of these core seminars. Core seminar content is available for free dowload at the CHBC website.)

- Strongly encourage parents' church attendance and accountability with others to foster spiritual growth through discipleship and the preaching of the Word.

- Planning times for our Pastor for Families to be available to speak with them and give advice.

- Encouraging teachers/caregivers to give deliberate, regular feedback to parents about their children.

- Hosting "Daddy" breakfasts and other informal, member-initiated meetings to encourage fathers in godly leadership of their families.

- Offering resources in the bookstall and library.

- Pastors mentioning and even giving out (for free) good books for families from the pulpit during announcement time.

- Giving out take home resources of what the children are being taught in their church classes so that parents can review and reinforce the concepts at home.

- Offering online curriculum resources and quarterly newsletter of what the children will be learning.

- Encouraging members to share honestly and deeply with each other about what is going on in their lives. Encourage them to truly support each other in what they are going through. Helping them make connections with others who are going through/have gone through similar seasons and issues with their children.

- Holding an annual book fair and giving out a resource of articles and good books for parents to use at home with their children. This book list is called Truths to Teach, Stories to Tell: Books and other resources for your family. We make it available through our website: www.capitolhillbaptist.org. It is also available on the praisefactory.org website. The booklists are substantial and updated annually as more good books come on the market. I have included some of our favorite books and some helpful articles from this book starting on p.99 as well as p.303 of this book.

Lesson #6: Questions for You in Your Ministry Setting:

1. How is your church like a sit-down, eat-in restaurant of spiritual food for your parents and children? How would you like to improve this?

2. What kinds of spiritual "doggie bags" do you send them home with?

3. Do you think parents are aware of good resources to use at home with their children? If not, what could you do to educate them better?

4. Is there an atmosphere of honesty about struggles and questions that parents have in raising their children? Why or why not? What could be done to improve this, if there is not?

Lesson #7: Be careful how you catechize.

No one can dispute that young children have an amazing ability to learn and memorize--often the quickest and easiest in their whole lives! Why not harness this skill for the sake of learning Bible truths?

Bible memory verses and catechisms are concise ways of putting a whole library of Bible truth in children's heads. While some people balk at the idea of helping children memorize concepts deeper than they can fully understand, others see the goal not so much as achieving full, immediate understanding in a young child today, but leaving it as a legacy in his head for the future. Many are the stories of conversions of even elderly people by truths memorized decades earlier in their childhood!

But on the other hand, don't exasperate your child! Yes, they may be little memory sponges, but you can harden their hearts and discourage them with the very truths you want them to love by forcing them to do too much, too soon...and in a format that just isn't appropriate or effective for them.

Remember: your point isn't just to check off the list that you taught these truths to your children. It's to try to make them stick in places where they will stay for years. Better to do less and do it well, than to think you've done it all and done it poorly or at the cost of a soft heart.

And don't forget: there is more than one way to skin a rabbit! Bible memory and catechism doesn't always have to take a recitation format. There are many Bible verses and catechism-like questions and answers put to song. There is now even a completely sung version of the Westminster Shorter Catechism. There are games you can play to help them learn, too. Look for things your kids love and ways they learn easily and try to harness them for your goal of feeding your kids with truth.

Lesson #7: Questions for You in Your Ministry Setting:

1. Do you emphasize the catechism of children at your church? Why or why not?

2. What blessings and what difficulties have your parents found in using catechisms with their children?

3. What resources have you found that help children who have difficulty with tradition forms of catechism?

4. How could you share with parents the benefits and the difficulties of catechizing their children?

Lesson #8: Be safe before you are sorry.

Develop a Child Protection Policy that protects both children and teachers. Develop it BEFORE you think you need it. It's never too early to put a policy in place. An incident of child abuse not only hurts little lives, but it can destroy your church and its gospel witness.

At our church, some parents of younger children choose to have their children in the worship service with them from their birth on up. Others have decided that the opportunity for them to have an undistracted worship and teaching time in God's Word at church helps them to better spiritually care for their family. As they are better equipped themselves, they have more to pour into their children.

So, our first goal is to provide safe, caring childcare for these parents, so that they are not worried about their children, but can focus on learning and worshipping God, themselves. This had led to the development of our child protection policy.

Some key points of this policy:

- Keeping to safe and effective teacher/student ratios, enlisting extra teachers or closing classes when the ratios are in danger of being exceeded.
- Enlisting team leaders for each group of children to help train less experienced workers.
- Assigning family numbers to each family which flash up on small display boards in the worship hall when a parent is needed during the service.
- Oversight of all childcare by our Pastor of Families, our Children's Ministry Administrator, and the Deacon of Children's Ministry.
- An interview process and background checks for all potential caregivers.
- Requiring child training classes and posting safety/evacuation procedures in all classrooms.
- Using numbered wrist bands and other sign-in/sign-out systems which identify both child and parent/s and make sure the children go home with the right adults.
- Enlisting volunteer hall monitors who are on alert for suspicious strangers and are available for emergency help within the classroom during Sunday School and church services.
- Requiring all teachers/caregivers to be a member at least six months before serving in direct contact ministry with the children. This gives us a chance to know them; and, gives them uninterrupted time getting to know people/the church before serving.
- Usually starting out new volunteers with basic nursery duty, then watching for signs of teaching ability (unless someone is already known to be a teacher, etc).
- Mentoring new teachers under the tutelage of experienced teachers who are teaching, whenever possible.

We consider ourselves successful if we have achieved just this goal...and we encourage our teachers with this fact, too. It is no small thing to help provide the children's primary spiritual caregivers (their parents) with a way to get a big, spiritually nutritious meal from God's Word and the encouragement of other believers. Kinda like a spiritual date-night. And yes, of course, we want our children to be well-taught in their classes while they are in our care. But, if everyone goes home happy, healthy and in one piece, with parents whose spiritual bellies are bulging out a little, that is a great accomplishment....and one with spiritual health benefits that can trickle down to even the youngest member of those families. Yes, safety is a job well done!

See the section on providing safe child care, starting on p.41.
- our Children's Ministry Care Training Session notes (we hold two training sessions a month on Sundays)
- a list of Children's Ministry Safety Resources
- a list of helpful safety tips
- our Application for Children's Ministry
- our Child Protection Policy

Some other tips we have used in helping teachers remember and keep to the child protection policy:
- Review one Children Protection Policy procedure each week with your teachers.
- Post regular used/commonly forgotten procedures in the classrooms.
- Quietly observe your teachers as they take the children to bathroom breaks, do check-in/check-out of children, or at other times when important policy procedures are used. If you notice they are not doing them, then find a chance to speak to them about it. Ask the teachers what you could do to help them follow through with the procedures more completely.

Some Helpful Resources:
- Children Desiring God workshops at their national conference (go to this conference or listen online)
- On Guard: Preventing and Responding to Child Abuse at Church by Deepak Reju (our Pastor to Families)
- Contact Children's Ministry staff at other churches who might be able to give you advice or let you come observe their procedures in action.

Lesson #8: Questions for You in Your Ministry Setting:

1. What parameters guide your current safety procedures? (insurance, child protection policy, church leaders, other?)

2. What teacher-student ratios do you use, if any?

3. Do you have emergency evacuation routes and procedures marked? Do the teachers know what the procedures are?

4. What do you consider the biggest safety risks in your ministry situation? How can you safeguard against these?

5. Do you have a child protection policy? When was it made? Is it up to date with the size and needs of your church now?

6. How do you screen children's workers?

7. How do you check in-check out…infants, preschoolers, elementary school kids, middle schoolers?

8. What failures in carrying out your child protection policy are most likely to occur? (don't check out children properly, forget the bathroom policy, etc.)? How could you remedy these?

9. What do you do if only one teacher shows up to care for children?

10. What about your building makes safety difficult? How do you work with these difficulties?

11. What resources have you used to decide upon your child protection policy? Who have you consulted with? Is there any issue that you wish you could find more information on?

12. What would ideal child protection policy look like at your church? What steps could you take to get there? How much would it cost?

13. Do you train your teachers/caregivers in the child protection policy? How? When? Do you give them refreshers? How? When?

14. Do you teachers follow child protection policy procedures? Why or why not?

15. Do parents know your church's child protection policy? Are they willing to carry it out?

16. Do many children have food allergies at your church? How does your church deal with them?

17. What kinds of special needs require special access or facilities? Are you able to meet those needs? What would you need to do to meet them?

Lesson #9: Practice finiteness. Start with less and do it well.

It's easy to want to provide a ton of programs for children. These programs are often seen as a drawing card for new families. If the kids are happy, the parents will stay at your church. But, I would caution you to start small and do that well. Don't just think of the programs that children enjoy or that parents might expect. Think of feeding the whole church well. Each one of those programs takes volunteers. The more programs, the more volunteers… or the more hours from the same volunteers. Those volunteers have their own spiritual needs and their own life obligations. You want to make sure that you aren't building a church of spiritually "fat" kids," but "starving" adults. This is why it is wise to have the church leaders make decisions about what children's programs the church will provide. Inform the leaders of the practical information they will need about volunteers needed, and what kind of commitment is expected in order for them to be able to truly decide what is healthy for the church.

This is especially hard in small church/church planting situations. I know of one pastor's wife, when their church was very small, led the only children's class there was. To make the situation even more complicated, this class took place during the church service. Other volunteers were few and far between. Needless to say, she started melting down. So, as hard as it was, this church decided to practice finiteness. They prayed for more volunteers, kept making the need known. But as they waited for the volunteer pool to grow, they chose to cut back the classes from weekly to every other week. This was as much as this woman could manage. Interestingly enough, more volunteers eventually did step forward and the class was once more offered weekly. This was a great decision!

That being said, what you do (and however often you do it), do it well! And this is certainly easier to do, if you when you aren't spread so thin! More on doing a good job to follow….

Lesson #9: Questions for You in Your Ministry Setting:

1. What programs does your church/ministry setting have for children?

2. When are these programs offered?

3. For what ages of children are they offered?

4. How would you prioritize your programs? Why?

5. What group of parents/children do you think are most vulnerable to not being well fed spiritually? What could you/what do you do to help support them, especially?

6. Do you have a hard time getting volunteers for all your programs or certain programs? Why?

7. Why might it actually be spiritually healthier if your church does not offer every program that parents might want or children might enjoy?

8. Why might it be better for families to leave nights free rather than offer another program?

9. How can we help support families, even if they are not at a program at church?

10. How do you care for the volunteers who care for your children, making sure they are not over-serving?

Lesson #10: Twirl with your swirls.

Life is a busy swirl for most families, but usually there is a discernible pattern to the swirl. Lesson #9 was a caution to start small and not try to do more than you can do well. This lesson is an encouragement to maximize what you do within those limits. This comes by taking a careful look at those discernible patterns in family schedules and figuring out how you can twirl along with the families in them.

Here are some examples of swirl patterns in children:

Toddlers and Preschoolers: Do better with morning activities or late afternoon after nap-time. Preschoolers frequently get very tired in the afternoons and fall apart in the evenings. You may have opportunities during weekdays to offer teaching time for preschoolers, while their moms (if they do not have to work) attend a day-time small group or Bible study.

Elementary School Age Children: Are usually busy with school during the day. Even weekday afternoons and Saturdays can be filled with music lessons, sports, or family time. Many churches offer programs on Wednesday nights when adult Bible study take place. Home-schoolers frequently are looking for an extra, outside supplement to their curriculum at home. You can offer classes to them during the school day. Sunday mornings or evenings are frequently the best times for classes for this age range. Some children have two, working parents (or are raised by a single parent) and may be after-school care. This can be a great time to reach these kids with the gospel. Elementary school children are off of school during the summer. This can be a great time for longer events, such as camps or VBS for these kids.

But it's not just family swirls that we need to think about. Your church: ministry schedule, resources available and facility type is another area where there is usually quite a swirl of activity. It's important to consider how you can work with what goes on at your church to make a great fit.

Here are some examples:

Ministry Schedule: You are a church (like us) that has only one, main worship service (i.e., if you miss the preaching, because you are caring for/teaching children during that time, there is no second service to catch what you missed.) Then, on one hand, you have a lot of children and potential teachers all at church at the same time, but you need to be careful how frequently these teachers serve and miss the service. So, you could offer Sunday School (before or after that worship service), and you will be reaching the children/supporting the parents, but at a time when volunteers will not be missing the preaching.

Resources Available: You found a curriculum you love, but it's very expensive or it requires a lot of teachers. That makes that curriculum "too expensive" (in money or in manpower) than your church can afford to spend. You might want to choose to find another curriculum that better fits these constraints.

Facility Type: Your church meets in a school and you have a lot of kids. You only have Sunday morning access. You have little storage space, but you do have a gym and great classrooms. You have a Sunday School program, but would really love to have some sort of second, missions-related program for your children. You choose to ask for use of the school during summer break (or even spring break) and have something more like a VBS-style missions program. Or, you offer smaller, back-yard Missions clubs held in homes of church members during summer break.

Working alongside who/what you have, rather than straining for what you don't have, will help you support families more effectively and more sustainably.

Lesson #10: Questions for You in Your Ministry Setting:

1. Who are you families? What are their typical swirl patterns?

2. Do the programs you offer them "twirl" with those patterns or do create more "swirl"?

3. What resources (teachers, money, staff time, etc) do you have plenty of? Which ones are tight?

4. What programs use most of your available resources? Do you think that are good "bang for your buck"? If not, what would you change?

4. What are your facitilities like? When can you use them? What kinds of programs work best in them? What difficulties do you face? Is there any way you can better use them, giving these difficulties?

5. Are there other programs you would like to offer, but have chosen not to? Why? Limited availability from families? Limited resources? Limited facilities? Is there any good way to incorporate the curriculum, but in a different format that better fits these "swirls"?

Lesson #11: Prepare the children to gather together for worship with the whole congregation.

"After this I looked, and behold, a great multitude that no one could number, from every nation, from all tribes and peoples and languages, standing before the throne and before the Lamb, clothed in white robes, with palm branches in their hands, and crying out with a loud voice, "Salvation belongs to our God who sits on the throne, and to the Lamb!" Revelation 7:9-10, ESV

I love this passage! I love this picture! The great, numberless gathering of God's people from every time, every tongue, every tribe, at last all together, praising God for their salvation through Jesus. This gathering is our goal. What an amazing experience that will be! Every Sunday, when we gather together as a whole congregation, we have a little dress rehearsal for that great Day.

These weekly dress rehearsals are not just encouraging for us. They can be a wonderfully attractive witness of the gospel for non-Christians and for our children. But how do we do this when they are sitting bored and fidgety through the singing and the prayers….let along the hour-long sermon (like at our church)? Do we just throw in the towel and give them their own, customized Children's Church, while we have our grown-up one…followed by their own, customized middle school service, then their own high school service…then their college fellowship at university? If so, when do they ever get to see the beauty of the body of Christ in this weekly dress rehearsal? When do they ever have their attention spans stretched to take in these bigger truths? Are we homogenizing our kids' worship experience in a way that does not point them to and prepare them for Revelation 7.

Or, do we take the hard line and just force them to sit and stand and listen, put on a happy face and like it?

Hmmm… No one wants to turn off kids from God and the gospel. So what do you do with the little ones who might not be old enough to sit through a long service or who are bored or even show signs of hating going to church because they cannot connect with the big words? What have we done to prepare them for the real local church—a body of believers that include people who are very different from us?

I think there are ways to both be sensitive to the limits of a child's attention span and level of understanding, and yet also to be progressively, deliberately preparing them to gather with the congregation as a whole in an understandable, hopefully memorable way as they grow up. And in doing so, always be keeping the goal a little bit of Revelation 7.

Here are some ways that we have done this at CHBC:

SUNDAY SCHOOL FOR EVERYONE
We offer Sunday School classes that do not over-lap with the worship services. Children can attend these, then attend all of the worship service. The middle school Sunday School teachers sometimes bring in the bulletin for the morning worship service and use it to go through the songs, Bible readings and sermon text before the kids go into the service.

MORNING WORSHIP SERVICE (We have only one so the whole church can gather together)
We do offer classes for preschoolers that run through the church service. Some parents bring their children into the worship service with them for the singing, prayers and reading of Scripture (about 45 minutes at our church), but sign them into their class for the sermon portion of the worship service (another hour). This exposes these children to the congregation gathered together in a way that most closely matches their attention span.

Our elementary school kids (K-3rd grade) join their parents for the first part of the service (singing, prayers, Bible readings), then some stay in for the sermon, while others are dismissed for Praise Factory Investigators (which takes place only during the sermon portion of the service.) Even those who do go to Praise Factory during the sermon, we are teaching them in ways which will better prepare them to stay in and gather with the rest of the congregation one day. We don't mind stretching the children's attention span a bit with the story length. We include hymns that we regularly sing in our worship services. And, the hymn activity involves not just learning to sing the songs, but takes a close look at the words and what they mean. This, in turn, helps the children better understand what they are singing in the worship services, which also helps them to gather with the church in a more meaningful way.

Children who are in 4th grade and higher are in the whole service, from beginning to end.

We also provide two worship bulletin (one for younger kids; one for older kids) that helps them interact with what's going on in the service, space to write down sermon notes and also gives them a coloring sheet and puzzle activity. Our Children's Ministry administrator and pastor of families create these each week, based on the music, Bible readings and Scripture passage being preached on. (a sample of two of our bulletins can found in G.)

As well as being able to sit in the worship hall with everyone else, we also provide special rooms with video feed just for parents with kids. This allows even parents with very wiggling, noisy kids to hear the service…and for them to help their children to participate in the service without being a huge distraction to others.

SUNDAY EVENING SERVICE
This 1.5 hour service is focused on sharing, prayer and singing, with a much shorter (15 minute) devotion on Scripture. Except for the long time of silence needed during the prayer time (20-25 minutes), it is an easier service for younger children to take part in. We provide a child care for pre-schoolers for the whole service; and, a class for children only K-2nd grade, that starts after the initial singing time (first 15 minutes) ends. Again, this is exposes K-2nd graders to part of the church service and all 3rd graders to all of it.

Lesson #11: Questions for You in Your Ministry Setting:

1. How are you helping children to prepare to gather with the congregation?

2. How can you help them learn more about what goes on during the worship services?

3. How could you help your parents help their children during the worship services?

4. What parts of the worship services do children regularly take part in?

5. Do you only offer children's classes during the church hour? The whole service? Just the sermon portion? What difficulties does that cause when children transition into the service? Is there anything you could do to help that transition?

Lesson #12: Pray! Pray! Pray! There are eyes that watch and minds that remember even when there seems to be no ears to hear.

Humans are big lovers of "Right Now"! But we serve a God to whom a thousand years is as a day. His plans are magnificent and big and they come about in His own, perfect time. And so, it's not surprise that while some children come to faith as children, there are many more who hear the gospel and learn the Bible, but who never come to faith until years, even decades later.

We are grateful for the encouragement of those children who become Christians at an early age! Yes, we are so grateful... both for their sake and the sake of those who pour their lives into teaching them in the things of God. We should pray for that fruit and thank God for that fruit.

But, we should pray just as much for those seeds sown by parents and teachers today, but that seem to simply lay dormant. It doesn't mean they are duds, just because they have not yet sprung to life. We serve a wonder-working, prayer-answering God! We must not give up. We must keep on praying!

Check your attitude! It is "What you see (right now) is what you get?" Mine so often reverts back to this, as I pray and pray for some and still they have not come to faith. One pastor friend said recently in a sermon: "How much are you praying for the lost? Have you given up? If God so willed to save everyone you prayed for this week, how many people would be saved?" It was a telling question. My impatience to see fruit now often turns into hopelessness and prayerlessness.

So, keep on being faithful! By God's grace, live out a godly life before the children. Let them see your relationship with the living God. Teach them all in the most memorable and understandable ways that you can. Don't give up doing your best! Don't give up praying! Pray for the parents, the teachers; pray for these little lives.

As Alfred Tennyson once said, "More things are wrought by prayer than this world dreams of."

The elders, children's ministry team, teachers and parents praying for the children, as you might expect. But we also encourage our whole congregation to regularly pray for families is by including the names of the children with the parents in a special section in the back of our membership directory. This helps reminds members like our college students or older singles, who might not usually think much of the children, to pray for them. Together, we support families!

So much of working with kids is like filling time capsules. Who knows when they will be opened by the Holy Spirit in a way that brings the truth of the gospel to life in a saving way? God has chosen to weave our prayers into the outworking of His great and glorious plans...even for these children.

Lesson #12: Questions for You in Your Ministry Setting:

1. Who regularly prays for the children and parents in your church?

2. How do you encourage people to pray? What else could you do?

3. Do you struggle with impatience or discouragement over children who have not yet become Christians? Does this show up in your prayers?

4. Do you know of anyone who heard the gospel as a child and many years later came to faith?

Lesson #13: Think outside of the boxed curriculum box.

Curriculum (almost) always needs customizing. It is but a set of tools, sitting in a toolbox, ready to be picked and worked with. Curriculum is a starting point, not a final product! It needs to be molded to fit your children, your teaching style and your teaching situation. The curriculum that you just purchased or downloaded needs a carpenter to really become useful... and that carpenter is YOU! It takes time, knowledge of your situation, and a bit of trial and error to make something that works well. Treat curriculum with the limitations it has and you will be on your way to building something beautiful with it. If you are looking for the perfect straight-out-of-the-box resource for your church, I doubt you will find it. I created the Praise Factory family of curriculums for use at our church, CHBC, and they STILL have to make changes and customize even more to fit our children, teachers, classrooms and parents!

Here are some steps that can help you customize a curriculum to best fit your ministry setting:

Step #1: Know Yourself (Your Church, Your Teachers, Your Families, etc.)
Think about your teachers' experience and teaching styles. Make sure you know the church leaders' vision for what they want the children to learn. Think about how much teaching time the teachers have each week; the pros and cons of their teaching environment; and, what teaching formats and activities best lend themselves to these parameters. Develop a good understanding of the families/children your are serving: their needs and abilities. How can you best support them, given what you know of them?

You may want to use the "Children's Ministry Questionnaire," found in Section 2 of this book. It has been created to help you get a good picture of your ministry setting and the families you are wanting to support. Discuss your answers as a group with your church leaders/children's ministry team. Ask God to give you a clear picture of where your church is and what He wants you to teach the children. The more you can understand about who you are wanting to teach, the better you will be able to customize the curriculum to reach that goal.

Step #2: Know the Curriculum
Read through a sample of the curriculum and any introductory materials a few times. Talk to someone who has used it already or observe it being taught. Get a good sense of what resources the curriculum includes and how they are used.

Step #3: Choose Your Resources
Now comes the "tools in the toolbox" part of your work. Review your answers to the questionnaire. Think about how to shape the curriculum resources to best fit your situation and your children. Is your session shorter than the time allotted in the lesson plan? Then take a highlighter and cut out elements. It is longer than the time alloted in the lesson plan? Think of what kind of resources you might be able to add to the curriculum to extend it. Are you using it for a VBS or another ministry setting different from the one it was originally intended for? Then you may need to re-group the resources into a rotation of activities. etc.

Step #4: Prepare Your First Session
Choose a sample session of the curriculum and prepare any Bible study, visuals, crafts, games or other resources you would need to teach your typical class. Notice how much time it takes to prepare these things. Are the instructions easy to follow? Are the resources required reasonable in price? Is the prep a do-able amount for your teachers? Do the activities seem to be a good fit for your teachers and kids? Do the activities seem like fluff or do they help reinforce the key teaching points?

Step #5: Make a Maiden Voyage
Try out your customized version of the curriculum on the kids. Our favorite way to try out a new curriculum is with a pair of very experienced teachers and a smaller group of children, when there is an opportunity to do so. This gives the curriculum its best test-run. Ideally, you want to give any curriculum a few sessions trial period. New curriculum is new curriculum. Teachers will be getting used to it as will the kids. The lesson plans for all three of the Praise Factory curriculum follow the same order, session after session. As this routine kicks in, it provides a structure helpful to teachers and children. But of course, it takes a number of sessions for the routine to become routine.

Step #6: Evaluate and Make Adjustments

As you test-run the curriculum, you will probably want to evaluate and make changes. Perhaps some activities typically take longer than anticipated. Perhaps your children would do better by switching the order suggested in the lesson plan.

Step #7: Train Others

Once you feel that you have adjusted the curriculum to a good fit for teacher and children, begin to teach others how to teach it, too. Ideally, this starts as a mentoring experience, with the teachers who have been teaching during the trial period lead the children and the new teachers observe. Gradually, you can hand over teaching to the new teachers, with you observing/aiding them. Do your volunteers a huge favor and always be looking for new help. Even the most eager teacher who gets no break will burn out. Many hands make light work...and work that keeps on working!

See Section 3: Eleven Steps for Making a Curriculum Custom Fit for even more information on this topic.

Lesson #13: Questions for You in Your Ministry Setting:

1. What are key factors about your teachers, parents, children, ministry setting and facilities that will affect what curriculum you use and how you use it?

2. Given what you have learned about your families and ministry setting, what characteristics are top priority for choosing and shaping a curriculum to best fit?

3. What kind of preparation work do you think your teachers should be expected to do? How much time do you think they will most likely commit/need to commit to prepare well for their class time?

4. Is there any of the preparation that can be done by someone on the children's ministry team (or other volunteer) besides teachers that would help make the teachers' load easier?

5. What are the greatest difficulties and greatest advantages to the curriculum you are trying out? Are any of them because the curriculum is new to teachers and children? How could you "fix" any of the persistent problems?

6. What would be the best way to introduce and train new teachers to use the new curriculum?

Lesson #14: Two Dead Men and a Diamond

As we develop or purchase curriculum the first three, key questions we ask are:

1. **Is it sound theologically? Is it God-centered?**
2. **Is it developmentally appropriate for the children?**
3. **Does it reinforce key truths about God in different ways?**

These questions are summarized by "Two Dead Men and a Diamond"

Dead Man #1: Martin Luther

Luther spoke of theology—the study of God—as not just dry, heady stuff, but how you live and how you die. Children want to learn real, solid truths about God because He created them to know Him. They want to know about the world, God and His great plans for the world and their lives. Teaching biblical truth is how they can know these things.

Dead Man #2: John Bunyan

Bunyan spoke of reaching people through the gates to their heart. We want to use every gate we can to reach the children. The eye gate, the ear gate, the hand gate, the feet gate, even the stomach gate. The more gates used, the better the chance for the learning time to be enjoyable, understandable and memorable.

A Diamond

The great Puritan preachers meditated upon a single truth from many different facets, seeking to expand their knowledge of God and the implications and applications of this knowledge to their lives. We strive to lead children in thinking upon God in ways that might expand their own understanding of Him, and help them see implications and applications of this knowledge to their lives. We find that curriculum which reinforces the same biblical truths in different ways and at different levels helps to achieve this goal.

See all nine of the questions we ask ourselves as we choose or create new curriculum starting on p.155.

Lesson #14: Questions for You in Your Ministry Setting:

1. What deep truths about God would you most want the children to learn?

2. What "gates" to the heart do your teachers/curriculum use? What gates might you add to these? Are there any gates that are consistently more effective with your children? Why do you think this is the case? Do most teachers realize which gates are most effective or is it just a few teachers? How could you write in these gates into the curriculum if they are not suggested?

3. How can you help the teachers think about these gates to the heart and develop their use with the curriculum you are using?

4. Does your curriculum provide opportunities for ideas to be reinforced or does it just "move on" to the next truth the next session? How could you provide repetition to help the children truly remember and understand each concept, yet keep the learning fresh?

Lesson #15: The remarkable results of repeating.

While it might sound boring to revisit the same Bible truth, verse and story, we have found that repetition allows children to actually understand and remember the truths we are teaching them.

Repetition can take come in a number of forms:

#1 Repeating a truth in different ways within the same lesson:
Such as teaching a truth, then singing a song about it, doing a craft that illustrates it or playing a game that includes questions that review the truth. Using different activities to repeat the same truth keep the learning fresh.

#2 Repeating a truth over multiple sessions:
Most curriculums take the take the one-new-concept-every-lesson approach, but we have found that if we repeat a truth over multiple sessions, the children are actually far more likely to remember it. Of course, this is exactly what is going on in their schoolrooms each week. No teacher would teach multiplication tables one day and assume the children have learned it. And don't most preschoolers drive their parents crazy by asking them to read the same story over and over and over again? There is a world of different between introducing a new concept and understanding it and retaining it.

#3 Repeating a truth at home:
By sending home a take home sheet of the truths or even copies of the story the children are learning in class, you provide an opportunity for them to be repeated and learned more deeply in families.

The Praise Factory curriculums repeat truths and even Bible stories for multiple lessons. Hide 'n' Seek Kids--for the youngest children-- provides five lessons on the same Bible truth, Bible verse and Bible story. Deep Down Detectives --for older preschoolers and early elementary--provides three lessons on the same Bible truth, verse and story. PFI--for elementary age children-- provides three lessons on the same Bible truth and verse, though it uses a different story for each of the three lessons. By using new activities each session, the children get the variety they also enjoy, while getting enough time to grasp the truths being taught. Take home sheets of the key concepts and even the stories are available to send home for the families to continue to learn from.

Lesson #15: Questions for You in Your Ministry Setting:

1. Do your children retain the truths you are trying to teach them?

2. Does the curriculum you use include repetition? How?

3. Are there ways more repetition might help your children better learn and remember the truths you want them to know? What would those be?

4. Does your curriculum provide take-home sheets? If not, how difficult would it be to create them from your resources?

Lesson #16: Think like a missionary!

Missionaries know that if they are to effectively share the gospel with people from another country, they will have to think cross-culturally. They spend time learning the language and the culture of the people they want to reach. They study the people they want to reach, trying to figure out how best to translate Biblical truths into understandable concepts. They look at themselves as communicators, the message they want to communicate, and the people they want to receive it and understand it. They know that all three parts of this chain need to be in place for them to make a connection.

This same cross-cultural way of thinking is very helpful when we want to communicate Biblical truths to children, too. Thinking about what we are like as teachers; understanding the message we want to communicate; taking time to understand what the children we teach are like and how they think, can help us to not just speak these truths to them, but help them understand them. Being aware of the developmental norms for a group of children can help us to give them activities that they enjoy and are suitable for their age.

You can find many great resources for what behavior and abilities to expect in preschoolers and elementary school children. See pp.255 and 289 for two papers on what to expect from preschool children and elementary age children can be helpful in reminding us how these little children think. They give a development snapshot of two through five year olds, as well as behavior to expect of these preschool age children as well as elementary school age children. This kind of information is important for curriculum developers as well as teachers to be familiar with and use as they work with the children.

Lesson #16: Questions for You in Your Ministry Setting:

1. What are the characteristics and developmental abilities of the children you are trying to reach?

2. What are some ways that the children you teach are different from you in their ability to think and understand?

3. What are some ways that the children you teach are different from you in activities that help them learn?

4. How do these differences in characteristics/developmental abilities affect how you present truth in an understandable way to the children?

5. What has helped you in getting a grasp of the differences and even barriers to communicating with the children in your class?

Lesson #17: Oh, I know that old story...or do I?" Fight Bible boredom in well-taught children.

How many times have you seen it? That glazed look or know-it-all expression; that groan or sigh that comes when you introduce the story of Daniel in the lion's den to a 3rd grader who has heard it from the time he was a two-year-old. I've seen it frequently. To make matters, worse, many times curriculum love to recycle the same Bible stories, year after year, creating a situation in which de-sensitization, not deeper appreciation, seems to be the outcome.

When you are faced with this situation, here are four things to consider doing:

#1 Dig in deeper yourself! Get a commentary, word-studies book, or a Bible backgrounds book on your passage; listen to a sermon; talk to a pastor; or, look online (be careful you find a reputable source!) Usually there are many interesting details you can add (about the city, the people, the word choices, etc.) that bring depth and life to a story that they have heard before.

#2 Sometimes use the Hebrew/Greek root name of the familiar people involved so the children won't hear the name and tune out immediately. For instance, Iobi is the Hebrew word for Job. Substitute Iobi and tell the story. It will let the children hear the story with new ears.

#3 Split the children into two groups, asking each group to write down the story, the best they can remember. Then read the story to them and give them another chance to modify their story to come closer to the real text. Read both teams' versions and decide who came closest to the actual text. Then, continue your class session with a discussion of the Bible truths and applications.

#4 Change how you present the story. For example, with the story of Esther, instead of reading and telling it at the beginning, make a set of props of key elements from the story and ask the kids to guess what story they come from. After they identify the story, have the children tell what each of the props had to do with the story. Ask them questions to help the kids tell the significance of each prop and a deeper, spiritual application. For example, if the king's scepter was one of the props, you could ask them to identify it as the scepter that the king had to hold out to accept someone who entered his throne room with asking. When you ask them the significance of this in the story, they could tell you that Esther asked Mordecai and the Jewish people to pray for the Lord to work in the king's heart so that when she went to see the king without asking, he would treat her favorably. The application questions that go with the scepter could be: Why did Esther ask the people to pray? What does this tell you about who Esther knew was even more powerful than the king? What should we do when we are faced with a seemingly impossible situation, against an enemy that seems to be too big for us? etc.

Lesson #17: Questions for You in Your Ministry Setting:

1. Do you have many children who have been well-taught? How often do you run into a bored attitude from children like these? What age does this boredom start to appear?

2. What have you done to help fight Bible boredom?

Lesson #18: Change your activities from time-fillers to conduits of truth.

Conduits of Truth

Praise God, there is a lot of curriculum on the market now that seeks to teach Biblical truths to children in an understandable, enjoyable and memorable way! However, we have found, especially in the response activity area, that you need to look closely to see if the activities actually help the children retain the key, biblical truths of the lesson we most want them to remember.

So, when we create or look at a curriculum, we are not only looking for enjoyable, age-appropriate activities, but at whether these activities are filled with truth or whether they just fill the time. Those which are filled with truth are what we call "conduits of truth." A conduit of truth activity is one that uses the enjoyable-ness of the activity to fill the children with the important truths of your lesson.

For example, if the lesson was on Noah's Ark and the children were asked to pair up and mimic animals entering the ark, the children may have a great time, but only go home making elephant noises. This game would not be a conduit of truth. But, if the children were asked to pair up and mimic animals entering the ark, but asked to freeze each time you blow a whistle, then you ask them a question related to the day's story for them to answer, then you have made the same game into a conduit of truth. You are using the enjoyable-ness of the activity to provide an opportunity to reinforce the biblical truths you want them to understand and remember.

Lesson #18: Questions for You in Your Ministry Setting:

1. What kinds of activities does your curriculum typically use?

2. Do the children enjoy them?

3. Do the children learn from them?

4. If they enjoy them, but do not learn from them, how could you change them to make them conduits of truth?

Lesson #19: Pray Bible-based, life-expanding ACTS prayers.

Using the ACTS structure for prayers has been one of the most surprisingly, remarkably effective tools we have encountered in teaching children to look at the Bible and learn more about who God is, who they are, themselves as sinners; Christ's work for sinners; and, how God wants us to live. And not only to help the children do this in class, but actually take this skill home and keep on using it.

ACTS is an acronym that stands for the four, basic ways we talk to God:
- Adoration (praising God for who He is)
- Confession (telling God about our sins and asking His forgiveness)
- Thanksgiving (thanking God for His many good gifts--especially those He's giving us through Christ)
- Supplication (asking God for what we need to live the way He wants us to live and to see His kingdom come)

We include an ACTS prayer with every Bible truth in all the curriculum we use, starting even with our two-year-olds. As the children get older, we continue to include the ACTS prayer, but we ask them to help think of an A, C, T, S from the Bible truth. This helps develop an ability to ask good questions about any Bible truth or Bible text. And, not just in any way...but in four, very important ways: Who is God? Who am I? Why do I need a Savior? What has God done, especially through Jesus that I am thankful for? And, how does God want me to live?

The ACTS format makes for an easy, ready-on-the-spot, spiritually-rich, thought-provoking devotion for families, too. Really, you can read any passage and ask these four questions and glean a lot of truth and good application from it.

Of course, the problem with introducing a structure to prayer is if the structure becomes a "must" instead of an "aid." To help avoid this mindset, we also make sure to pray with the children in ways that are not structured like this, to help them understand that prayer is talking to God and He does not require a certain format to listen and answer!

Lesson #19: Questions for You in Your Ministry Setting:

1. When do you pray with the children in your ministry setting?

2. Have you ever used the ACTS prayer format with them?

3. How could you introduce children and families to this prayer tool?

4. What cautions would you give to them about over-use of this tool?

Lesson #20: Don't throw out the baby with the bathwater! Be a pirate!

A little bit of pirate-ing from other sources can go a long way in "fixing" a curriculum's weaknesses. Few, if any, curriculums will have everything you want, just the way you want it. One curriculum might have fun activities, but they are fluffy, time-fillers. Another one may have outstanding teaching, but many workbook/seat-work activity... and you have a bunch of wiggle monkeys! Yet another may have great teaching and good activities, just not enough. A fourth might have great activities, but the truths presented are very shallow or moralistic. Is there any way to use curriculums like these?

Many times, yes! Here are some suggested fixes for different problems?

1. Not theologically sound.
Re-write, if possible. Sometimes, a curriculum is just too off-base to work with, though.

2. No regular presentation of the gospel.
Include a copy of the gospel, appropriate for the children's age group in the teacher's binder and/or add it to the lesson plan.

3. Too much seat-work.
Add games such as the Praise Factory games (see pp.) along with your own discussion questions to be used with the games to combine movement with reinforcement of the truths learned. Save the seat-work for a take-home sheet or for the opening minutes of the next Sunday's session as children are arriving into class. A great way to reinforce truths from the previous week!

4. Don't like the order in the lesson plan.
Switch it around!

5. No parent hand outs for review and discussion at home.
Save some of the seat-work and give it out as a take home instead. Type up the Bible passage used and a few discussion questions for the parents to use with their children to review at home. Or, give them a memory verse to learn. Or, give them a coloring sheet and type the Bible passage and discussion questions on the back for the children to take home.

6. The curriculum presumes too much reading or writing ability.
Teacher reads passages instead of the students. Teacher takes the questions from a written assignment and uses them in a game, instead. (See praise factory games.)

7. Not enough activities.
Add crafts, music or games from other sources, along with your own discussion questions, to combine movement with reinforcement of the truths learned.

Two particular good resources for adding extra games: Great Games for Preschoolers and Great Games for Elementary School Children are two resources available through www.praisefactory.org. They each contain dozens of games that can be used in any Bible story or with any Bible verse.

Lesson #20: Questions for You in Your Ministry Setting:

1. What do you like about your current curriculum?

2. Are there any areas that need "fixing"? What are they?

3. How could you keep what you like and fix what you don't like?

Lesson #21: Skip the chaos! Plan your transitions between activities.

Last time I checked, kids are not mind readers. Furthermore, if given the chance, they will do things in a way you didn't expect, and often times, in a way that is disruptive to the learning environment. So, help them by telling them what you want them to do before they do it. A great example is transition from one activity to another within the class. For example, say they have been sitting in chairs listening to a story and next they will be going over to tables to do a craft activity. Before they move, tell them where you want them to go, how you want them to go there and what you want them to do (or not do) when they get there. You might say, "Class, next we are going to do a craft activity over at the tables. When I tell you to get up, I want you to quietly walk over to the tables and sit down. Please do not touch any of the coloring supplies. When everyone is settled, I will tell you what to do next." These instructions make it clear what the children should do and make it clear what mis-behavior is. It won't take care of all your problems, but it will certainly help some of them.

Appendices I and J, at the back of this book, include two articles that help teachers manage transitions and many other common classroom scenarios.

Lesson #21: Questions for You in Your Ministry Setting:

1. When are your children most likely to misbehave in class? Are they predictable? Are they a pattern? Do you set clear expectations during these times before they happen? How do you respond to them?

2. Does the children's behavior vary depending on the training of the teacher in charge? What is the difference between how the best teacher manages the class and how the worst teachers manage it? How could you teach the worst teachers these techniques or establish the best teacher's strategies as regular rules or write them into the curriculum you use?

3. What are the transition points in your curriculum? What could you do to help the children make these transitions more smoothly? How could you introduce these ideas to your teachers?

Lesson #22: Skip the chaos! Teach with a predictable schedule.

A predictable schedule is like an extra helper that is always present in your classroom.

Kids love doing and seeing new things, but they thrive in predictability. Why not give them both? Create a regular structure for your classes that both teachers and kids come to expect. Fill that structure with rich learning experiences that bring the truths you are teaching to life. And, you will find that even when a different teacher teaches, the familiar structure helps create continuity that in turn helps create a great learning environment.

Lesson #22: Questions for You in Your Ministry Setting:

1. What is the session time like for your ministry setting?

2. Is there a regular order to what activities happen when?

3. If there is not, what benefit might there be to creating one?

4. If you do try to create one, what order would be most helpful?

5. Have you observed a certain order being better with the children? Why was that better?

6. Have you observed a certain order being worse with the children? Why was it worse?

7. If you use a rotation of teachers to teach the children, does everyone use the same schedule? How does this make teaching more difficult? How could you systematize the schedule from teacher to teacher?

Lesson #23: The Triple Crown of Teaching

The Triple Crown is considered by many to be the greatest accomplishment in thoroughbred racing. And rightly so, only twelve horses in the last one-hundred years have been able to do it. It takes pedigree, training and versatility...not to mention being at the right place, in the right weather, at the right time, experts say. It is a summary of greatness as the same horse, in the same year, wins the Kentucky Derby, then the Preakness, and finally, the Belmont Stakes.

I think there's a Triple Crown of teaching, too--a summary of great teaching. I'm putting this lesson at the end of the curriculum and teaching section because of that. And the good news it, this Triple Crown is fair more attainable; you can try for it every time you teach; and there's no horse to clean up after (though probably quite a few children).

Here's my Triple Crown:
Crown #1: Teaching that is Faithfully Understandable
Here is my Kentucky Derby: the sort of first race of the Triple Crown. This is teaching that is true to the God's Word. And, that is presented in a way that the children can grasp. You won't even get out of the starting gate if you leave God's Word behind. We have to make sure we aren't just teaching moralism or what we would like the Bible to say. The children (like us) need the gospel if they are to be saved. That means teaching them about the Great and Good God who created them and is king over them and is worthy of all their worship. That means understanding they are sinners who rebel against this Great and Good King and face His eternal judgment. That means knowing about Jesus, the Son of God, the perfect Savior who came to pay for the sins of all who turn from their sins and trust in as their Savior. Who died on the cross and who rose from the dead in victory on the third day. And this means, hearing the call to repent of their sins and trust in Jesus, themselves. And, as they do so, to live the rest of their lives, not their own way, but God's way and with His help. Yes, we must be faithful to teach all of this, displayed through every page of the Bible.

But to be faithful AND to present it in a (usually simplified) way that children can understand is the half to this challenge. It is something that takes prayer, and practice...and some training certainly does not hurt! Like Lesson #16 reminded us, we might know truth, but we have to think about who we are telling it to, if we want them to know it, too. Children, especially preschoolers and younger elementary-aged children, don't understand abstract ideas like we do. They are very concrete thinkers. That makes some ideas tricky to get across to them. The two papers on what to expect from preschool children and elementary age children (also mentioned in Lesson #16,) can be helpful in reminding us how these little children think. These start on pp.255 and 289..

Crown #2: Teaching that is Enjoyably Rich
Winning the Kentucky Derby is just the first trophy need. Next comes the Preakness: teaching in a way that the children enjoy, yet is deeply rich with Biblical truth. "Enjoyable" is usually not so hard to come by. Most every curriculum has it. Most every teacher can figure that out (even just bring cupcakes to class and see if that doesn't up the enjoyable factor!). But enjoyable that is rich in truth take a bit more forethought. It means thinking about what those children enjoy doing AND what you want them to do and marrying them right there in your classroom. These are the "Conduits of Truth" from Lesson #18. Don't settle with being everyone's favorite teacher because you are fun or funny! Use all that is enjoyable in you and all that the kids enjoy to display truth and bring them back to it again and again.

And that thought, of course, brings us to the crunch race, the Belmont Stakes:

Crown #3: Teaching that is Deeply Rememberable
We cannot be the Holy Spirit. We cannot save the children we teach. But, by God's grace, we can leave a testimony and a trail in their hearts. The testimony of the truths of God's Word. The testimony of His work in the lives of person after person after person through every page of the Bible. And, the testimony of His work in our lives, who He is living in right before them, right now. And the trail of how to come, find and know this great God through faith in Christ.

We want to teach children truths today in a way that it might stay in their minds the rest of their lives. Who knows what day is the day of salvation for any child in our class? How wonderful to think God can use us to plant seeds ready to spring up into salvation, in His perfect timing!

How do we do this? Well, like the Triple Crown, you won't get to the Belmont Stakes and get to try for the Triple Crown if you didn't first win the Kentucky Derby and the Preakness first. So, you need to strive to teach in an understandable way. (You cannot believe that which you do not understand). And, when you use enjoyable activities to help reinforce those truths they are learning, that repetition will help cement the ideas in place. And lastly, you need to keep on persevering in these things and in prayer.

By the time those three-year-old thoroughbreds get to the Belmont Stakes, tiredness is becoming a factor. Athletes train to peak for the "big race." These horses have to train to peak for three big races that take place over six weeks. So with us, perhaps we can pull off these wonderful, enthusiastic ideals for one or two sessions, but what do we do to stay the course to the end? It is by God's grace! So we must pray for ourselves and pray for the children. Ask God to help you to be faithful week after week you teach. Ask Him to help you better understand the children and better understand His truth..and how to make a connection. Ask Him, by His Holy Spirit, to be making that connection, even when you are not sure that you know how to. Ask Him to show you how to make good conduits of truth with enjoyable activities. Ask Him to use your time with the children to plant many seeds...and plant them deep and securely. Ask Him to bring them to life.

There's a wonderful way this analogy breaks down. Any horse that attempts the Triple Crown and fails is forgotten. But with our Triple Crown of teaching, we know that God is Himself at work in us to will and to act according to His good purposes. We know that He has given us good works He prepared for us in advance...even teaching these children. We know that He can do imaginably more than we can think or ask for the glory of His name. We know that all things work for the good for those who love God and are called according to His purposes. We know that all our righteousness is as filthy rags. Our work with the children may never reach full Triple Crown proportions... or at least not every week. But God is faithful and He is at work! Yes, we should continue to strive for the prize, but we can be confident that because of who God is, He will use even our most feeble attempts to do great things, for His glory, for our good and for the good of the children we teach! Press on!

Lesson #23: Questions for You in Your Ministry Setting:

1. Do your parents/teachers have a good understanding of the Bible truths they are called to teach to the children? If not, how could they learn them better? How could you help them?

2. Do your parents/teachers feel confident in conveying Bible truths in a way that is understandable to their children? Are there resources that could help them grow in this skill? How could your curriculum help your teachers improve in this?

3. Are there key, Biblical truths that you, your teachers or your curriculum avoid? If so, why? What benefit would it be to include them? What harm does it do to leave them out? How can you add them into the curriculum in a way that is appropriate for the children?

4. What do your children enjoy doing?

5. Do the teachers know what the children they teach enjoy doing? How does know this/would knowing this help them teach the children better?

6. How could you use the things the children enjoy doing to help reinforce the truths you teach?

7. Does the curriculum you use incorporate the enjoyable things the children do? Does it do it in a way that is only enjoyable, or that makes it a conduit of truth?

8. What helps you to persevere in your work in children's ministry?

9. What is hardest for you to keep persevering in doing in children's ministry? What about your volunteers, in general?

10. How does your curriculum help you persevere?

11. How do the church leaders help you persevere?

12. How has God been faithful to answer your prayers for perseverance?

13. How likely are you /your teachers to pray for the children's families and teachers during the week?

14. How has God been faithful to answer your prayers for the families? teachers?

Lesson #24: A few, good men are hard to come by...
...but they go a long way!

Most Children's Ministry programs have a high percentage of women volunteers and a low percentage of men volunteers. God uses women to do wonderful things in Children's Ministry.. at least I hope so, because, of course, I'm a woman!

But… there is something very special that happens when men help in Children's Ministry. We have seen it over and over again. Perhaps it's seeing them tenderly care for the children. Perhaps it's the authority and leadership their presence brings to the classroom. Perhaps it's because there tends to be less of them volunteering. Perhaps it's that extra reflection of the loving Heavenly Father that a godly man can give. I can't say I have anything really solid to go on here, but I know it's true.

Not only is it good for the children in the classroom, but it's great for the men, too. We have found that Children's Ministry is a wonderful place for men to develop their teaching skills (and maybe one day become a small group leader or even a pastor). We have seen man after man grow in his teaching ability with the children and before long, be asked to teach the adults in some capacity. And, it is great for men who hope to be fathers one day or who are fathers already and who want to grow in their understanding of children of various ages. It's even been good for men looking to find a wife (Yep! Many a dating relationship, then marriage has had its first spark as teachers teach together.). And lastly, we have seen men grow in their own relationship with God as His child, as they work with the children. It has grown their understanding of what it means to be a child: their needs, the way they think; and their dependence upon others to take care of them.

How do you get men to serve? Here's a few ways we do it:
- The pastors preach and encourage it from the pulpit.
- The church leader who oversees Children's Ministry (the pastor of families, in our case) calls men and asks them to serve.
- We use men in our Children's Ministry leadership—specifically, the deacon of Children's Ministry. We make sure that he is a godly, SINGLE (yes, single) male—and usually we choose a men who is fairly clueless, but very willing to learn, about Children's Ministry when he starts. As he serves the Children's Ministry every week, other men—even those hard to get single men—see him serve and are much more willing to serve themselves. He has been effective in getting men volunteers than the women on our team. And, because he, himself, comes to serve in Children's Ministry with little or no experience and survives…even thrives, he can make a powerful case to other single men to do the same.
- We provide mentoring situations so that they know will have help learning what to do.
- We provide novice-level, short term volunteer opportunities so they can dip their toe in the water and try it out, instead of throwing them in the deep end and refusing to give them a helping hand out for a whole Sunday School year.

Lesson #24: Questions for You in Your Ministry Setting:

1. Do you have difficulty getting men to serve in your ministry setting? Why?

2. Have you asked (many) men why they don't serve?

3. What could you do to get rid of any of your men's barriers to serving?

4. What do/what could your church leaders do to encourage men to serve in Children's Ministry?

5. Do you have any men who do serve who could share with the congregation and encourage other men to serve, too?

6. What fruit have you seen from men serving in Children's Ministry... in the children's lives? in men's lives? in families' lives?

Lesson #25: Care well for your teachers and they will come back.

Teaching is a big responsibility and often a tiring one. Many teachers burn out from frustration or lack of support. We try to train our teachers so they will be well prepared. And, we try not to overtax them by asking for a commitment from them that is greater than is reasonable or spiritually good for them. Here are ways we try to care for our teachers....and it helps them be ready to come back again and again.

#1 We Mentor Our Teachers

We try to mentor all new teachers, so that they see a teaching model before they start teaching themselves. This gives us a chance to observe their teaching before they teach to see if they are suited to teach. And, it allows them to try out teaching before committing to a class. As new teachers watch more experienced teachers, they can become familiarized with the curriculum and with effective teaching skills. This brings both greater continuity to the classroom and greater success among new teachers, which in turn helps our children learn.

#2 We Model Teach for Our Teachers

At least once a year, we model-teach in each classroom. We walk the teachers through lesson preparation before class, then have them watch us teach the lesson. Afterwards, we talk about what went well and what could have gone better. This give-and-take of loving criticism fosters an atmosphere of humility and teachability as well as helps us become better teachers. As teachers (and perhaps even more importantly as fellow believers in community together), we think it is important to model soliciting, giving and receiving this kind of healthy criticism. How will we grow if we are not willing to ask others to help us see not only areas in which we do well, but also those in which we need to grow?

#3 We Observe and Encourage Our Teachers

We try to observe teachers at least once a year. The point is not to be the perfection police, but to encourage them. Yes, often this also provides opportunites to give helpful feedback that will make for a better teaching and learning experience. If it causes too much anxiety in the teachers to be observed, we resort back to model teaching.

#4 We Teach Classroom Management Skills As Well As Provide Teacher-friendly Curriculum

We try to carefully choose materials that will help our volunteer teachers understand what to teach and how best to teach it. We also give our teachers tips on how to manage children's behavior in ways that help everyone learn and foster respect for the teacher and for the other students.

#5 We Have Our Teachers Teach in Teams Bigger than They Need

We form teams of teachers that partner together/switch off teaching a particular class of children. A typical team of Sunday School teachers at CHBC commits to one year of teaching. But because they are part of a team of four teachers, with only two teaching any week, they are really teaching twenty-six Sundays rather than all fifty-two Sundays of the year. This allows for teachers to teach a full year without getting burned out and provides built-in substitutes. In our other classroom settings, we have 2 to 6 teachers teaching at a time (depending on class sizes and ages of children). This also allows less experienced teachers to partner and learn from more experienced teachers, making hands-on teacher training a regular part of the classroom experience. It also creates the opportunity for teaching responsibilities within the classroom to rotate from week to week.

#6 We Train Our Teachers

Once a year, we hold training sessions for particular groups of teachers, such as preschool teachers, or elementary school teachers. We also have coordinators who oversee the large number of volunteer teachers who teach in the Praise Factory preschool and elementary school classes. A coordinator helps train new teachers for two, non-consecutive months a year (non-consecutive so that they do not get burned out, themselves!). They also help other teachers prepare and often team teach with them these months. The encouragement, advice and model-teaching of these coordinators often makes the difference in everyone's experience in the classroom. And, often makes the difference in whether a new teacher signs up for other teaching opportunity! Coordinators like these are simply invaluable!

#7 We Give Our Teachers Deacon Support

Each Sunday, our Deacon of Children's Ministry faithfully checks in with our Sunday School teachers and Praise Factory teachers (both preschool and elementary classes). He is on hand to find any needed supplies, extra volunteers or other help a teacher might need. He keeps an eye out for issues that would be important for the rest of the Children's Ministry team to know about, usually communicating these through a weekly e-mail. A deacon volunteers for three years. This long term commitment allows the deacon to gain quite a bit of institutional knowledge as well as becomes a familiar, reliable face to teachers and parents.

#8 We Limit Our Teachers

Out of spiritual care for the teachers, the elders have set limits on how much any one member can spend teaching the children.

First of all, any volunteer who works directly with children must have been in membership for 6 months. This is so they are well-fed, well-adjusted, and well-known before serving. Their spiritual health is a priority.

For approved, child-care volunteers who have been members at least six months:

Childcare teachers:	Volunteer 1 Sunday a month
Sunday School teachers:	Volunteer 1 year at a time, on a team of 4 to allow for substitutes
Worship Service teachers:	Volunteer for 2 nonconsecutive* months a year
Hall monitors:	Volunteer 1 Sunday a month
Children's Ministry Deacon:	Volunteer for 3 years

#9 We Are Willing to Shut Down Programs or Change Age Limits on Them to Protect Our Teachers

Because we have only one Sunday morning service and one Sunday evening service, the elders are especially careful about how much time members spend away from regular preaching. If we have a consistent, month after month, lack of volunteers, our elders may suggest that we shut down a particular program or change the age limits (such as changing a program for K-4th graders to K-3rd graders, making less volunteers needed to teach the class) for a time.

They have decided that this action is best for the spiritual welfare of the teachers, who too many times are asked to miss yet another service just to keep a program going--to their own spiritual detriment. We want to support our parents, but not at the expense of over-taxing and under-feeding of the rest of the body. Our elders have developed an order of priority of programs, making child care for infants and toddlers during the two Sunday morning and evening services the top priority.

Lesson #25: Questions for You in Your Ministry Setting:

1. What programs does your church/ministry setting have for children?

2. How many teachers are required to teach each session?

3. How do you support your teachers? Mentoring? Modeling? Observing? Training? Teams of teachers? Deacon support? Limit the time they serve? other? What works best? What else would you like to do?

4. What are the typical problems your teachers run into in their classes? How could they be helped with those?

5. Do you have much teacher burn-out? How do you group your teachers to teach? Do you build in a way for them to have a break?

6. How do you get substitutes for your teachers? Do they find them or do you?

7. Do you frequently run short on the number of teachers you need?

8. Do you frequently depend upon a small group of teachers to teach over and over again without giving them a break?

9. Do you have teachers who are not getting an opportunity to be well-fed themselves?

10. If you were to shut down or limit a program/s to better serve your volunteers, which one/s would they be? Why? What programs are most crucial to serve the families in your ministry setting?

The Children's Ministry Questionnaire

about this questionnaire

This questionnaire is a gleaning from questions included in previous section: <u>Twenty-Five Lessons Learned in Children's Ministry at CHBC</u>. They are the ones we most frequently ask people when they are thinking through customizing a curriculum to fit their situation. Ideally, each member of your Children's Ministry team/church leadership would answer these questions individually first, then meet together to discuss them. We hope they provide you with solid insight that will help you in choosing and customizing whatever curriculum you are considering.

The questions are grouped into eight categories:
- Ministry Foundations
- Children
- Classroom
- Teachers
- Facilities and Resources
- Parents
- In the Worship Service
- New Curriculum
- Ministry Reflections

A Word of Caution:

This questionnaire is like going to the doctor for your annual physical. You go because you want to get a complete picture of your health, even if it means that you see some things you don't like. Chances are you are about to see some things you really like and some things that you don't like. That will always be true, this side of heaven. **That is why at the bottom of each page we have included two questions: "What can I thank God for? What can I Ask God to help us do?"** These are reminders that God has been good and used us--even us--to bless others. And, that with His help, we can become an even greater blessing to them.

Use the findings from this questionnaire to thank God for what He has done. Use them as points of prayer. And, use them to humbly, with God's help, one step at a time, to work towards even better service to the families and to the Lord.

The Children's Ministry Questionnaire

MINISTRY FOUNDATIONS:

1. What is your setting for teaching kids? (VBS, AWANAS, after school program, school, Sunday School, Children's Church; Church evening program, outreach to non-Christians, English as a second language group.

2. Do you have a statement of faith that provides a foundation for the truths you believe and teach? If not, what are the Biblical truths that under-gird your ministry?

3. Do you have a mission statement for what you hope to do within this ministry? If not, what would it be?

4. Who provides leadership over your Children's Ministry? Have the church leaders provided guidance as to what they want the children to learn?

5. What staff support (paid or volunteer) does your Children's Ministry have? What do they do?

6. Do you have a child protection policy? Is it enforced? How do you screen prospective teachers?

Highlights from this page:
What can I thank God for in what He's done already?

What can I ask God to help us do?

CHILDREN:

7. How many children do you usually have in total? What's your break-down by age/grade?

8. Describe, in general, the children who come/you hope will participate in this program and their parents. Are they well-taught or have they never heard the gospel... or something in between?

9. What are the children like, developmentally/academically? How well can they read or write? Do they tend to like seat work or are they active? Are there children who have needs that will need special assistance? What kind?

10. Do the same children attend regularly or do you have many one-off attendees? If many one-off attendees, why?

CLASSROOM:

11. When do/you will you meet with the children (day of week, time of day, etc)? How long is your teaching period?

12. How do you split up the children in their classes? Do you combine children with very different development abilities (such as pre-schoolers and elementary age kids/ readers and pre-readers) into the same class? What are those different abilities you are trying to accommodate? What has worked well?

Highlights from this page:
What can I thank God for in what He's done already?

What can I ask God to help us do?

13. How likely are behavior problems to seriously disrupt the class time? What types? Do your teachers feel confident and well-equipped to meet these problems? What has been done to improve the issues or to help the teachers?

14. What kind of schooling do these children receive (public, private, home-school; Christian/secular)? Has this affected how/when/what you teach the children? In what ways?

15. Do the children understand what they as they learn in class? Do they enjoy what they do in class? Do they remember what they've learned?

TEACHERS:
16. Describe your teachers: (younger/older; enthusiastic/worn-out; spiritually mature/immature; dependable/unreliable; experienced/inexperienced, show up late/early, etc.)

17. How do you get new teachers to volunteer? For what period of time do they volunteer?

18. How do you train new teachers?

19. If a teacher needs a substitute to teach for them, how do they get one? Is this frequently a problem? Why?

20. How much prep is a teacher required to do to be ready to teach? How much prep work does the Children's Ministry staff do? Are teachers usually reliable in doing the prep work they are called to do? How much is a good amount to ask the teachers to do?

Highlights from this page:
What can I thank God for in what He's done already?

What can I ask God to help us do?

FACILITIES & RESOURCES:

21. What are your facilities like? Do you have storage? Can you put visual aids up on the walls?

22. What is your budget for Children's Ministry resources like? What equipment/resources do you have on hand already?

23. Are you frequently faced with a limited resources--money, teachers, space, time, equipment, etc? If so, what resources are you lacking? How does this affect what you do?

PARENTS

24. How well-equipped are the parents in their role as primary spiritual care-givers of their children? Do you feel like your children's programs are carrying the majority of the weight or only supporting what the parents are doing? What has been done to try to better equip the parents, where needed?

25. How involved are most parents in what their children are learning in class? What kind of take home resources would you like to give out with the new curriculum? What have you sent home previously? Do parents use them? Why or why not?

26. Do you communicate with parents? What form does that contact take? (email; phone; in person; etc). What do you try to tell them? Are they very responsive? Why or why not?

Highlights from this page:
What can I thank God for in what He's done already?

What can I ask God to help us do?

IN THE WORSHIP SERVICE:

27. Do your children sit through the entire worship service with their parents? Why or why not? If not, what is provided for them? What ages? For what portion of the service (whole service: just the sermon; etc.)?

NEW CURRICULUM:

28. What do you most like about your current curriculum? What would you most like to change? What an ideal curriculum look like for your situation?

29. When do you want to start the new curriculum?

30. Do you have any/many "load-bearer" teachers; that is, teachers willing to invest lots of time and energy into your current program or would be willing to do this with a new program?

Highlights from this page:

What can I thank God for in what He's done already?

What can I ask God to help us do?

SUMMARY MINISTRY REFLECTIONS

31. What are some things to thank God for in your ministry setting? Who has it been most effective in reaching with the gospel? What are some things you would love to improve, with God's help?

ADDITIONAL THOUGHTS, COMMENTS, & QUESTIONS:

Eleven Steps to A Custom Curriculum Fit

Eleven Steps to a Custom-Fit Curriculum

1. GET TO KNOW YOURSELF!	Any curriculum is but a set of tools in the teacher's hands. It is a starting point, not a final product! It needs to be molded to fit your children, your teaching style and your teaching situation. Your knowledge of your church leaders' vision for teaching the children/supporting families; the pros and cons of your teaching environment; and, a good knowledge of the families/children and their needs and abilities all work together to make a more understandable, enjoyable learning connection. If you start out by taking time to get to know who you are, you will make a better curriculum for all involved.
	Ask God to give you a clear picture of where your church is and what He wants you to teach the children and consider using one or more of these ideas to get to know yourself better:
	1. BRAINSTORM: Simply get your Children's Ministry team/church leaders together and talk about who you are. Write down your description.
	2. THE CHILDREN'S MINISTRY QUESTIONNAIRE (Section 2) Provide more structure for your team's thoughts and discussion by using the "Getting to Know You" Questionnaire." Ideally, have each member of your team/church leader involved go through the questions and answer them on their own. Then, bring everyone together and discuss your reflections.
	3. THE TWENTY-FIVE LESSONS DISCUSSION QUESTIONS (Section 1) Have your team/church leaders read through the twenty-four lessons and write down/ discuss their answers to the questions that follow each section. This might be the most time-intensive option, but you might glean even more insight through it.
2. GET TO KNOW THE CURRICULUM!	Take a good look through whatever curriculum/s your team is considering. Read the introductions; a few lesson plans; and check out the curriculum website (if there is one). For each curriculum you are considering, fill out the Curriculum Questionnaire (included on the next two pages) to create an overview by which to compare the curriculums to each other.

New Curriculum Questionnaire

Fill out one of these questionnaires for each of the curriculums you are looking at. This will provide a great overview to aid your curriculum comparisons and decision-making.

1, Curriculum Name: _____

2. Publisher: _____   3. Suggested Age Range: _____

4. Suggested Ministry Use (Sunday School, VBS, etc): _____

5. Curriculum Type: (Bible Study; Old Testament/New Testament Overview, Theology, Missions, etc.):

_____

6. Format (Hard Copy/Download): _____

7. Resources you need to use this curriculum: _____

_____

8. Is it single use or repeat use curriculum: (uses workbooks that have to be purchased again; have to pay each time you download or for an annual membership; or, gives you permission to make copies after your initial purchase, etc.)

_____

9. Cost of Set Up: _____

10. Cost of Maintaining the Curriculum: _____

11. How many sessions of curriculum are available? _____

12. What are the lesson plans like? Scripted or bullet-points? _____

13. How easy are they to follow? _____

14. Does the curriculum elements follow the same order/structure each lesson? What is it? _____

_____

15. How hard would it be to train teachers in this curriculum? _____

_____

16. Would an inexperienced teacher or a younger Christian be well-equipped to teach them, or only an experienced or more mature Christian?

_____

_____

_____

New Curriculum Questionnaire

17. Do they include a devotional for teachers? _____

18. How sound are the Bible truths? How deep are they? _____

_____

19. Are the Bible truths appropriately explained for the age group they are intended? _____

_____

20. What kinds of visual aids/props are included? _____

_____

21. What kind of activities included? _____

_____

22. What learning styles are the activities most suited for? _____

23. Are the activities time-fillers or are they "conduits of truth" which help reinforce the key truths taught?

_____

24. Are the teacher prep steps clearly listed and easy to follow? _____

25. What kind of prep must be done for the typical session? What kind of prep work is it? _____

_____

26. Are there any take home resources? What kind? _____

_____

Any other thoughts/comments/questions?

Eleven Steps to a Custom-Fit Curriculum, continued

3. CHOOSE IT!	Now comes choose and customize work. Review your reflections from the Get to Know Yourself Questionnaire. Then, look over the Curriculum Questionnaires you filled out for the curriculum/s you are considering. Based on this information, which curriculum looks best for your needs?
4. CUSTOMIZE IT!	Once you have narrowed it down to the curriculum you think fits best, it's time to start making a fit. Look through the curriculum and ask yourself questions like: • Does the curriculum follow the same basic order each lesson? What is that order? How is it different from your current curriculum? • What elements fit your teachers best, just they way they are? Which ones do not? How can you make them a better fit (re-writing/training/modeling/removing/practice/etc)? • What elements are like what you do now and would be easy for the children to get used to? • What elements might take a bit more time for them to get adjusted to? How can you make them a better fit (re-writing/training/modeling/removing/practice/etc)? • How does the time alloted for the curriculum compare with the time you have? What would you need to change to make it fit? • How is the curriculum's intended use different from how you will be using it? What changes in order/what you do/how you do it should you make? • (For instance, are you using a Sunday School curriculum for VBS? Then you may need to re-group the resources into a rotation of activities. etc.) • Who will do the prep for the lessons? How much will teachers do and how much will something on the Children's Ministry team or another volunteer do? Get some paper, or better yet, go to a whiteboard. Write down what is currently down in the class/es who will be using the new curriculum. Star what elements you like or want to change. Make a copy of the first lesson of the new curriculum. Write up on the board the elements of that lesson in order. Look at the lesson segments (such as Opening activity, Bible story, response activity). Think of them as building block that can be moved around. Based on what you know about your teachers, children, time constraints, etc., make any necessary shifts in the order of lession elements. Maybe you won't make any changes. Maybe you will switch many activities. Maybe you will take some out or even see that you need to add some extras in.

5. PREPARE FOR THE TEST RUN	Take your changes and make a new cut and pasted version of the first lesson of your new curriculum and prepare it. This will be what you use in your next step: the test run with the kids. Prepare any visual aids, games and crafts you will use in the lesson. Make copies of any take home resources. Now you are ready to try it out! If at all possible, test run the curriculum a few times before handing it over to your teachers. This will allow you to try it out and adjust it to make a better fit before you start to train other teachers to use it.
6. TRY IT!	Try out your customized version of the curriculum on the kids. Our favorite way to try out a new curriculum is with a smaller group of children (of the more-likely-to-be-well-behaved variety), when there is an opportunity to do so. This gives the curriculum its best test-run. Ideally, you want to give any curriculum a few sessions'Ev trial period. New curriculum is new curriculum. There's no getting around the learning curve. Teachers will be getting used to it as well the kids. You will get a better sense for your fit if you try it more than once.
7. EVALUATE AND ADJUST IT!	As you test-run the curriculum, you will probably want to evaluate and make changes. Reflect on how the teaching session goes, after each of your test runs and make any necessary changes. As you get closer to a good fit, add in more conditions like the typical classroom--such as your crazier kids, etc. See how the curriculum works with these new elements. Make more changes until you feel good about your fit.
8. SIGN POST IT!	Once you have figured out what works best for your children and those teaching the curriculum, put sign posts in place in the classroom. If you found that certain activities work better in a certain part of the room (such as games or craft time), put up a sign on the wall near that area indicating that. Or, put down a rug where you want to have Circle Time, if the curriculum uses one. If the curriculum follows a set time schedule, display the schedule on the wall in large print so a teacher can with just a glance know what he/she should be doing. If particular resources are used in the curriculum, store these and signpost these, too, so that even the newest teacher can easily find what he/she needs.

9. CHOOSE YOUR LOAD BEARERS	Once you feel that you have adjusted the curriculum to a good fit for teacher and children, begin to teach others how to teach it, too. Ideally, this starts as a mentoring experience between you and another teacher (preferably two) who are willing to learn the curriculum inside and out, until they can teach it well themselves and later train others in it, too. I call these teachers, "load-bearers," because they will share the weight of implementing the new curriculum. Have your load-bearers first come observe you as you teach the curriculum. Have them read any introductory materials as well as the curriculum lesson plan you will be teaching from before they observe. After class, de-brief with them about the session. Have them continue to come for a number of sessions. Gradually give them more and more of a teaching role each session, until they teach the curriculum completely, themselves.
10. ADD OTHERS	With your load-bearers in place and confident in the curriculum, you can now begin to look for more potential teachers to be trained. Follow the same steps as you did with the load-bearers: have them read any introductory materials and the lesson plan before they observe a session. De-brief with them afterwards and gradually add them into the teaching experience.
11. WANT MORE IDEAS? GO SEE IT!	Find other churches that use the same curriculum and ask them if you can come observe the curriculum in action. Very helpful!

'6

Guidelines for Teaching Preschoolers

TABLE OF CONTENTS

About This Paper

This paper was developed by Jennilee Miller and Connie Dever for the teachers and Preschool Coordinators at Capitol Hill Baptist Church. While some elements are applicable to only our church's preschool department, most are of a broader use.

Why Working with Preschoolers Matters

"We will walk together in brotherly love, as becomes the members of a Christian Church; exercise an affectionate care and watchfulness over each other and faithfully admonish and entreat one another as occasion may require."

"We will endeavor to bring up such as may at any time be under our care, in the nurture and admonition of the Lord, and by a pure and loving exempt to seek the salvation of our family and friends."
-- Capitol Hill Baptist Church Covenant

Playing with dolls, reading stories, singing songs, giving out snacks, settling squabbles and potty breaks. These are among the normal activities that take place in the preschool classes each week. They may seem trivial or even tiresome, sometimes. They certainly may seem to have very little to do with fulfilling the covenant promises we make to each other as members. But in fact, these activities are of great importance. Those that are willing to serve the preschoolers are part of an important work, not only in proclaiming Christ to the next generation, in building up and bringing unity among church members, and even in growing as Christians, themselves.

How can such small tasks bear such great fruit? Let's look at each and find out.

Proclaiming Christ to the Next Generation

Deuteronomy 6:4-7, NIV
"Hear, O Israel: The LORD our God, the LORD is one. Love the LORD your God with all your heart and with all your soul and with all your strength. These commandments that I give you today are to be upon your hearts. Impress them on your children. Talk about them when you sit at home and when you walk along the road, when you lie down and when you get up."

God made people busy. God made people with lots of daily needs. Nowhere do we see this more, perhaps, than with preschool children. They are in perpetual motion. They are in perpetual need of help from others…except when they are sleeping. This passage from Deuteronomy 6 reminds us that it is not just children's bodies that are in constant motion and need. Their hearts are spiritually in constant motion and need, too. It is an encouragement not to relegate the spiritual training of children to a particular time of devotion in the morning or evening, but to see the daily events of life as opportunities for spiritual training.

While the spiritual raising of children is primarily the task given to parents, we as members have an opportunity to partner with the parents in this great task. In the few hours we have each week to be with the preschoolers, we intersect with their lives. It is our opportunity to fill the little events of their day with stories and songs of God, and model lives that seek to love God and others in all that we do.

Building Up and Bringing Unity among Church Members

When you serve the preschoolers, you are not only serving them by being with them, you are also serving them by allowing their parents opportunities to grow spiritually through the teaching and preaching of the Word. Some parents choose to keep their children with them through the worship services. But many choose to let other members teach and tend to their children in the preschool classes while they go to Core Seminar Classes *(Sunday School a la CHBC)* and/or the worship services for a time of undistracted teaching and worship. As parents listen and grow, they become better equipped to be godly parents as well as godly people. Sharing in the same teaching and worship with other members fosters unity as we grow and worship together. Do the math: 100+ preschoolers + 200 parents...that's some 300 people you serve when you serve in the preschool department. A three for one deal! That's hard to beat!

Growing as Christians, Ourselves

Working with children is great for the children. It's great for the parents. But that's not all. It's great for you! Seasoned teachers will tell you: "What you teach, you learn." Seasoned parents will tell you: "Caring for children grows your appreciation for God's care for His people and your dependence upon Him."

Volunteering with our preschoolers, on a weekly or even monthly basis, can provide you with an opportunity to learn more about God yourself as you teach them about Him. And, it can be a great way to grow in your reliance upon God for grace to live godly lives before them, as well as wisdom to teach and train them well.

Teaching Biblical Truth to Preschoolers

Teaching Biblical Truth in Safety

The top priority of all of our children's ministry programs is to provide a safe environment for children to learn and play while their parents attend Core Seminar classes *(Sunday School a la CHBC)* or the worship services. To this end, require all potential children's workers to:

- Attend a Childcare Training Class
- Go through a Screening/Application Process
- Learn and adhere to our Child Protection Policy procedures

Child training classes

This class is led by one of the Deacons of Child Care or the Pastor of Families and Children. Child Training Classes take place about two or three times a month, immediately after the morning worship service. Attendees learn about the Child Protection Policy and why it is so important that we follow it carefully. The class takes about one hour. For more information, contact the Children's Ministry Administrator, at Capitol Hill Baptist Church, (202) 543-6111.

Screening/application process

As another precaution, all potential children's workers must fill out a Children's Ministry Workers Application. This application requests basic information about each worker, as well as questions about your previous experience working with children. It also asks for a number of references that will be contacted and questions related to any criminal offenses or instances of abuse. Each person's name is also submitted to the Department of Justice Screening System which does a background check for similar offenses. All application information is treated with the utmost confidentiality by
the Pastor of Families and Children. While it may feel awkward to have to ask such questions, they are a necessary part in achieving our goal for a safe environment for the children. For further information about this process, please contact Deepak Reju, the Pastor for Families and Counseling at Capitol Hill Baptist Church.

Child protection policy

Our child protection policy have been developed around two key principles:
1. No one adult should be alone with one child at any time.
2. When in doubt, call a hall monitor or a parent.

It includes the use of:
- Matching wristbands for all children and their parents so that the right children go home with the right adults
- Red wristbands for children with special allergy alerts
- A family number identification system which flashes up on number boards in the worship hall' if a parent is needed during the worship services
- Procedures for taking boys and girls to the bathroom
- What to do in an emergency or when an accident occurs

The full Child Protection Policy is reviewed in the Child Training meetings and is also available in the church office and on the church website.

Teaching Biblical Truth Developmentally Appropriately

Successful teaching involves conveying truth from teacher to student in a way that is understandable and memorable. A teacher needs to not just know the truth he wants to teach, but what his students are like in order to achieve this goal. Here are brief descriptions of what 2-5 year olds that may help you know how to best teach our children.

TWO YEAR OLDS

A Snapshot of Two Year Olds
- Full of life and curiosity
- Can be very stubborn and demanding
- Growing awareness of capabilities of their mind, body and language, but with only a fledgling skill level in the use of them

Speech and Communication Skills
- 2's may only start out with a fairly limited vocabulary and 2 word sentences but develop into 3-5 words sentences by the end of the year.
- Pronunciation may be difficult to understand by others not familiar with the child.
- Are able to understand most of the speech in your regular conversation, even with other adults by the end of the year

Play and Socialization
- Largely plays alongside other children, but not with them (this is called parallel play)
- Playing with others begins to develop by the end of the year
- Loves to imitate others' speech and actions
- Begins to engage in pretend play

Emotional/Intellectual Development
- Can have rapid, emotional swings from very happy to very sad
- Can be destructive and throw things when angry
- Has a hard time control his impulses
- Often tests limits and rules
- Many enjoy answering "no" when asked to do something, even when they mean "yes"
- Their perspective of the world is largely "me-centered"
- Starts to show consideration of the feelings and needs of others
- Can be very willful, yet still have a strong desire to please adults
- Frequent separation anxiety when parents leave
- May often act shy around new people
- Wants to try to do tasks by themselves

Fine Motor Skills
- Fine motor skills gradually develop. Learns to hold crayon and make basic strokes.
- Can make a low stack of blocks

Large Motor Skills and Other Physical Milestones
- Runs, jumps, begins to climb and may even be able to pedal a tricycle
- Enjoys rolling, throwing, and catching a large ball
- By 2 ½ years, many are ready to begin toilet training

Classroom Skills and Behavior
- Enjoys simple stories, action rhymes and songs over and again. Tries to sing along.
- Extremely short attention span, especially for structured group activities
- Largely engages in individual activities rather than group activities
- Has a hard time sitting still for long periods
- Often plays with the same toy for more than a few minutes
- Enjoys pouring, sifting, sorting, moving things
- Does best with simple 1 step directions

THREE YEAR OLDS

A Snapshot of Three Year Olds
A year of growing confidence in use of body, language and socialization

Speech and Communication Skills
- Expanding vocabulary and sentences (up to 6-word sentences) though with grammar errors
- Speech becomes clear enough to be understood by many people
- Stuttering may develop in the child's language

Emotional/Intellectual Development
- Enjoys asking who, what, where, and especially why questions
- Many still enjoy testing limits and rules, particularly to see the adult's reaction.
- Separation anxiety largely gone
- Seeks the approval of adults
- Often enjoys helping
- Enjoys laughing and acting silly
- Often looks for and thrives under praise

Play and Socialization
- Is able to get along better with other children. Less "me-centered. Learning to cooperate, take turns and share (with promptings)
- Begins to notice typical roles of their gender and engages in pretend play using them.
- Plays with groups of other children her age, but still enjoys playing alongside other children (on his own)
- Pretend play become much more complex. Expands into stories. Can include imaginary friends.
- Moves between the world of real people/friends and pretend people/friends. May have a hard time differentiating between what is pretend and what is real. Even G rated movies can be scary because they seem so real.

Large Motor Skills and Other Physical Milestones
- Growing confidence in ability to use body. Walking, running, jumping, climbing come easily, with little thought
- Balancing on one foot or standing on tiptoes still difficult
- Can kick a ball
- Can use the toilet by himself

Fine Motor Skills
- Fine motor skills are developing. Can hold a crayon with confident grip. Older three's often are able to make simple drawings of shapes, animals and people with a few body parts. They can use child's scissors fairly well.
- Can dress self and feed self with spoon and fork
- Can put on shoes, put not tie them

Classroom Skills and Behavior
- Enjoys hearing familiar stories, doing familiar action rhymes and singing familiar songs. Will often ask for the same stories, action rhymes and songs again and again.
- Enjoys short books and stories
- Does best with activities/games in which everyone is busy at the same time, rather than waiting for their turn.
- Growing attention span for group activities, but still quite short.
- Enjoys moving and dancing to music. Can sing a simple song
- Enjoys simple puzzles, playing with play dough, matching games
- Enjoys acting like different animals (hop like a rabbit, slither like a snake, etc)
- Likes to count things
- Does best with simple, 1 step directions
- Loves follow the leader games
- Thrives under praise

FOUR YEAR OLDS

A Snapshot of Four/Five Year Olds
- Most are confident in their ability to use body, communicate and socialize with others
- They like to talk and make plans
- They are often excited and happy

Speech and Communication Skills
- Vocabulary is expanding rapidly to include a few thousand words.
- Sentences can be fairly complex.
- Speech gets quite clear, though the pronunciation of some letters may still not be completely correct. Many fewer grammatical errors. Asks many "how" and "where" questions. Can answer many why" questions.
- Most talk with adults with greater ease and have learned to look them in the eyes when speaking.
- Often likes to talk and can carry on extended conversations with adults and others.

Emotional/Intellectual Development
- Asks "why" questions a lot!
- Boasting, lying, name-calling may begin
- Begins to understand danger and become fearful. Fears may center around loud noises, the dark, animals and strangers
- May begin to experience feelings of jealousy
- May be quite bossy
- Seeks adult approval
- May begin to misbehave to get attention
- Many 5's like to take risks
- Understands and respects rules. Wants others to respect them, too

Play and Socialization
- Regularly plays with other children. Best friends become very important.
- More in tune with the feelings and needs of others. May take them into consideration in their actions and words.
- Expects to share and take turns. Usually does so without adult help.
- Makes up games with simple rules to play with others.
- In group play, one child is usually the leader who organizes the other children and what they will play.
- May exclude other children from playing with the group.
- Their imagination and ability to engage in pretend play continues to expand, but they are more able to differentiate between pretend and real life.
- Likes collecting things

Large Motor Skills
- They are quick and confident with most body movements. They develop the ability to do somersaults and skip. 5's like to test their physical strength.
- Fine motor skills are more developed. Begins to tie shoes, dressing self and brushing teeth.
- Catches a ball, move up and around obstacles easily. 5's begin to be able to throw a ball overhead.

Fine Motor Skills

- Can draw simple patterns and shapes and print (some) letters. Enjoys painting with a paintbrush, cutting and pasting.
- Likes to count and sort objects.
- Can stack high towers of blocks
- Can use a spoon, knife and fork

Classroom Skills and Behavior

- Can begin to learn to raise hand to answer a question, rather than blurting out comments.
- Can understand and follow multistep rules.
- Growing ability to play games in which they must wait their turn.
- Enjoys mastering a skill, idea or story. Enjoy getting to share their ability/information with others.
- Still enjoys listening to familiar stories, doing familiar action rhymes and singing familiar songs repetitively.
- Enjoys dancing and moving to music. Often can sing fairly well.
- Expanding attention span for structured group activities
- Can organize objects from smallest to largest
- Can recognize and maybe write his own name
- Can recognize familiar words, like "Stop" on a stop sign. Some 5's begin to identify letters of the alphabet, sound out letters and do simple reading.
- Can follow multi-step directions
- Loves play-acting and role-playing
- Enjoys creating and telling their own stories
- Loves follow the leader games
- Can tackle more complex puzzles and games
- Likes to thread beads, form shapes out of play dough, including simple animals and people
- Likes to count.
- 5's can understand yesterday, today and tomorrow
- 5's like to plan and build more elaborate pictures, buildings, scenes
- Loves nonsense rhymes

Resources used: http://www.nncc.org/Child.Dev/ages.stages, parenting.ivillage.com/

Teaching Biblical Truth through Play

Preschoolers learn through play! They learn to compare things; they learn how things work; they learn to imagine and create; they learn how to use their bodies and minds. Preschool play is a beginning of the answer to God-given command for humans to fill and subdue the earth, as these little children first discover and learn to use the bodies and the world around them. But preschool play does more than that. Preschool play lays the foundation for teaching them about God, the Bible and His glorious plans for His people. How? As they develop abilities to compare objects, they are developing skills which will help them discern between right and wrong. As they learn how things work, they are developing skills which can help them understand the cause-and-effect of their actions upon others and God's holy response to them. As they imagine and create, they are being prepared to understand that God has plans for His world and has created it for His glory. As they learn how to use their bodies and minds, they are being prepared to be able to serve and love God with all their heart, mind, soul, and strength and to love others as themselves.

Playtime also can provide you with time to talk to the children about the Bible truths they learned as their hands are busy or to re-create what they have learned in their play. Their interactions with other teachers and children allow opportunities to speak to them about God's holiness and forgiveness, and about His good laws to obey Him and love others.

Yes, playtime is an important time in any preschool program! We should pray that God would use it to prepare these children to do great things for His glory one day!

Teaching Biblical Truth through Structured Instruction

As important as play time can be in laying a foundation of skills on which to place future understanding of God's truth, preschoolers are ready even at the age of two to begin to hear and understand God's truth now. This is done with age-appropriate amounts of structured teaching time and activities.

Teaching Two Year Olds

Two year olds have a very, very limited attention span for group teaching, say about five minutes. Keep it short. Keep it simple. And keep it moving. Incorporate movement and use plenty of visuals. Use an interesting tone of voice.

Two year olds love repetition. It's how they learn. About the time you are perhaps getting beyond bored with a story or concept, your two year olds are beginning to really love it. They love to be able to participate and predict what will happen, so they thrive on routine and hearing the same stories again and again.

Change activities frequently. Tell a little story, then sing a song incorporating movement. Prioritize what you want to teach them, realizing that you may only get to a small portion of what you would like to do with them.

Having the children sit together for a short Circle Time can be quite a chore in itself. They will probably wiggle around, even when they are sitting together. Don't be discouraged by this! You can't make a two year into a five year old… at least not without waiting three years! These first attempts at teaching group behavior are so important for preparing them for group learning in the future.

Use carpet squares. Two year olds are not used to sitting in a circle time, so having a clearly defined area in which to sit helps them learn that circle time is a time for them to sit still and listen & participate.

Use wisdom with the lessons. If you are on week one of a new month and have five new two year olds, you should probably limit your circle time to five minutes of activities.

Train two's to transition from activities. Make it a game (move to circle time by hopping like a bunny, creeping like a caterpillar, etc) or a race.

Typical Classroom Skills and Behavior
- Enjoys simple stories, action rhymes and songs over and again. Tries to sing along.
- Extremely short attention span, especially for structured group activities
- Largely engages in individual activities rather than group activities
- Has a hard time sitting still for long periods
- Often plays with the same toy for more than a few minutes
- Likes to learn about new things by tasting, touching, smelling, listening, etc.
- Enjoys pouring, sifting, sorting, moving things
- Does best with simple 1,2 or 3 step directions

Summary: Key Goals for Teaching Two's
- Keep children safe
- Teach them truth from God's Word
- Help ease separation anxiety
- Acclimate children to functioning & participating in a group,
- Give no more than 2 or 3 step directions
- Train them to sit still for 5+ minutes in structured group story time

Teaching Three Year Olds

Three year olds are growing in their ability to sit still and to be interested in structured group activities for longer periods of time. However they are still very young and still very new to the concept of structured group learning. Proceed with lots of visuals, movement and an interesting voice. Keep your expectations low for their attention span, especially with the youngest threes.

Change activities frequently. Tell a little story, then sing a song incorporating movement. Prioritize what you want to teach them, realizing that you may only get to a small portion of what you would like to do with them.

This is another important year for beginning good group behaviors. Within Circle Time, this is a good age to begin really working on taking turns talking and raising their hands. They will often forget to raise their hands (I mean... when else are they practicing this. They don't have to raise their hand to talk to their parents or friends), but be patient and persistent to help train them.

The more familiar you are with the lesson, the more comfortable you will be keeping your eyes on the kids instead of your teaching binder, which significantly helps your ability to manage the children.

Don't feel chained to the lesson plan! The classroom is not a theatrical performance where teachers follow a script word-for-word. Gauge how well children are engaging. Do you have a handful of boys with excess energy that would benefit from a quick, impromptu game of "Duck, Duck, Goose" or "Simon Says" to get out some of their energy so they can listen to the lesson? Does the lesson seem to be running long and your kids are loosing interest? Shuffle things around, and perhaps do the game right after the story, and then get back to the music at the end of class.

Typical Classroom Skills and Behaviors
- Enjoys hearing familiar stories, doing familiar action rhymes and singing familiar songs. Will often ask for the same stories, action rhymes and songs again and again.
- Enjoys short books and stories
- Does best with activities/games in which everyone is busy at the same time, rather than waiting for their turn.
- Growing attention span for group activities, but still quite short.
- Enjoys moving and dancing to music. Can sing a simple song
- Enjoys simple puzzles, playing with play dough, matching games
- Enjoys acting like different animals (hop like a rabbit, slither like a snake, etc)
- Likes to count things
- Does best with simple, 1 step directions
- Loves follow the leader games
- Thrives under praise

Summary: Key Goals for Teaching Three's
- Keep children safe
- Teach them truth from God's Word
- Grow children in their ability to function & participate in a group
- Give them no more than 3 or 4 step directions
- Sitting still for 10+ minutes in structured group story time

Teaching Four/Five Year Olds

Four and five year olds are beginning to hit their stride. They are getting more confident in their ability to communicate with others and more used to group behaviors. Their attention span allows them to sit in a group for longer periods of time. But, preschoolers are still preschoolers. You still want to incorporate lots of visuals, movement and use an interesting voice as you teach.

By the time a child is four, they are familiar with the group-norm of raising their hand when they want to talk. Because they are not usually in large groups, it's easy for them to forget, yet it is a great habit to encourage. You can encourage children by lavishing the positive reinforcement when they do raise their hand. "Oooh! I love how Lisa is raising her hand because she has something to say! What a good example! Thank you, Lisa." If you have lots of blurting out going on and you have just asked the kids to raise their hand when they have something to say, you can be lighthearted with them and say "Wow! I hear a lot of noise right now, but my ears just can't listen because no one has raised their hand and so all I hear is 'blah blah zzzzzzz blah wooooo.' What should we do? I know someone has something good to say?" When children correctly raise their hands, immediately encourage and compliment them.

Typical Classroom Skills and Behavior
- Can begin to learn to raise hand to answer a question, rather than blurting out comments.
- Can understand and follow simple rules. Many fives can understand and follow multi-step rules.
- Growing ability to play games in which they must wait their turn.
- Enjoys mastering a skill, idea or story. Enjoy getting to share their ability/information with others.
- Still enjoy listening to familiar stories, doing familiar action rhymes and singing familiar songs repetitively.
- Enjoys dancing and moving to music. Often can sing fairly well.
- Expanding attention span for structured group activities
- Can organize objects from smallest to largest
- Can recognize and maybe write his own name
- Can recognize familiar words, like "Stop" on a stop sign. Some 5's begin to identify letters of the alphabet, sound out letters and do simple reading.
- Can follow multi-step directions
- Loves play-acting and role-playing
- Enjoys creating and telling their own stories
- Loves follow the leader games
- Can tackle more complex puzzles and games
- Likes to thread beads, form shapes out of play dough, including simple animals and people
- Likes to count.
- 5's can understand yesterday, today and tomorrow
- 5's like to plan and build more elaborate pictures, buildings, scenes
- Loves nonsense rhymes

Summary: Key Goals for Teaching Four's/Five's

- Keep children safe
- Teach them truth from God's Word
- Grow children in their ability to participate and share in a group
- Following 3 or 5 step directions
- Sitting still for 10-15 minutes in structured group story time

Teaching Biblical Truth by Training Behavior

Key Principles
1. Children are Foolish by Nature
"Folly is bound up in the heart of a child," Proverbs 22:15

We can expect foolish behavior from children in the classroom.

2. Responding to Foolish Behavior is an Important Part of Our Teaching
Since we can expect foolish behavior, we can plan how to use foolishness to train children in the biblical truths we hope they will learn from our lessons. Foolish behavior fills the pages of the Bible; and, it often fills the lives of our children. Why? Because foolish behavior is the outworking of foolish, sinful hearts. We enjoy good behavior from our children because it makes our jobs as teachers easier and more effective. But, it is important to remember that our primary objective in all our teaching is to help the children learn about the Creator God, see their sinful, rebellious hearts, understand the consequences of their sin; and turn to Jesus as their Lord and Savior. We can use their foolish behavior and our teaching as opportunities to point out foolish behavior, its consequences and our need for a Savior. As you prepare your lesson, ask yourself: What foolish behavior do I see the people in this story exhibiting? What wise behavior? Do any of these behaviors look like the heart issues or actions of the children in my class? What questions could I ask them to help them see these issues/actions and apply them to their lives? How could I point the children to their own heart issues and their own need of a Savior through this story and the issues/actions highlighted, as well as, of course, through any foolish classroom behaviors?

3. Training and Turning of Hearts and Actions
As we address foolish behavior in our classroom, it is important to think about how we change. Any kind of training takes time, even more so the training of behaviors overflowing from sinful hearts. Since children are by nature foolish, then we need to help train them in wise behavior, encourage them to turn away from it. We need to make sure they understand how they are to act (through learning classroom rules as well as through learning biblical truths in our lessons). We also want to lead them to see their sinful hearts, ask God for forgiveness, and for the Holy Spirit's help to change both their hearts and their actions. We need to be praying for God to be at work in the children even during the week. How easy it is to forget the children until Sunday morning when we are faced with teaching them again! What opportunities we waste when we do this!

How important it is that we also remember that changed behavior does not necessarily mean changed hearts! Changed hearts are a work of the Holy Spirit alone! We also should pray that God would make us gentle, wise and consistent in our training of the children.

4. Train and Turn Only with Great Compassion, Gentleness and Graciousness
Behavioral problems, especially with "repeat offenders", can be very frustrating. It is very, very important that we only train and turn with compassion, gentleness and mercy. Not only can this often help a situation more quickly resolve (cf. Proverbs 15:1 "A gentle answer turns away wrath and a harsh word stirs up anger."), but when we act and speak from a heart of compassion, gentleness and graciousness, we reflect our merciful and loving Father to the children. Pray that God would fill your heart with His mercy and love as you deal with any behavior issues. Then of course there's the work that God will do in our heart and lives as we ask Him to cultivate this attitude in ourselves. Be aware of growing frustration on your part. If you feel that you cannot speak or act towards a child with the right attitude, it would be better to leave the situation to another teacher.

5. An Ounce of Prevention is Worth a Pound of Correction

out of temptation's way
When you become familiar with the children in your classroom, you will become aware of the things that typically tempt them. You may prevent many mishaps by looking over your lesson plans and classroom for situations, objects, etc. that will tend to draw out misbehavior and adjusting them accordingly. Do you have a group of especially wiggling children? Look for ways to add in more movement. Do you have some very competitive children? Change the games to be group cooperation games rather than team vs. team. Are there things in the room that regularly distract? Find a place to put them away.

working as a team
When one teacher is leading the teaching, the other teacher(s) should be actively looking for ways to facilitate focus and learning. This includes everything from noticing if the lead teacher needs a dry erase marker and bringing it to him, hold visuals, etc. to sitting next to a wiggly child, to quietly pulling aside a child who has a behavioral issue. Whenever possible, avoid the lead teacher interrupting his teaching to deal up with these issues. It will be distracting the other students and be more embarrassing to the student who is struggling.

6. Choosing your battles
Issues which must be addressed each time
- Safety issues
- Pattern behaviors that reflect heart
- Issues that affect feelings of another child
- Deliberate disobedience

Issues in which you can choose your battles
- Classroom training (like raising hands, etc.)

7. A Note about the Children of Visitors
Children of visitors may face extra anxiety in child care. They are surrounded by new teachers, new children and are in a new setting. While the above guidelines are useful for all children--visitors or regular attenders--you may need to spend a little extra time and show an extra measure of patience with the visiting children in most issues. However, issues of safety or physical harm must be treated with the same immediate response as with the children of members.

8. We Serve the Children Best by Partnering with Their Parents
The Lord has primarily given parents the honor and challenge of nurturing and admonishing the children we teach in our classroom. By gleaning from their knowledge and experiences of their children, we can learn how to best teach them and train them. By sharing with them both encouragements and concerns, we may be able to help them to better understand and shepherd their children.

engaging with parents
Parents appreciate a report on how their child did during class, so don't be afraid to touch base with them with a one-sentence feedback. "Mikey did a great job answering questions during Circle Time." "I could tell Katie really liked our songs today." "Ask Lewis to tell you what grasshoppers had to do with our story today."

If you had a discipline issue that warranted time out, you should tell the parents about it, even if you feel like the issue was resolved.

Don't be afraid to ask parents for advice about their children. If you have had trouble with a particular child (be it girl drama, throwing, not participating) or if you simply feel perplexed, share your observations with the parents and humbly ask if they have any suggestions on how you can help their child.

When a parent has left a child in your care, they have temporarily transferred their authority to you in the care of their child. However, the teacher is still not the primary caregiver or the one primarily accountable to the Lord for the shepherding and training of that child. We can partner with the parents helping to train, encourage and correct (when needed) a little one, but sometimes, you may find a "tough cookie" who does not respond to your correction. In these situations, where you cannot help turn their heart from sin, or their behavior from a behavior that is persistent and distracting or even harmful to the class, it is very appropriate that you have the hall monitor call the parents to your room to help. While we, as teachers, of course want to extend grace and understanding when possible, we also need to realize that we do not benefit the child (or his/her parents) when we ignore consistent issues, hardening hearts, etc.

encouragements

Dismissal time can be a particularly wonderful time to share encouragement. Share signs of spiritual growth or turning away from tempting behaviors. Tell the parents what their child learned that day. Even if you had trouble with behavior earlier in class, share ways that the child acted positively during your time with them. If possible, make these encouragements with the child present. Even small comments make a big difference to a parent and a child. An encouraging e-mail or a card to your children or parents can have an even greater impact.

concerns

Dismissal time can also be a time to share lesser concerns (or give a brief behavior update for on-going issues already addressed). However, since conversations about behavior concerns may bring up delicate issues that are usually better discussed out of earshot of child or other parents, a brief comment after class, followed up by a conversation at a later time is often best. Sharing concerns about the children we teach can be difficult. Perhaps you are not a parent yourself and have little experience with behavioral issues except as you volunteer at church. Perhaps the child is new to the class or a visitor and you do not know the child or the parents. Perhaps you think you observe a serious problem. Perhaps the thought of talking to any parent, no matter how well you know them, is a terrifying thought. While you are right to humbly consider your shortcomings, we would encourage you to ask God to help you speak to the parents. Pray that He would give you the right words to say and that your words would be well-received. Use words that describe what you have observed of the child instead of those that make judgments about the child or the parents. Make sure to express your gratitude for the parents and the child and your desire to serve them. Feel free to talk to the Pastor for Families about concerns you have either about the child or about speaking to parents. He is here to help you.

insights

Since the parents spend most of the week with their children as we have them for an hour or two a week, it is easy to see how we can greatly benefit from their insights into their children. They very likely have already observed issues or giftings that we see in the children and can give us helpful tips in how to train or encourage the child. Their insights can help us teach the children better and often save lots of time in figuring out how to train them.

prayer

Nothing is done well without prayer! We are God's servants and need His Holy Spirit to work in both our hearts and the hearts of our children and their parents. He delights in the praise of children. He gives parents their children as a good gift. And He gives us the opportunity to glorify Him in speaking words of truth and living that reflect Him. And, for a few hours each week, He gives us this opportunity to do before and to serve children and their parents. We need His Spirit to be at work in us all. He is the One True Turner and Trainer of Hearts. He is the Shepherd who shepherds the parents and the children. He is the Giver of Wisdom and the Producer of the Fruit of Love, Gentleness and Patience. Pray with the other teachers before class for both the instruction and the behavior and hearts of the children. Pray during class with the children, that God would be at work in you all. Pray after class, to thank God for how He answered your prayers and about insights into the children you received during the time. Take home your class list and pray for the children and parents during the week. Look ahead to the topic of the next week's lesson and begin to pray it for all of you. In conclusion: PRAY!

Common Behavior Scenarios by Age

TWO YEAR OLDS

separation anxiety
Separation anxiety is a developmentally normal and expected part of being a two year old. Follow the parents lead when they know what is comfortable, though most experts recommend that "sneaking off" is not always helpful for teaching a child to make a healthy transition.

Tips for easing a child into a classroom
- Tell them what they're going to be doing in class
- Have a specific toy or book in mind that you think they'll like. Tell them about it, or show it to them before they come into the class.
- Stoop down to communicate w/ them on eye-level. You are less scary when you aren't so big
- Invite parents in to help them settle their child into an activity. Generally, parents should make their exit within about 5 minutes, so as to not prolong disruption of class/teaching that may occur when they leave.
- Don't forget about the windows in your room. if the distractions of the toy shelf hold no interest for an upset child, try walking them to the window and point out cars, trees, people on the street, animals, houses, colors, etc.
- If a child grows increasingly inconsolable after 5 - 10 minutes, have the hall monitor page the parents for assistance.

- If a child is brand new to the class and struggling with separation anxiety, invite to stay in the room for the duration of class to help them get used to their environment (but do not leave a parent alone with the other children)
- When Sunday School transitions to Church Hour, teachers should try to overlap for at least a few minutes and make the departure of Sunday School teachers as quiet as possible.

a child won't participate
If they're not being disruptive, but quietly listening, consider what might make them feel more comfortable to participate.

a child refuses to come to circle time, especially if they want to play:
Give a child two choices: "You may come sit on a carpet square with the group, or you may sit in a chair at the table. But, it is not play time and no one may play with the toys. Would you rather sit on the carpet or on a chair?"

a child disobeys

As with all things, consider the heart. Did the child disobey because they were confused or didn't understand what the teacher was asking? Teacher should clarify. Did they understand and willfully disobey? Start by explaining the problem and giving a warning. "Timmy, Mrs. Miller said it was Katie's turn to play with the dump truck, but then you took the truck away from her. That made her sad AND it was disobeying Mrs. Miller. We are learning to share, and if you will not share, Mrs. Miller will need you to sit in time out." If a similar thing happens again, repeat your little speech, and say "Mrs. Miller warned you that if you took toys from someone else again that you would sit in time out. Please come sit in this chair until I tell you it's time to play again."

note about time outs for two year olds

Two minutes is an appropriate amount of time for a 2 year old time out. Longer than that and you loose the teachablility of the moment.

Before letting a child return to the group, have a conversation. "Timmy, do you remember why you sat in time-out?" "You took a toy away from Katie, and then you took a toy away from another friend. This is not good sharing, and one of the ways we can show love to other people like God has loved us is to be kind. Are you ready to play with your friends and share? Let me pray for you that God would help you to obey 'God, thank you for giving us friends to love. Please help Timmy to love his friends and share with them. Amen." Dismiss Timmy to play, and then (hopefully within 5 minutes or so), "catch" Timmy being good and encourage him in the way he is obeying and sharing with friends.

THREE YEAR OLDS

a child won't participate:
If they're not being disruptive, but quietly listening, consider what might make them feel more comfortable to participate. Would giving that child a special role help them? Perhaps you can ask them to be your special helper and let them sit next to you and hold up the big question signs.

a child refuses to come to circle time, esp. if they want to play:
Give a child two choices "You may come sit on a carpet square with the group, or you may sit in a chair at the table. But, it is not play time and no one may play with the toys. Would you rather sit on the carpet or on a chair?"

a child disobeys
As with all things, consider the heart. Did the child disobey because they were confused or didn't understand what the teacher was asking? Teacher should clarify. Did they understand and willfully disobey? Start by explaining the problem and giving a warning. "Timmy, Mrs. Miller said it was Katie's turn to play with the dump truck, but then you took the truck away from her. That made her sad AND it was disobeying Mrs. Miller. We are learning to share, and if you will not share, Mrs. Miller will need you to sit in time out." If a similar thing happens again, repeat your little speech, and say "Mrs. Miller warned you that if you took toys from someone else again that you would sit in time out. Please come sit in this chair until I tell you it's time to play again."

note about time outs for three year olds
Three minutes is an appropriate amount of time for a 3 year old's time out. Longer than that and you loose the teachability of the moment.

Before letting a child return to the group, have a conversation. "Timmy, do you remember why you sat in time-out?" "You took a toy away from Katie, and then you took a toy away from another friend. This is not good sharing, and one of the ways we can show love to other people like God has loved us is to be kind. Are you ready to play with your friends and share? Let me pray for you that God would help you to obey 'God, thank you for giving us friends to love. Please help Timmy to love his friends and share with them. Amen." Dismiss Timmy to play, and then (hopefully within 5 minutes or so), "catch" Timmy being good and encourage him in the way he is obeying and sharing with friends.

a child throws something
This warrants an immediate time out. Kneel down so you are eye level with the child and explain "we never, ever throw things in our classroom. It is not safe and someone could get hurt. Because this is very serious, you need to come sit in this time out away from your friends for a little bit so you can calm down. Mrs. Miller will come back in 3 minutes and see if you are ready to go back and play." After 3 minutes, go back to the child and see if they can articulate why they are in time-out (this can be hard, especially for young 3 year old, so you may need to help them with the words.) Remind them that we do not throw toys in our classroom and that if it happens again, you will call Mommy or Daddy right away. if they are ready to go back and play, briefly pray with them that God would give them kindness toward their friends as they play.

FOUR/FIVE YEAR OLDS

a child won't participate

If they're not being disruptive, but quietly listening, consider what might make them feel more comfortable to participate. Would giving that child a special role help them? Perhaps you can ask them to be your special helper and let them sit next to you and hold up the big question signs.

a child refuses to come to circle time, esp. if they want to play:

Give child two choices: "You may come sit on a carpet square with the group, or you may sit in a chair at the table. But, it is not play time and no one may play with the toys. Would you rather sit on the carpet or on a chair?"

a child disobeys

As with all things, consider the heart. Did the child disobey because they were confused or didn't understand what the teacher was asking? Teacher should clarify. Did they understand and willfully disobey? Start by explaining the problem and giving a warning. "Timmy, Mrs. Miller said it was Katie's turn to play with the dump truck, but then you took the truck away from her. That made her sad AND it was disobeying Mrs. Miller. We are learning to share, and if you will not share, Mrs. Miller will need you to sit in time out." If a similar thing happens again, repeat your little speech, and say "Mrs. Miller warned you that if you took toys from someone else again that you would sit in time out. Please come sit in this chair until I tell you it's time to play again."

a child throws something

This warrants an immediate time out. Kneel down so you are eye level with the child and explain "we never, ever throw things in our classroom. It is not safe and someone could get hurt. Because this is very serious, you need to come sit in this time out away from your friends for a little bit so you can calm down. Mrs. Miller will come back in 4/5 minutes and see if you are ready to go back and play." After 4/5 minutes, go back to the child and see if they can articulate why they are in time-out (you may need to help them with the words.) Remind them that we do not throw toys in our classroom and that if it happens again, you will call Mommy or Daddy right away. If they are ready to go back and play, briefly pray with them that God would give them kindness toward their friends as they play.

girl drama

By age four, the girl-drama phenomenon begins to emerge (sometimes even earlier). Whereas a four year old boy is more likely to just chuck a dump truck at his friend when he's mad, the ways of a girl are much more under-the-radar and catty. Because there's no blood with a hurled word or attitude, it's easy to let this slide, but we do our little gals no favors when we don't address it.

note about time outs for four/five year olds

Four/five minutes is an appropriate amount of time for a 4/5 year old's time out. Longer than that and you loose the teachability of the moment.

Before letting a child return to the group, have a conversation. "Timmy, do you remember why you sat in time-out?" "You took a toy away from Katie, and then you took a toy away from another friend. This is not good sharing, and one of the ways we can show love to other people like God has loved is to be kind. Are you ready to play with your friends and share? Let me pray for you that God would help you to obey 'God, thank you for giving us friends to love. Please help Timmy to love his friends and share with them. Amen." Dismiss Timmy to play, and then (hopefully within 5 minutes or so), "catch" Timmy being good and encourage him in the way he is obeying and sharing with friends.

Proactive measures

If you have a few girls known for their drama with each other, proactive separate them, especially during lesson time. When you do see them being kind to each other, encourage them in it. It is good to even pray with them and praise God that you see them reflecting his kindness in the way they are treating each other.

Reactive measures

When something does happen (usually it is an unkind comment or exclusion), take the time to teach the girls about what God-honoring friendship looks like. Speak to them individually, and try to help them see how their words and actions affect others. Try to help them identify how they would feel if their friend treated them that way. Encourage apology and reconciliation AND then give them instruction on how to play together in kind way (be it sharing toys, taking turns, listening to each other, etc.)

CLASSROOM EXPECTATIONS: Classroom Learning Expectations

Reasonable Learning Expectations
- God answers prayers to help children learn
- God answers prayers to help you teach the children well
- God answers prayers to work in the children's hearts
- Children can learn important things about God
- Children can know God and desire to please Him
- Children learn best when doing a variety of activities within a familiar structure
- Children can learn best when first given a model or example
- Children learn best when you give them clear instructions
- Children learn best with review and reinforcement
- Children can participate cheerfully

Unreasonable Learning Expectations
- You can teach well without preparing in advance
- You can teach well without asking for God's wisdom and grace
- You will teach without mistakes
- The best teaching is only about transferring information and not about heart or behavior issues
- Children can sit still as long as adults
- Children do not need to move
- Children learn well in a lecture format
- Children enjoy all activities the same amount
- All children will have equal ease or difficulty in doing activities
- Children of all ages will be able do the same things and act the same way
- Children will know what to do without your clearly communicated instructions
- Giving directions once will be enough for the children to know what to do You only need to teach a child something once for them to know it, understand it and remember it
- Children learn best with review and reinforcement
- Children can participate cheerfully
- You only need to teach a child something once for them to know it, understand it and remember it

Expected Behavior Goals, by Age

NOTE: All these behaviors will only come with lots of coaching and prompts within each session! Be patient and consistent!

TWO YEAR OLDS
Introducing these classroom behaviors:
- Sitting (ok, really just basically staying) on carpet squares during circle time activities about 5 to 7 minutes
- Learning to share comments and toys
- Learning to take turns
- Listening to the teacher
- Obeying the teacher

THREE YEAR OLDS
Working towards a pattern of these classroom behaviors:
- Listening to the teacher
- Obeying the teacher
- Sitting (staying) on carpet squares during circle time activities about 7 to 10 minutes
- Sharing comments and toys
- Introducing raising hands to make comments and answer questions
- Taking turns

FOUR/FIVE YEAR OLDS
These classroom behaviors fairly well established
- Listening to the teacher
- Obeying the teacher
- Sitting (staying) on carpet squares during circle time activities about 10 to 13 minutes
- Sharing comments and toys
- Raising hands to make comments and answer questions
- Taking turns

Responses to Behavior Issues

1. Give the "Look"
- This can take place without stopping the class
- At this point, it may be helpful for a co-teacher to position themselves near the child
- The "look" becomes more effective as children get older and become more perceptive to body language. Some preschoolers will not be attuned to the "look" and so be patient with them if they miss the non-verbal clue you're trying to give them.

2. Give a Warning
- Stop teaching and give warning for specific behavior
- Alternatively, a co-teacher can give a warning for specific behavior while the lead teacher is teaching

3. Have a Private Conference
- For 2 and 3 year olds, explain to the child why you wanted to talk to them. Explain your expectation & follow the other points below.
- For 4 years and up, you can ask child if they can tell you why you have called them aside. Ask the child if they can explain what it is about their behavior that is unacceptable
- Tell child what you expect
- Give the child a warning of what their consequence will be if the repeat the same behavior
- Briefly pray with the child/ren involved before returning to the group
- Foster reconciliation with others involved
- Praise child for changes in behavior you see
- Speak to parents at end of class if behavior is a pattern

4. Remove from Activity
- Give them some "time out" to cool off and consider behavior (5 minutes is an appropriate time out)
- Remind the child of expectations before they can continue to participate in the activity
- You may need to ask the hall monitor to step into your class while you remove the child
- Speak to parents at pickup time

5. Call for the Parents to remove child from class immediately
- Call for the hall monitor to get the child's parent(s)
- Have another teacher or the hall monitor step into your class while you speak to the parents
- Tell the parents what behavior you expect, what steps you took to correct it, and what the child's response has been
- Call Deepak Reju, Jennilee Miller, or a Deacon of Children's Ministry if you need help

6. Communicating with Parents
- Speak to parent about notable issues or concerns (parents need to be know about and/or may have good advice)
- Speak to parents at the end of class if pattern behavior is IMPROVING!!!

7. Discuss and pray about any major issues or patterns after class
- Pray for God's wisdom for both the families and the teachers.
- Speak with a member of the Children's Ministry team about particularly troubling situations that you have questions about or that seem to not be resolving.

Expected Behavior Tips

1. Pray for God's help, both before class and with the class...and don't forget to pray afterwards, both thanking Him for how He worked and asking Him for more help, based on what you saw that day.

2. Give Clear, Specific Expectations of Expected Behavior
- Give these at the beginning of class, or at the beginning of each section (Opening Large Group Time, Small Group Time, Closing Large Group Time)
- Tell them how you will deal with their misbehavior (for example, "If you cannot share the toys in our room with your friend, then you will need to sit in a chair and take a break from playing."

3. Do not ignore flagrant disobedience of clearly explained behavior expectations. Be willing to wait for obedience.
- Do not just plow ahead and speak over the children or ignore their behavior.
- Disobedience does typically multiplies rather than disappears when ignored
- Remind the children of behavior expected.
- Do not be afraid to stop your activity and wait until they are cooperating.

4. Prepare the children for transitions between activities with clear instructions. Many difficulties in behavior arise during transitions; partly because we do not give clearly tell children how we want them to behave.
- Tell them WHEN you want them to move
- (for example, "When I say "go" I want you to...."
- Tell them HOW you want them to move
- (for example, "When I say "go", I want you creep like a little mouse…"
- Tell them WHERE you want them to move
- (for example, "when I say "go," I want you creep like a little mouse and walk quietly and sit down on a carpet square...")
- Review with them WHAT YOU WANT THEM TO DO

Important Guidelines for Preschool Teachers

Come Observe!

Especially if you have never taught the 2-5's before, we encourage you to come up and observe our classes in progress. This is a great way to see what preschoolers are like and what each of the different volunteer opportunities involves. Contact Gio Lynch about scheduling a visit.

Choosing Months to Teach

Please be careful to choose months in which you will be available all Sundays. We understand there may be times when this is not possible, but it is extremely important for continuity's sake to try to keep the same teachers in place all month. Structure and repetition is important to preschoolers.

Finding a Substitute

- The Children's Ministry Administrator and the Deacon of Children's Ministry are available to help you find a substitute.
- It is important that you choose someone who has taught in the preschool department before.
- Often times, you can get someone assigned a different month to switch a week with you. (They teach a week for you and you teach a week for them).
- Please let the rest of the team know who your substitute is. It may affect their preparations.
- Please do NOT use the unofficially CHBC Google Group to find subs!! This is an important part of our Child Protection Policy. There is a special Google Group expressly for the purpose of Children's Ministry. If you would like access, the Children's Ministry Administrator would be happy to give you access.

Preparing to Teach

- Read through your first week's curriculum before Sunday. There are sometimes things that you need to get ready and Sunday morning may be too late to get them done adequately. There may be questions you need to ask someone else regarding content, activity or supplies.
- Pray during the week for your teaching and the children's learning during the session.
- It is also extremely important that you pray as a group before the session.
- Feel free to contact Jennilee Miller or Gio Lynch with your questions.

OPPORTUNITIES TO SERVE

Two Year Olds

2's Sunday School
SERVE: As one of four teachers for one year. The four teachers teach as teams of two, splitting up the year's worth of teaching among the two teams. This system helps prevent burn-out and has built-in substitute teachers, when needed.
TEACH: The Sunday School hour includes a brief time of teaching using a very short version of Teach, Take & Tell.

2's Sunday Morning Service
SERVE: Once a month.
TEACH: The worship hour time is devoted solely to play time.

2's Sunday Evening Service
SERVE: Once a month.
TEACH: The evening service time is devoted solely to play time.

Three Year Olds

3's Sunday School
SERVE: As one of four teachers for one year. The four teachers teach as teams of two, splitting up the year's worth of teaching among the two teams. This system helps prevent burn-out and has built-in substitute teachers, when needed.
TEACH: The Sunday School hour includes teaching time using Teach, Take & Tell.

3's Sunday Morning Service
SERVE: For two, non-consecutive months (such as May and October, but not May and June). This is so that volunteers do not miss too much of their own "spiritual feeding."
TEACH: The worship hour time is a continuation of Teach, Take & Tell.

3's Sunday Evening Service
SERVE: Once a month.
TEACH: The evening service time is devoted solely to play time.

Four/Five Year Olds

4/5's Sunday School
SERVE: As one of four teachers for one year. The four teachers teach as teams of two, splitting up the year's worth of teaching among the two teams. This system helps prevent burn-out and has built-in substitute teachers, when needed.
TEACH: The Sunday School hour includes teaching time using Big Questions & Answers for little people.

4/5's Sunday Morning Service
SERVE: For two, non-consecutive months (such as May and October, but not May and June). This is so that volunteers do not miss too much of their own "spiritual feeding."
TEACH: The worship hour time is a continuation of Big Questions & Answers for little people.

4/5's Sunday Evening Service
SERVE: Once a month.
TEACH: The evening service time is devoted solely to play time.

Classroom Management Suggestions for Elementary School Age Children

Classroom Management Suggestions For Elementary Age Children

Dear Teachers,

Thank you so much for volunteering to teach our children! We have developed this tip sheet to give you some ideas about how to deal with common classroom management situations. We hope that it helps both you and your students to better learn about God and to love one another.

Child Protection Issues

Key Principles
1. No one adult should be alone with one child at any time.
2. When in doubt, call a hall monitor or parent

Some Scenarios:
A boy needs to go to the bathroom
A male teacher or the hall monitor (always male) should accompany the boy and another boy of similar age to the bathroom. The adult stands outside the door and makes sure the children have washed their hands before returning to the classroom. If teacher leaves, hall monitor should be called to take place in classroom until their return.

A girl needs to go to the bathroom
A woman teacher takes the girl and another girl of similar age to the bathroom. Teacher stands outside the bathroom door and waits. Hall monitor takes teacher's place in their classroom until they return.

A child gets badly hurt, significant nosebleed, throws up, etc.
Call for hall monitor to page parents. Write up incident on an injury report sheet. Inform parents when they pick up their child.

A child gets slightly hurt (a cut requiring a band-aid)
Use the first aid kit to clean and cover any small wound. Write up incident on an injury report sheet. Inform parents when they pick up their child.

A child's parents do not show up to pick up their child within 15 minutes of the end of session
Call for hall monitor's assistance in finding the children's parents. If the hall monitor is not reachable, send one teacher to find the child's parents or contact the Children's Ministry Administrator. Make sure that there are two teachers or certified children's workers with the remaining child as he waits for his parents to collect him.

Behavior Management

Key Principles
1. Children are Foolish by Nature
"Folly is bound up in the heart of a child," Proverbs 22:15, NIV, 1985
Therefore, we can expect foolish behavior from children in the classroom.

2. Responding to Foolish Behavior is an Important Part of Our Teaching
Since we can expect foolish behavior, we can plan how to use foolishness to train children in biblical truths we hope they will learn from our lessons. Foolish behavior fills the pages of the Bible; and it often fills the lives of our children. Why? Because foolish behavior is the outworking of foolish, sinful hearts. We enjoy good behavior from our children because it makes our jobs as teachers easier and more effective.

But, it is important to remember that our primary objective in all our teaching is to help the children learn about the Creator God, see their sinful, use their foolish behavior and our teaching as opportunities to point out their rebellious hearts, understand the consequences of their sin; and turn to Jesus as their Lord and Savior. We can use their foolish behavior and our teaching as opportunities to point out foolish behavior, its consequences and our need for a Savior. As you prepare your lesson, ask yourself: What foolish behavior do I see the people in this story exhibiting? What wise behavior? Do any of these behaviors look like the heart issues or actions of the children in my class? What questions could I ask them to help them see these issues/actions and apply them to their lives? How could I point the children to their own heart issues and their own need of a Savior through this story and the issues/actions highlighted, as well as, of course, through any foolish classroom behaviors?

3. Training and Turning of Hearts and Actions
As we address foolish behavior in our classroom, it is important to think about how we change. Any kind of training takes time, even more so the training of behaviors overflowing from sinful hearts. Since children are by nature foolish, then we need to help train them in wise behavior, encourage them to turn away from it. We need to make sure they understand how they are to act (through learning classroom rules as well as through learning biblical truths in our lessons); as well as lead them to, see their sinful hearts, ask God for forgiveness and the Holy Spirit's help to change both their hearts and their actions. We need to be praying for the children during the week to this end. How important it is that we remember that changed behavior does not necessarily mean changed hearts! Changed hearts are a work of the Holy Spirit alone! We also should pray that God would make us gentle, wise and consistent in our training of the children.

4. Train and Turn Only with Great Compassion, Gentleness and Graciousness
Behavioral problems, especially with "repeat offenders", can be very frustrating. It is very, very important that we only train and turn with compassion, gentleness and mercy. Not only can this often help a situation more quickly resolve (cf. Proverbs 15:1 "A gentle answer turns away wrath and a harsh word stirs up anger."), but when we act and speak from a heart of compassion, gentleness and graciousness, we reflect our merciful and loving Father to the children. Pray that God would fill your heart with His mercy and love as you deal with any behavior issues. Then of course there's the work that God will do in our heart and lives as we ask Him to cultivate this attitude in ourselves.

Be aware of growing frustration on your part. If you feel that you cannot speak or act towards a child with the right attitude, it would be better to leave the situation to another teacher.

5. An Ounce of Prevention is Worth a Pound of Correction

out of temptation's way
When you become familiar with the children in your classroom, you will become aware of the things that typically tempt them. You may prevent many mishaps by looking over your lesson plans and classroom for situations, objects, etc. that will tend to draw out misbehavior and adjusting them accordingly. Do you have a group of especially wiggling children? Look for ways to add in more movement. Do you have some very competitive children? Change the games to be group cooperation games rather than team vs. team. Are there things in the room that regularly distract? Find a place to put them away.

working as a team
When one teacher is leading the teaching, the other teacher(s) should be actively looking for ways to facilitate focus and learning. This includes everything from noticing if the lead teacher needs a dry erase marker and bringing it to him, hold visuals, etc. to sitting next to a wiggly child, to quietly pulling aside a child who has a behavioral issue. Whenever possible, avoid the lead teacher interrupting his teaching to deal up with these issues. It will be distracting the other students and be more embarrassing to the student who is struggling.

6. The Child that Will Not be Trained and Turned
Sometimes a child refuses to change in a particular situation. Sometimes there is a pattern of behavior and heart issues that becomes apparent. In these cases, you need to be speaking to the parents about what you observe. Usually this can be done after the session during sign-out time. In extremely rare cases, you may need to call the hall monitor to page the parents immediately. Be sensitive as to whether this is a conversation that should take place in the child's presence or not. As a guideline, one time issues may be best addressed with the child present, while patterns may be best addressed without the child. If in doubt, speak to the parents privately and they can decide whether to discuss the matter further with the child present. decide whether to discuss the matter further with the child present.

General Guidelines for Behavior Issues: Children of Visitors

How Visitors Are Different
Visitors are not familiar with the class rules and may come from non-Christian families. So much of our training and turning is based on knowledge of our families, our rules and the relationship we have with the children. Since little if any of these elements are in place with visitors, they must be treated differently. On the other hand, we do not want to let visitor's bad behavior set the tone for our class, be left unaddressed, and certainly not allow harm to either children or teachers. Sometimes this makes for a tricky balance.

Special Principles for Behavior Issues of Visitors

1. Forbear as long as possible with behavioral issues of visitors
2. Use positive reinforcement as much and as long as possible
3. Try to give cues to a visiting child through a whispered comment rather than removing them for a conversation
4. Contact the parents through the hall monitor if the situation escalates and/or becomes unmanageable

Common Scenarios with Visitors

Lack of cooperation in the group
Give them two or three choices of things they can do, such as: sitting quietly, helping you, or taking part in the activity. Your goal to help the visitor be obedient in a comfortable way (given their new setting), while maintaining focus to stay on the group activity.

Disrespectful behavior or speech
Instead of taking the child aside, have a teacher come along side the child and whisper to them: "That sounded pretty unkind/disrespectful, etc. Please don't say that/do that, etc." If behavior persists, then give the child a warning that they will not be able to stay in the class if they keep on doing that. Call the parents via the hall monitor and page system, if situation escalates to an unmanageable distraction.

If they change behavior, praise them, especially in front of their parents at the end of the session.

In Praise Factory: Older and younger children from the same family want to stay together
Let the children stay together! Put them, if possible, in the group of the younger child. If the children visit consistently for three or four weeks, consider transitioning them to their own groups. You can do this best by speaking to the parents privately at the end of a session, asking them how their children are enjoying the program. If they are still feeling pretty new, leave them together. If they seem to be happy and settled, tell the parents that you would love the children to be with their own age group so that they can establish closer friends with the other children their age. If parents are happy for this to happen, ask them if they would speak to their children about this. If the children seem ready after this conversation with their parents, then go ahead and split them. If not, wait a few more weeks and reassess. It works best to put the older child in the younger child's group, since frequently the younger child's transition is more difficult and the older child will want to be with their age group sooner.

The Child that Will Not be Trained and Turned
Sometimes a child refuses to change in a particular situation. Sometimes there is a pattern of behavior and heart issues that becomes apparent. In these cases, you need to be speaking to the parents about what you observe. Usually this can be done after the session during sign-out time. In extremely rare cases, you may need to call the hall monitor to page the parents immediately. Be sensitive as to whether this is a conversation that should take place in the child's presence or not. As a guideline, one time issues may be best addressed with the child present, while patterns may be best addressed without the child. If in doubt, speak to the parents privately and they can decide whether to discuss the matter further with the child present.

Learning Expectations for Elementary School Age Children

Reasonable Learning Expectations

- God answers prayers to help children learn
- God answers prayers to help you teach the children well
- God answers prayers to work in the children's hearts
- Children can learn important things about God
- Children can know God and desire to please Him
- Children learn best when doing a variety of activities within a familiar structure
- Children can learn best when first given a model or example
- Children learn best when you give them clear instructions
- Children learn best with review and reinforcement
- Children can participate cheerfully

Unreasonable Learning Expectations

- You can teach well without preparing in advance
- You can teach well without asking for God's wisdom and grace
- You will teach without mistakes
- The best teaching is only about transferring information and not about heart or behavior issues
- Children can sit still as long as adults
- Children do not need to move
- Children learn well in a lecture format
- Children enjoy all activities the same amount
- All children will have equal ease or difficulty in doing activities
- Children of all ages will be able do the same things and act the same way
- You only need to teach a child something once for them to know it, understand it and remember it
- Children will know what to do without your clearly communicated instructions
- Giving directions once will be enough for the children to know what to do

Behavior Expectations for Elementary School Age Children

Reasonable Expectations

- God will hear and answer our prayers for help in teaching and training the children
- God will use the class time with the children to support what the parents are teaching at home
  Children can keep from touching and teasing each other during class
- Children can keep quiet and listen while others speak
- Children can sit, stand, move appropriately (sit up in one place: stand in place; walk, not run, to where you want them to go)
- Children can raise hand for permission to speak
- Children can obey directions, cheerfully and in a timely manner
- Children can change their behavior when corrected
- Children can participate cheerfully
- Children can improve in behavior and obedience
- Children appreciate encouragement when you see even small improvements
- Children can learn the classroom rules and learn how to put them into practice

Unreasonable Expectations

- You will not need to pray for God's wisdom and help with the children
- You can change a child's heart by correcting his behavior
- You will be able to handle all behavior issues without the parents' aid
- Teaching the children the classroom rules will necessarily bear the fruit of good behavior
- Children will not act foolishly or willfully
- Children are not sinners
- Children will never disobey
- Children will act the same every class time
- All children have equal ease or difficulty behaving as expected
- Children will not need reminders of expected behavior
- Children will know what behavior you expect of them without your clearly communicated expectations
- Telling the children expected behavior once will be all they need to hear it
- A verbal warning is always sufficient to correct behavior

Tips for Better Classroom Behavior

Reasonable Learning Expectations

1. Pray for God's help, both before class and with the class...and don't forget to pray afterwards, both thanking Him for how He worked and asking Him for more help, based on what you saw that day.

2. Give Clear, Specific Expectations of Expected Behavior
- Give these at the beginning of class, or at the beginning of each transition point between activities.
- Tell them how you will deal with their misbehavior (for example, "If you cannot show respect during game time you will be asked to leave the group and sit on a chair to the side of the room.")
- A child should raise his/her hand and wait for the teacher to call on him/her, when they have a question or comment

3. Do not ignore flagrant disobedience of clearly explained behavior expectations.
- Be willing to wait for silence and compliance.
- Do not just plow ahead and speak over the children or ignore their behavior.
- Disobedience does typically multiplies rather than disappears when ignored
- Remind the children of behavior expected.
- Do not be afraid to stop your activity and wait until they are cooperating.

4. Prepare the children for transitions between activities with clear instructions.
Many difficulties in behavior arise during transitions, partly because we do not give clearly tell children how we want them to behave.

- **Tell them WHEN you want them to move** (for example, "When I say "kitty cat" I want you to...."
- **Tell them HOW you want them to move** (for example, "When I say "kitty cat", I want you to put your hands on your head and walk quietly to....")
- **Tell them WHERE you want them to move** (for example, "when I say "kitty cat," I want you to put your hands on your head and walk quietly to the other room...")
- **Tell them WHAT YOU WANT THEM TO DO or NOT DO WHEN THEY GET THERE** (for example, "When I say "kitty cat," I want you to put your hands on your head and walk quietly to the
-    other room and sit at the craft tables. Put your hands in your laps and do not touch the snack.")
- **Review with them WHAT YOU WANT THEM TO DO before you ask them to do it** (for example, "How should you go into the other room? What should you do when you get there? etc.)

Behavior Management Steps

1. Give the "Look"
- this can take place without stopping the class
- at this point, it may be helpful for a co-teacher to position themselves near the child

2. Give a Warning
- stop teaching and give warning for specific behavior
- alternatively, a co-teacher can give a warning for specific behavior while the lead teacher is teaching.

3. Have a Private Conference
- ask child why you have called them aside
- ask the child if they can explain what it is about their behavior that is unacceptable
- tell child what you expect
- ask the child if s/he can correct behavior on their own, or does s/he need your help
- briefly pray with the child/ren involved before returning to the group
- foster reconciliation with others involved
- praise child for changes in behavior you see
- speak to parents at end of class if behavior is a pattern

4. Remove from Activity
- ask child why they have been removed (follow guidelines above)
- give them some "time out" to cool off and consider behavior (5 minutes is an appropriate time out)
- remind the child of expectations before they can continue to participate in the activity
- you may need to ask the hall monitor to step into your class while you remove the child
- speak to parents at pickup time

5. Call for the Parents to remove child from class immediately
- call for the hall monitor to get the child's parent(s)
- have another teacher or the hall monitor step into your class while you speak to the parents
- tell the parents what behavior you expect, what steps you took to correct it, and what the child's response has been..
- call Deepak Reju, Jennilee Miller, or a Deacon of Children's Ministry if you need help

6. Communicating with Parents
- speak to parent about notable issues or concerns (parents need to be know about and/or may have good advice)
- speak to parents at the end of class if pattern behavior is IMPROVING!!!

7. Discuss and pray about any major issues or patterns after class
- Pray for God's wisdom for both the families and the teachers.
- Speak with a member of the Children's Ministry team about particularly troubling situations that you have questions about or that seem to not be resolving.

Common Behavior Scenarios

Children Lie Down on Carpet

- If is it quite a few children, you may want to make a general reminder about the behavior expected. This can be done in a fun way, such as: "I see a number of slouchers and loungers on the carpet today. Get up, sleepy heads! Let's see if everyone can sit straight up by the time I count to "3".
- If a child/children persist in behavior, catch the child's eye and give the look. Make a sit up gesture with your hand and when child obeys, give them a mouthed "thank you."
- If the child still persists in lying down, then it is time for a child to be taken aside for a private conversation by one of the supporting teachers, while the lead teacher keeps teaching. Based on the conversation, the child can either be allowed another chance on the carpet, or asked to sit in one of the chairs along the side.
- All of these steps, except the first general reminder, are best done by a teacher other than the teacher leading the teaching, if at all possible. This allows the rest of the teaching time to continue and is less embarrassing for the child.
- If behavior persists after this, pull the child aside again and speak to them. If behavior is slow to turn, but is turning, try to continue to work with the child. Notice and praise even small changes in behavior. If behavior cannot be turned at all, then you will need to call the hall monitor and ask for the parents to pick up the child from class. You will at very least need to talk to the parents when they come to pick up their child at the end of the session.

Children keep whispering to each other

- If is it quite a few children, you may want to make a general reminder about the behavior expected. This can be done in a light way, such as: "I hear a lot of extra noise as I am trying to talk. Let's see if we can be quiet enough to hear the children playing in the floor below us, the wind blowing in the trees, etc. "When everyone is quiet, say, "Thank you, children, for being so quiet. Now, let's continue."
- If a child/children persist in behavior, catch the child's eye and give the look. Make a "shh" gesture with your hand and when child obeys, give them a mouthed "thank you."
- If the child still persists in talking, then it is time for a child to be taken aside for a private conversation by one of the supporting teachers, while the lead teacher keeps teaching. Based on the conversation, the child can either be allowed another chance back with the group but seated next to a teacher and away from the other friends; be asked to sit in one of the chairs along the side, separated from the friend(s) they have been talking to; or, be given a 5 minute "time out" before returning to class (and then seat them next to a teacher and away from friends).
- If behavior persists after this, pull the child aside again and speak to them. If behavior is slow to turn, but is turning, try to continue to work with the child. Notice and praise even small changes in behavior. If behavior cannot be turned at all, then you will need to call the hall monitor and ask for the parents to pick up the child from class. You will at very least need to talk to the parents when they come to pick up their child at the end of the session.
- All of these steps, except the first general reminder, are best done by a teacher other than the teacher leading teaching, if possible. This allows the rest of the teaching time to continue and is less embarrassing for the child.

Children do not want to fully participate

- This is a tricky one! Often this behavior is seen in the oldest children who are being to feel too big to do the activity. The trouble is that their indifference quickly spreads to other children.
- If it is tiredness and an infrequent behavior, then don't worry about it. You may try to re-engage the child by asking them a pointed question or a suggestion that helps draw them back into the activity. You can ask them to help you by holding a sign or some other way.
- If this appears to be a pattern rather than just a one-off occurrence, then it may be time to speak to the child about it in a private conversation and find out what is behind their behavior. Their answer will make a difference in how you respond to the situation. If they are feeling "too big," you may want to give them a way to assist you in leading the group. Or, you may want to talk to the parents: it may be time to encourage the child to sit in the service. This is not an infrequent occurrence with the older children.
- Visitors often do not feel as comfortable to participate with a new group of children. Help them feel at ease. Do not be surprised if they do not participate as fully as the other children. As long as they do not disrupt your class, allow them to watch quietly.

Children keep blurting out answers or comments without raising hand and being called on

- Make a general reminder of behavior expected. Say something like, "I hear voices, but I'm only calling on people whose hands are raised and are waiting quietly to be called on."
- Often times this behavior shows up in excited children who still need practice in raising their hands and waiting. Sometimes, however, it is done in defiance.
- If a child/children persist in behavior, catch the child's eye and give the look. Point to your hand and mouth "Raise your hand" to the child. If they respond with a raised hand, mouth "thank you."
- If the child still persists in blurting out, position an assisting teacher near the child, who can give them gentle, quiet reminders. If you have no assistant available, such as in Small Group Time, ask the child to come sit next to you. This allows you to quietly prompt the child with less disruption to the class.
- If the behavior still persists, then it is time for a child to be taken aside for a private conversation, preferably by an assisting teacher while the lead teacher keeps teaching. Based on the conversation, the child can either be asked to have a time out for 5 minutes or so; or, allowed back in the teaching time, but seated next to a teacher.
- Unless you think this behavior is coming from defiance, show the utmost patience and encouragement. You may find it helpful to speak to the parents about the behavior, if it continues as a long-standing difficulty. It will be good information for them to know and they may have good advice for you.
- If behavior persists after this, pull the child aside again and speak to them. If behavior is slow to turn, but is turning, try to continue to work with the child. Notice and praise even small changes in behavior. If behavior cannot be turned at all, then you will need to call the hall monitor and ask for the parents to pick up the child from class. You will at very least need to talk to the parents when they come to pick up their child at the end of the session.

Children blurt out inappropriate comments

- Most of the time, the children are blurting out answers related to your question or story. Sometimes, though, they are inappropriate "wise cracks" or "complaints." These comments come from a very different issue than the simple need to learn to raise one's hand.
- Respond to the child's wise crack comment make before the group something like this: "Charlie, we all like to laugh, don't we? And we want to have fun. But it is never good to make fun of someone else (if the wise crack made fun of someone else) or, but as much as I hope you have fun in Praise Factory, I want you to learn. This is our teaching time. If you have a good comment, answer or question to contribute, I am happy to take it. But please keep any other remarks to yourself. Thank you." If another child has been hurt by the child's comment, it will be good for an assisting teacher to take the two children aside and help them ask forgiveness and reconcile.
- Respond to a child's vocal complaint (before the group) something like this: "Charlie, we all like to have fun and always do just what we want to do. I certainly hope that I hope you have fun in Praise Factory, but I want you to learn even more than have fun. This is our teaching time. If you have a good comment, answer or question to contribute, I am happy to take it. But please keep any other remarks to yourself. Thank you."
- If behavior persists after this, pull the child aside again and speak to them. If behavior is slow to turn, but is turning, try to continue to work with the child. Notice and praise even small changes in behavior. If behavior cannot be turned at all, then you will need to call the hall monitor and ask for the parents to pick up the child from class. You will at very least need to talk to the parents when they come to pick up their child at the end of the session.

Child raises hand to answer question and instead relates a totally unrelated incident

- Children get so excited about things! Perhaps their bodies are in your class, but it was their birthday yesterday, and they are dying for an opportunity to tell about the new bike they were given.....right in the middle of your serious question about why Jesus died on the cross! This is a part of childhood that is both endearing and sometimes frustrating!
- As the child starts telling the group their unrelated exciting news, try to break in as soon as you can and say something like, "Charlie, it sounds like you had some really exciting things happen yesterday. I really want to hear them, but could we wait until the break (or some other time you can think of in the near future), when I can hear all about them? Thanks." Then continue with your teaching.
- If child persists in telling the story, have an assistant teacher take the child to the side and speak to them in a private conversation.

Children push each other

- Depending on where this happens, this can be very, very dangerous! All too many times, it happens on the top row of the risers or on the stairs. Even if it happens on the floor, though, it can be a small action that leads to a serious injury.
- Immediately take aside the children involved in the incident and have a private conversation with them. Help them reconcile any issue between them. Help them to understand what serious consequence could have occurred from the push. This is best done by asking the child something like, "Charlie, if Ryan had fallen down when you pushed him, what might have happened? Help the child/ren understand the consequences that could have happened from their behavior. Warn

the child/ren that this behavior cannot be tolerated at all and that their parents will be called if it happens again.

- If the behavior occurred on the risers, have the child/ren sit on the floor or on a chair near a teacher for the remainder of the activity. At very least, you want to separate the children.
- If the behavior occurs again during the same session, call the hall monitor to send for the parents.
- While the taking aside of the children is best done by a teacher other than the teacher leading the teaching, it is such a potentially dangerous action, that it is worth making a point of this conduct with the whole class.

2018
CHBC Bookfair
Booklist

AGE CODE:

1 Ages 0-3 (Baby/Toddler/Young Preschooler)
2 Ages 3-5 (Older Preschooler)
3 Kindergarten – 2nd Grade (Early Elementary)
4 3rd Grade – 7th (Older Elementary/Preteen/Middle School)
5 Grades 8th – 12th (Teens/High School)

NOTES: We have spent many hours going through these books. HOWEVER… that doesn't mean that we didn't miss something. Also, it takes your knowledge of your own children to discern the best, most appropriate books for them. Hope you enjoy these books!

A FEW, OTHER SPECIAL CODES:

NC: Non-Christian Book
PC/AG: Presumes Conversion/Add the Gospel
Always be on the watch out for needing to add the gospel. We mainly chose Christian books that do NOT presume conversion, but that include the gospel. However, there were a few good books that we included, that were not Christian books, but had really great resources. Or, were Christian books, but did presume conversion and did NOT include the gospel.

WHERE TO FIND THESE BOOKS:

Christianbook.com
Wtsbooks.com
Amazon.com
Cumberland Valley Bible and Book Service (CVBBS)
Matthias Media
Good Book Company (GBC)
Truth 78
Christian Focus Books (CF)
Tenofthese.com

Apologetics

4,5 The Bible Is God's Word—the Evidence Catherine Mackenzie
4,5 Case for Christ for Kids Lee Strobel
4,5 Case for Creation for Kids Lee Strobel
4, 5 Case for Grace for Kids Lee Strobel
2,3 Inspector Smart and the Case of the Empty Tomb Michael J. Tinker GBC
4,5 Is God Anti-Gay? Sam Alberry
4,5 Jesus Rose from the Dead—the Evidence MacKenzie
5 What Makes Us Human? Mark Meynell
5 Where Was God When that Happened? Christopher Ash
5 You Asked William Edgar

Bibles

Note: Ordered from Easiest to Understand/Message Emphasis Translations to More Exact (and More Difficult) Translation

NLT (New Living Translation):
2,3 Holy Bible for Little Hearts and Hands (Very small size, but very small print)
3,4,5 NLT Teen Slimline (Nice size print)

NIrV: (New International Readers Version)
1,2,3,4 NIrV Beginner's Bible
2,3 Giant Print NIrV
1,2,3,4 NIrV, Gift Bible, Leathersoft, Blue by Zondervan
3,4 NIrV, Study Bible for Kids, Hardcover

NIV: (New International Version)
3,4 The Action Bible Study Bible (NIV) Cariello, Sergio

HCSB/CSB: (Holman) Christian Standard Bible
2,3 Read to Me Bible for Kids
2,3,4 HCSB Illustrated Study Bible

ESV: English Standard Version
1,2,3 Big Picture Bible David Helm
3,4,5 Family Devotional Bible
4,5 Follow Jesus Study Bible
3,4,5 Holy Bible for Kids

Special Codes: **NC:** Non-Christian Book   **PC/AG:** Presumes Conversion/Add the Gospel

Bible Hybrids
(Portions of Actual Bible Translations, But Not Every Word)

3,4   Day by Day Bible   Karyn Henley
1,2,3   Day by Day Early Readers Bible Karyn Henley
1,2,3,4   God's Good News NLT (with short devotional remarks by Billy Graham)
4,5   The Third Day   Alex Webb-Peploe (Easter Story from the Gospel of Luke)

Bible Stories and Storybooks

Compilations of Bible Stories

2,3,4   365 Bible Stories   Mary Batchelor
3,4   365 Great Bible Stories   Carine MacKenzie
3,4   The Action Bible Storybook Cariello, Sergio
4,5   The Action Bible: God's Redemptive Story [Picture Bible] Cariello, Sergio
1,2,3   The Beginner's Bible Zonderkids Karyn Henley
1,2,3   Beginner's Gospel Story Bible Kennedy, Jared
1,2   The Bible in Pictures for Toddlers Ella Lindvall
1,2,3   The Big Picture Story Bible   David Helm
1,2   The Candle Bible for Toddlers Juliet David
1,2   A Child's First Bible   Kenneth Taylor (BB)
2,3   The Christian Focus Story Bible   Carine MacKenzie
2,3   The Christmas Story Carine MacKenzie
2,3   The Easter Story   Carine MacKenzie
1,2,3   Little Hands Story Bible   Carine MacKenzie
1,2   Little Words Matter Bible Storybook (BB)
       In Spanish: Libro de Historias Biblicas (BB)
3,4   The New Children's Bible   Anne de Vries
1,2,3   Read Aloud Bible Stories: Ella K. Lindvall
- Volume 1
- Volume 2
- Volume 3
- Volume 4
- Volume 5
2,3,4   When God Says It—He Does It   Carine MacKenzie

NOTE: Jesus Storybook Bible
I am confident that the Lord has used this very, very popular book in great ways, BUT I NEVER recommend it. I think Lloyd-Jones' creative license goes too far. And, if a number of places, she (probably unintentionally) presents bad theology. So, praise God for the good He does through this book, but please consider branching out to other storybook Bibles.

Special Codes: **NC:** Non-Christian Book   **PC/AG:** Presumes Conversion/Add the Gospel

Individual Bible Stories

2,3 Bible Alive Series (dozens of different, individual Bible stories, I simply chose the David ones as examples)
- David the Fugitive: True Friendship   Carine Mackenzie
- David the King: True Repentance   Carine Mackenzie
- David the Shepherd: A Man of Courage   Carine Mackenzie
- David the Soldier: A Man of Patience   Carine Mackenzie

2,3 Bible Time Series (dozens of different, individual Bible stories, I simply chose the John the Baptist one as an example)
- John the Baptist
- And many more

2,3,4 Hall of Fame Series: Catherine MacKenzie
- Hall Of Fame: Old Testament
- Hall Of Fame: New Testament

1,2,3 Stories from Jesus Series: Catherine MacKenzie
- The Good Shepherd: Luke 15: God Rejoices
- The Good Traveller
- The Wise and Foolish Servants
- The Wise and Foolish Builders
- The Wise and Foolish Bridesmaids

Tales that Tell the Truth Series
- 1,2,3 The Friend Who Forgives: A True Story about How Peter Failed and Jesus Forgave Dan DeWitt
- 2,3,4 The One O'Clock Miracle   Alison Mitchell
- 3,4   The One O'Clock Miracle Coloring Book   Alison Mitchell
- 1,2,3 Two Fat Camels   Douglas Sean O'Donnell

Bible Studies, Bible Memory, Reference Resources, and Activity Books

3,4,5 66 Books in One: A Guide to Every Book of the Bible   Paul Reynolds (Christian Focus)
1,2,3 Alby's Amazing Book   Echeverri Catalina
1,2,3 Beginning with God
4,5   Engage (various volumes) Good Book Company
3,4,5 Exploring the Bible: A Bible Reading Plan for Kids David Murray
4,5   How the Bible Can Change Your Life Josh Moody
3,4   Mark's Marvellous Book: Learning about Jesus Through the Gospel   Mann, Alan
3,4   Meet Jesus in Mark   Matthew Sleeman
4,5   My Bible Journal   Mary J. Davis
3,4   That's Not What the Bible Says Bill Ross
3,4   The Whole Story of the Bible in 16 Verses Bruno, Chris

Special Codes: **NC:** Non-Christian Book   **PC/AG:** Presumes Conversion/Add the Gospel

316

Bible Memory (also see Music)

2,3,4   The Big Picture Bible Verses
2,3,4,5   Fighter Verse Sets   Truth78
2,3,4   Fighter Verse Coloring Books
1,2,3,4,5 Fighter Verse Songs
2,3,4   My 1st Book of Memory Verses   Carine MacKenzie

Reference Resources

3,4,5   66 Books in One: A Guide to Every Book of the Bible Paul Reynolds   Christian Focus
3,4,5   Action Bible Handbook
3,4,5   The Bible Explorer   Carine MacKenzie
3,4   The Bible Explorers Guide   Zonderkids
3-5   Bible Infographics for Kids: Giants, Ninja Skills, a Talking Donkey, and What's the Deal with the Tabernacle? Harvest House Publishers
         The Bible Story Handbook   Walton, John H.; Walton, Kim E.
         Show Them Jesus: Teaching the Gospel to Kids   Jack Klumpenhower

Activity Books

1,2,3   Colour the Bible Book 4: Matthew - Mark (Colour the Bible) MacKenzie, Carine
1,2,3   Bible Names: Presenting Gospel Truths to Little Children Using Bible Names and Their Meanings

Board Books

A Child's First Bible   Kenneth Taylor

All About God's Animals Series: Janyre Tromp
All about God's Animals: Colors
All About God's Animals: Around the Water

Baby Believer Books:
- Bible Basics   by Danielle Hitchen
- From Eden to Bethlehem: An Animals Primer (Baby Believer®) by Danielle Hitchen
- Let There Be Light: An Opposites Primer (Baby Believer®) by Danielle Hitchen
- Psalms of Praise   Danielle Hitchen and Jessica Blanchard

Banner of Truth Series:
- The Man Who Preached Outside
- The Woman Who Helped a Reformer
- The Woman Who Loved to Give Books
- The Doctor Who Became a Preacher

Christmas Carols for Kids: A Sing Along Book (with CD)   Shiloh Kids

---

Special Codes: **NC:** Non-Christian Book   **PC/AG:** Presumes Conversion/Add the Gospel

Famous Bible Stories (Christian Focus):
*   Adam & Eve
*   Joseph's Coat
*   Baby Moses
*   And others

Fit Together Shapes Books from Tommy Nelson:
*   Count My Blessings: A 1,2,3 Boardbook
*   Noah's Very Noisy Zoo

God Gave Me Series (Christian Focus):
*   God Gave Me Hearing   Catherine MacKenzie
*   God Gave Me Sight   Catherine MacKenzie
*   God Gave Me Smell   Catherine MacKenzie
*   God Gave Me Taste   Catherine MacKenzie
*   God Gave Me Touch   Catherine MacKenzie

God's Little Ones Series by Tommy Nelson:
My First Words Bible Boardbook
and more books in this series

"God Made" Board Books (Christian Focus):
*   God Made Animals   Una Macleod
*   God Made Colors   Una Macleod
*   God Made Food   Catherine MacKenzie
*   God Made Me   Una Macleod
*   God Made Time   Catherine MacKenzie
*   God Made Weather Catherine MacKenzie
*   God Made the World   Una Macleod

I Am: The Names of God   Diane Stortz

I Can Say to God Series: Catherine MacKenzie
*   I Can Say: I Love You
*   I Can Say: Sorry
*   I Can Say: Thank You
*   I Can Say: Please

I Prayed for You   Jean Fisher

Learn About God Board Books (Christian Focus):
*   God Has Power MacKenzie, Carine 3.59
*   God Is Faithful (Learn About God, Board Book) MacKenzie, Carine
*   God Is Kind (Learn About God, Board Book) MacKenzie, Cairne
*   God Knows Everything (Learn About God, Board Book) MacKenzie, Carine

Lift the Flap Bible Stories for Young Children   Andrew J. DeYoung

*

*   Special Codes: **NC:** Non-Christian Book   **PC/AG:** Presumes Conversion/Add the Gospel

Little Words Matter Series (B & H):
- 100+ Little Bible Words Board Book
- Thank You, God, from A to Z
- Little Words Matter Bible Storybook
- Libro de Historias Biblicas
- 1, 2, 3 God Made Me
- And more (including in Spanish)

Mi Primera Biblia (The Toddler Bible)   Bethan James, Yorgos Sgouros

Peek-A-Boo Bible: 4 Board-Books   MacKenzie, Catherine

A Special Baby Carine Mackenzie

Catechisms, Worship, Prayer, Family and Personal Devotions

Catechisms

2,3,4	The Big Book of Questions and Answers Sinclair Ferguson
2,3,4	My 1st Books and More (My 1st Book) Carine MacKenzie; Ross, Philip
2,3,4	My 1st Book of Questions and Answers Carine MacKenzie
2,3,4	The New City Catechism for Kids: Children's Edition
2,3,4,5	The New City Catechism: 52 Questions & Answers for Our Hearts & Minds (use with Children's Edition)
4,5	The New City Catechism Devotional: God's Truth for Our Hearts and Minds
1,2,3,4,5	Westminster Shorter Catechism Full Set Music

Hymnals/Songbooks

1,2,3,4	25 Hymns Every Child Should Know: 25 Hymns Sung by Kids with More Than 100 Pages of Printable Sheet Music Karen Mitzo Hilderbrand, Kim Mitzo Thompson
1,2,3,4	Christmas Carols for Kids a Sing a long book Karen Mitzo Hilderbrand, Kim Mitzo Thompson (CBD)
1,2,3,4,5	Hosanna Loud Hosannas Student Hymnal
1,2,3,4,5	Hosanna Loud Hosannas Student Hymnal Piano Accompaniment
1,2	My First Hymn Book Clare Simpson
1,2	My First Hymnal 75 Favorite Bible Songs and What They Mean Karyn Henley

Worship Resources

	Family Worship in the Bible, in History and in Your Home Donald S. Whitney
3,4	My Church Notebook: Come Into His Presence Truth78
3,4	My 1st Book about the Church Carine MacKenzie
	Parenting in the Pew Robbie Castleman
1,2,3	What Is the Church? Mandy Groce
2,3,4	Words about God: To Help You Worship Him Nicholas Choy

Special Codes: **NC:** Non-Christian Book   **PC/AG:** Presumes Conversion/Add the Gospel

Prayer

3,4 40 Days Series: (Missions/Praying) Trudy Parkes
- 40 Days, 40 Bites
- 40 Days, 40 More Bites

1,2 I Can Say to God Series: Catherine MacKenzie (Board Books)
- 1,2 I Can Say: I Love You
- 1,2 I Can Say: Sorry
- 1,2 I Can Say: Thank You
- 1,2 I Can Say: Please

1,2   I Prayed for You   Jean Fisher (Board Book)
3,4   My Kid's Prayer Journal 100 Days of Prayer and Praise Lettering Design Company
3,4,5 Windows on the World (Old Version)   Jill Johnstone, Daphne Sprackett (Missions/ Praying)
3,4,5 Windows on the World (New Version)   Molly Wall (ed.); Jason Mandryk (ed.)   (
        Missions/ Praying)
2,3,4 What Every Child Should Know About Prayer Nancy Guthrie

Family Devotions

1,2,3,4,5 Bible Reading With Your Kids: A Simple Guide for Every Father   Jon Nielson
3,4,5   Exploring Grace Together: 40 Devotions for Families Elyse Fitzpatrick, Jessica Thompson
3,4   Indescribable 100 Devotions about God & Science Louie Giglio
3-5   Listen Up: 10-Minute Family Devotions on the Parables, Family Devotional Marty Machowski
2,3,4   Long Story Short 10-Minute Family Devotions Marty Machiowski
2,3,4   Old Story New 10-Minute Family Devotions Marty Machiowski
PC/AG 4,5 One Year of Dinner Table Devotions and Discussion Starters Nancy Guthrie
3-5   Wise Up: Ten-Minute Family Devotions in Proverbs Marty Machiowski

Personal Devotions/Christian Living
(Sometimes presumes knowledge of gospel and/conversion)

2,3 Berenstain Bears Series:
- Faith Gets Us Through
- Give Thanks
- Go to Sunday School
- Say Their Prayers
- Faithful Friends
- And the Forgiving Tree
- And a Job Well Done
- Kindness Counts
- Gives Thanks
- And the Golden Rule
- And the Joy of Giving
- The Very First Christmas
- 5 Minute Inspirational Stories: Read-Along Classics
- And the Easter Story

Special Codes: **NC:** Non-Christian Book   **PC/AG:** Presumes Conversion/Add the Gospel

3,4,5 101 Devotions for Girls: From the Lives of Great Christians (Daily Readings) Rebecca Davis
3,4,5 101 Devotions for Guys: From the Lives of Great Christians (Daily Readings) Rebecca Davis
1, 2,3 Beginning with God Series (Good Book Company) Boddam Whetham & Alison Mitchell
4,5 Between Us Girls Trish Donohue (go through it with mother/mentor)
5 Even Better than Eden: 9 Ways the Bible's Story Changes Everything about Your Story Nancy Guthrie
4,5 Girl Talk Carolyn Mahaney & Nicole Mahaney Whitacre (go through it with mother/mentor)
3,4 Hope for Each Day: 365 Devotions for Kids Billy Graham
4,5 My Bible Journal Mary J. Davis
4,5 Engage (various volumes) Good Book Company
PC/AG 2,3,4 Girls Just Like You: Bible Women Who Trusted God (Daily Readings) Jean Stapleton

PC/AG 2,3,4 God, I Need to Talk to You Series: (these are also in Spanish)
- About Being a Bad Sport
- About Whining
- About Lying
- About Vandalism
- About Video Games
- About Healthy Eating
- About Bedtime
- About Homework
- About My Parents
- About School
- About Cheating
- About Stealing
- About Bad Manners
- About Greed
- About Feeling Sad
- About Bad Words
- About Laziness
- About Hurting Others
- About Sharing
- About Paying Attention
- About Disrespect
- About My Bad Temper
- About Bullying
- About Talking Back

4,5   Hanging in There   John Dickson
4,5   How the Bible Can Change Your Life Josh Moody
PC/AG 3,4   How to Be a Bible Beauty Catherine MacKenzie
4,5   How to Be Your Own Selfish Pig   Susan MacAulay
PC/AG 3,4   How to Have a Bible Make-over 4.49 Catherine MacKenzie
PC/AG 5   Keeping Your Cool (Teen's Dealing with Their Anger Biblically)   Lou Priolo
PC/AG 4, 5   Love Is Loving Others God's Way   Laura Martin
PC/AG 2,3,4   My ABC Bible Verses from the Psalms Susan Hunt and Richie Hunt
3,4,5   My Kid's Prayer Journal 100 Days of Prayer and Praise Lettering Design Company
PC/AG 5   Sipping Saltwater   Steve Hoppe
PC/AG 4,5   True   Sarah Bradley

Special Codes: **NC:** Non-Christian Book   **PC/AG:** Presumes Conversion/Add the Gospel

Christmas

Definitely more of a PG level of excitement. Use with elementary/middle school age children. They are very good at helping the children see the birth of Jesus through different eyes. (But some of the devotion reflections at the end of each chapter need to be edited or skipped…. but the stories are so good, even without the devotionals.)
- Jotham's Journey
- Tabitha's Travels

Church History and Missions

Activity Books

Biographies

3,4 Building on the Rock Series: Joel R. Beeke and Diana Kleyn
- How God Used a Snowdrift and other Devotional Stories
- And many others in this series

Special Codes: **NC:** Non-Christian Book   **PC/AG:** Presumes Conversion/Add the Gospel

3,4 Christian Biographies for Young Readers Series:

- Augustine of Hippo (Christian Biographies for Young Readers) Simonetta Carr
- Athanasius (Christian Biographies for Young Readers) Simonetta Carr
- Marie Durand (Christian Biographies for Young Readers) Simonetta Carr
- And many more

3,4   The Church History ABCs: Augustine and 25 Other Heroes of the Faith
        Stephen J. Nichols and Ned Bustard
3,4   Reformation ABCs: Augustine and 25 Other Heroes of the Faith Stephen J. Nichols and Ned Bustard
5   Christian Heroines: Just Like You? Catherine MacKenzie
2,3,4 Everyone a Child Should Know Clare Heath-Whyte
3, 4,5 God's Timeline: The Big Book of Church History Linda Finlayson
5   Gold from Dark Minds: The Journey to Conversion of 6 Famous Christians Irene Howat

3,4,5 Hidden Heroes Series (Christian Focus) Rebecca Davis

- Lights in a Dark Place: True Stories of God at Work in Colombia
- With Two Hands: Stories of God at Work in Ethiopia
- The Good News Must Go Out:
- Living Water in the Desert:
- Return of the White Book:
- Witness Men: True Stories of God at Work in Papua, Indonesia

4,5 History Lives Series (Christian Focus) 5 Volumes in the Series

- Brandon and Mindy Withrow full series
- Volume 1: Perils and Peace Chronicles of the Ancient Church
- Volume 2: Monks and Mystics Chronicles of the Medieval Church
- Volume 3: Courage and Conviction Chronicles of the Reformation Church
- Volume 4: Hearts and Hands Chronicles of the Awakening Church
- Volume 5: Rescue and Redeem Chronicles of the Modern Church

3,4 Light Keepers Series Irene Howat

- Light Keepers for Boys: 5 Volume Box Set
- Light Keepers for Girls: 5 Volume Box Set
- Ten Girls Who Made a Difference
- Ten Girls Who Made History
- Ten Boys Who Made History
- Ten Boys Who Made a Difference
- Ten Boys Who Changed the World
- Ten Girls Who Didn't Give in

3,4 Missionary Stories on Safari Lorna Eglin

3,4 RiskTakers Series

- Adventure and Faith, Book 1   Linda Finlayson
- Facing Lions J.R. Williamson; R. M. Freedman
- Fearless and Faithful Linda Finlayson
- Danger and Dedication Linda Finlayson

Special Codes: **NC:** Non-Christian Book   **PC/AG:** Presumes Conversion/Add the Gospel

2,3 Little Lights Series: Catherine MacKenzie
- Eric Liddell: Are You Ready?
- Mary Slessor
- Lottie Moon: What Do You Need?
- Helen Roseveare: What's in the Parcel?
- Hudson Taylor: Can Somebody Pass the Salt?
- George Muller: Does Money Grow on Trees?
- C.S. Lewis: Can You Imagine?
- Corrie ten Boom: Are All of the Watches Safe?
- Little Lights Set 1
- Little Lights Set 2

4,5 Tales of Persia: Missionary Stories from Islamic Iran   William Miller

3,4 Torchbearers Series:
- Danger on the Hill: Margaret Wilson Martyr for Christ   Catherine MacKenzie
- Jim Elliot: He is No Fool   Catherine MacKenzie
- Nate Saint: Operation Auca Catherine MacKenzie
- Titanic: The Ship of Dreams: John Harper of the Titanic Catherine MacKenzie

3,4,5 Trailblazer Series: Various Authors Christian Focus (Over 40 Titles)
- George Muller: Children's Champion
- Isobel Kuhn: Lights in Lisuland
- Hudson Taylor: An Adventure Begins
- Helen Roseveare: On His Majesty's Service
- Adoniram Judson: Danger on the Streets of Gold
- Eric Liddell: Finish the Race
- Gladys Aylward: No Mountain Too High
- Paul Brand: The Shoes that Love made
- Richard Wurmbrand: A Voice in the Dark
- John Newton: A Slave Set Free
- Isobel Kuhn: Lights in Lisuland
- John G. Paton: South Sea Island Rescue
- Amy Carmichael: Rescuer By Night
- Mary Slessor: Servant to the Slave
- And many more

Special Codes: **NC:** Non-Christian Book   **PC/AG:** Presumes Conversion/Add the Gospel

Education, Special Topics, and Hands-On Activities

Homeschool

The Big Book of Home Learning   Mary Pride (Preschool/Elementary; Junior High/High School)
NC Complete Book of Homeschooling Resources A-Z   Rebecca Rupp
For the Children's Sake Susan Macaulay
NC Home Learning Year by Year   Rebecca Rupp
The Homeschooling Handbook Mary Griffith
Teaching from Rest: A Homeschooler's Guide to Unshakeable Peace   Sarah MacKenzie
The Gospel for Moving Targets: Helping Active Children Grow in Grace   Nancy Snyder

Favorite Other Books

4,5 Streams of Civilization Mary Stanton and Albert Hyma
- Volume 1
- Teachers Guide
- Test Packet
- Volume 2
- Teachers Guide
- Test Packet

NC 2,3 Teach Your Child to Read in 100 Easy Lesson Siegfried Engelmann

Fun Activities

NC 1,2 The Arts and Crafts Busy Book Trish Kuffner
NC 2,3,4 The Children's Busy Book Trish Kuffner
NC 1,2 The Toddler Busy Book Trish Kuffner
NC 1,2,3,4 150+ Screen-free Activities   Asia Citro
NC 1,2 Play and Learn Toddler Activity Book   Angela Thayer

Science and Creation

3,4 Big Bible Science Erin Greene
3,4,5 Case for the Creator   Lee Stroebel
NC 2,3,4 The Curious Kids Science Book Asia Citro

1,2,3 God Made Something Series (Find the Animal)   Penny Reeves
- God Made Something Funny
- God Made Something Tall
- God Made Something Enormous
- God Made Something Amazing
- God Made Something Strong
- God Made Something Clever
- God Made Something Beautiful
- God Made Something Quick

3,4 Indescribable 100 Devotions about God & Science Louie Giglio

---

Special Codes: **NC:** Non-Christian Book   **PC/AG:** Presumes Conversion/Add the Gospel

Special Needs

NC How-To Homeschool Your Learning Abled Kid: 75 Questions Answered: For Parents of Children with
NC Learning Disabilities or Twice Exceptional Abilities by Sandra K. Cook
NC Learn to Read for Kids with Dyslexia (Activity Book)
NC Putting on the Brakes: Understanding and Taking Control of Your ADD or ADHD Children Patricia Quinn, Judith Stern
NC Smart But Scatttered (Executive Function Skills) Peg Dawson, EdD Richard Guare, PhD
NC Smart But Scatttered for Teens (Executive Function Skills) Peg Dawson, EdD Richard Guare, PhD

Personality

1-5 Personality Plus for Parents: Understanding What Makes Your Child Tick Florence Littauer
1-5 Understanding Your Child's Personality by David A. Stoop

Stories to Help Kids (Learning Difficulties)

NC 2,3 Adventures of Everyday Geniuses:
- Keep Your Eye on the Prize Barbara Esham
- If You're So smart, How Come You Can't Spell Mississippi Barbara Esham
- Last to Finish A Story about the Smartest Boy in Math Class Barbara Esham
- Mrs. Gorski, I Think I Have the Wiggle Fidgets

NC 2,3,4 The Alphabet War: A Story about Dyslexia Dian Burton Robb
NC 2 I See Things Differently A First Look at Autism Pat Thomas
NC 3,4 Marvin's Monster Diary ADHD Attacks! Raun Melmed

NC 2,3,4 Special Stories Series: Kate Gaynor
- A Birthday for Ben (Deafness)
- A Friend Like Simon (Autism)
- Freddie's Super Summer (Down Syndrome)
- Tom's Special Talent (Dyslexia)

Helping Kids with Anxiety and Other Common Biblical Counseling Issues

CAREFUL: PC/AG 2,3,4 Good News for Little Heart Series:
- Zoe's Hiding Place: When You Are Anxious David Powlison
- Jax's Tail Twitches: When You Are Angry   David Powlison
- Buster's Ears Trip Him Up: When You Fail   Ed Welch

NOTE: These books apply gospel truth to these issues, but fail to clearly state that they are truths for Christians. Kids need to know the gospel. No where in this book (as of the first printing) is the gospel presented. Biblical counseling must always include the gospel. There was talk of rectifying this issue in the 2nd printing of the books. I don't know if it was taken care of or not.

PC/AG 4,5   Keeping Your Cool: A Teen's Survival Guide Priolo, Lou
4,5   Get Outta My Face! How to Reach Angry, Unmotivated Teens with Biblical Counsel   Horne, Rick
4,5   Get Offa My Case: Godly Parenting of an Angry Teen   Horne, Rick

---

Special Codes: **NC:** Non-Christian Book   **PC/AG:** Presumes Conversion/Add the Gospel

God's Beautiful Plan of Diversity

1,2,3,4 God Made Me and You: Celebrating God's Design for Ethnic Diversity Shai Linne
    (There's music you can download, too)
2,3,4 God's Very Good Idea Trillia Newbill

Sexuality, Abuse, Courtship/Dating

5 Diary of a Teenage Girl: Caitlin Series   Melody Carlson
- Becoming Me
- It's My Life
- Who Am I?
- On My Own
- I Do!

5 Diary of a Teenage Girl: Chloe Series Melody Carlson
- My Name Is Chloe
- Sold Out
- Road Trip
- Face the Music

1,2,3,4 God Made All of Me: A Book to Help Children Protect Their Bodies Holcomb, Justin
God's Design for Sex Series: Brenna and Stan Jones
- 2,3,4 The Story of Me
- 3,4 Before I Was Born
- 4,5 What's the Big Deal
- 4,5 Facing the Facts

5   Letters to a Romantic: On Dating   Sean Perron
5 Openness Unhindered   Rosario Butterfield
5 Secret Thoughts of an Unlikely Convert Rosario Butterfield
4,5 Raising Teens in a Hyper-Sexualized World: Help for Christian Parents   Huie, Eliza
1,2,3,4 Wonderfully Made (Conception to Birth)   Danika Cooley

Wise Use of Technology/Protecting Against Pornography

1,2,3,4   150+ Screen-free Activities   Asia Citro
2,3 Good Pictures, Bad Pictures, Jr. Kristen A. Jenson
4,5 Good Pictures, Bad Pictures Kristen A. Jenson
Plugged In Parenting   Bob Waliszewski
Tech-Savvy Parenting   Brian Housman

Manners

1,2,3,4 Manners Can Be Fun   Munro Leaf
1, 2,3,4 How to Speak Politely Munro Leaf
1,2,3,4 How and Why to Behave Munro Leaf

Special Codes: **NC:** Non-Christian Book   **PC/AG:** Presumes Conversion/Add the Gospel

Fiction with a Christian Message

3,4,5 Rwendigo Tales: Myhre, Jennifer
- A Bird, a Girl, and a Rescue
- A Chameleon, a Boy, and a Quest
- A Forest, a Flood, and an Unlikely Star

4,5 Binding of the Blade Series L.B. Graham (5 Books in Series)
3,4,5 The Chronicles of Narnia, Boxed Set   Lewis, C. S
5   Diary of a Teenage Girl : Caitlin/Chloe Series   Melody Carlson (honest look at the longings, struggles and dependence upon God as these two girls face high school life and beyond. Emphasis is on courtship and saving yourself for marriage, growing in the Lord)
4, 5   Dragon Seed Machowski, Marty

1,2,3 The Emily Stories: Carmichael, Stephanie; Green, Jessica 19.99 (Split up) (Matthias Media)
- The Birthday Party
- Grumpy Day
- Over the Fence
- The Rag Doll

4,5 Escape from Danger (Faith Finders Series—Day One Publications, UK) Gill Jacobs

4 Two Worlds Books (Africa Stories)
- A Girl of Two Worlds Eglin, Lorna
- A Boy of Two Worlds Eglin, Lorna

4,5 Heaven, How I Got Here: The Story of the Thief on the Cross Colin S. Smith Christian Focus
3,4   Los Tres Árboles - Bilingüe (The Tale of Three Trees - Bilingual Ed.) Angela Hunt
3,4   The Family Pilgrim's Progress: Adapted from John Bunyan's Classic   Jearn Watson (Christian Focus)
4,5 The Pilgrim's Progress: John Bunyan's Original Story
2,3   Queen Victoria's Request Jeff Anderson
4,5 Screwtape Letters   Lewis, C. S.
4,5 Taken, Book 1 (The Quest for Truth Series) Eastman, Brock D.
2,3,4 Wise Words: Family Stories That Bring the Proverbs to Life   by Peter J. Leithart

Other Fiction

3,4   The Little House Collection Box Set (Full Color) [Box set]   Wilder, Laura Ingalis
1,2   Motor Goose Nursery Rhymes that Go   Rebecca Colby
2,3   Pooh Library original 4-volume set (Pooh Original Edition)   Milne, A. A.
2,3 Three Tales of My Father's Dragon   Gannett, Ruth Stiles

Gospel

2,3,4 Gumtree Gully
3,4   How God Changes People: Conversion Stories from the Bible Carine MacKenzie
2,3,4 My 1st Book about the Gospel Carine MacKenzie
      Show Them Jesus: Teaching the Gospel to Kids Jack Klumpenhower
1,2   This is the Gospel Amanda Williams
1,2,3 What Is the Gospel? Mandy Groce
2,3,4 When Santa Learned the Gospel Camilleri, Simon
2,3,4 Who Will Be King (various languages)
      Your Child's Confession of Faith   Dennis Gunderson

Gospel

Songbooks

1,2,3,4   25 Hymns Every Child Should Know: 25 Hymns Sung by Kids with More Than 100 Pages of Printable Sheet Music Karen Mitzo Hilderbrand, Kim Mitzo Thompson
1,2,3   Christmas Carols for Kids a Sing a long book Karen Mitzo Hilderbrand, Kim Mitzo Thompson (CBD)
1,2,3,4,5 Christmas Carols for a Kids Heart Joni E. Tada, Bobbie Wolgemuth
1,2,3,4,5 Hosanna Loud Hosannas Student Hymnal
1,2,3,4,5 Hosanna Loud Hosannas Student Hymnal Piano Accompaniment
1,2   My First Hymn Book Clare Simpson
1,2 (3)   My First Hymnal 75 Favorite Bible Songs and What They Mean Karyn Henley

Getty Hymn CD's

- 1-5 Family Hymn Sing
- 1-5 For the Cause
- 1-5 In Christ Alone

1,2,3 Hidden in My Heart Series

- Volume 1
- Volume 3
- Volume 3

Bible Stories, Bible Truths:

1,2,3,4 J Is for Jesus
1,2,3,4 Praise Factory Investigators   music and Sing along book Constance Dever

1,2,3 Rain for Roots Series:

- Big Stories for Little Ones
- Waiting Songs
- The Kingdom of Heaven Is Like This

1,2,3   Songs for Samplings Dana Dirksen

Special Codes: **NC:** Non-Christian Book   **PC/AG:** Presumes Conversion/Add the Gospel

Bible Verses

1,2,3,4   Hide 'em in Your Heart: Volumes 1 & 2 Steven Green
1,2,3,4,5 Fighter Verse Songs   78Truth (Children Desiring God)
1,2,3,4   Praise Factory Bible verse Songs Free downloads of over 200 Bible verses set to music
           (praisefactory.org)
1,2,3,4   Seeds Family Worship CDs 1-10

Fiction/Historical Fiction Stories:
- 2,3,4 Adventures in Odyssey
- The Adventure Begins
- Up in the Air
- Under the Surface
- Discovering The Odyssey
- Ultimate Road Trip
- Bible Eyewitness Collection
- Silver Celebration
- And many more

Catechisms
1,2,3,4,5 Westminster Shorter Catechism in Song set of 4

Audio Books

2,3,4 Children's Wonder Bible Over 500 stories, songs, etc. for kids to listen to. Especially catering to
       the go-to-bed with a story crowd. Little, hand-held device with re-chargeable battery.
       Great Ipad-less choice.

Podcasts:
Renewing Your Mind:
R.C. Sproul Reading his books: The Prince with the Dirty Clothes, etc.

Librivox
Has free audiobooks of public domain classics. Quality of reader can be hit or miss.

Audible
There are too many to list. Use the books on this list to search for audio versions.
Here are some I found …

2,3 Theology/Redemptive History
- The Biggest Story DeYong Audio
- The Biggest Story DeYong DVD
- The Garden, the Curtain and the Cross   Laferton, Carl; Echeverri, Catalina

Non-Fiction Audio Books:
5 Unbroken Laura Hillenbrand

Special Codes: **NC:** Non-Christian Book   **PC/AG:** Presumes Conversion/Add the Gospel

Bible Stories

1,2   Beginner Bible Audio
3,4,5   The Action Bible Devotional Jeremy Jones
3,4,5   The Action Bible Jeremy Jones
2,3   God's Good News (Billy Graham)
1,2,3   Berenstain Bears Storybook Bible
2,3,4   The Bible Comes Alive Your Story Hour Sound effects, old classic! English and Spanish Versions

Parenting

Pregnancy

Waiting in Wonder Growing in Faith while You're Expecting   Catherine Claire Larson

Babies/Toddlers

NC Secrets of the Baby Whisperer   Tracy Hogg
NC **CAREFUL** Secrets of the Baby Whisperer for Toddlers   Tracy Hogg
This secular book has some great ideas for communicating with your child. However, as you might expect, it has no place for spanking. Use it as a helpful side resource that supplements (but does not replace) Christian books on parenting.

Preschool

NC **CAREFUL** _How to Talk so Little Kids Will Listen: A Survival Guide to Life with Children Ages 2-7
       by Joanna Faber
This secular book has some great ideas for communicating with your child. Use it as a helpful side resource that supplements (but does not replace) Christian books on parenting.

NC New First Three Years of Life: Completely Revised and Updated   Burton L. White
This secular book is based on Dr. White's 37 years of actual observation and research of the developmental stages children 0 to 3 years go through. He gives very commonsense tips everything from best toys to buy to dealing with many common issues parents face with their child. Interestingly, Dr. White's observations about what works best with children echoes much of biblical wisdom. Use it in combination with other Christian books on parenting.

Grade School

The Heart of Anger Lou Priolio
Workbook for the Heart of Anger: Practical Help for the Prevention and Cure of Anger in Children
       Lou Priolio
NC **CAREFUL** How to Talk So Kids Will Listen & Listen So Kids Will Talk   Adele and Joanna Faber
This secular book has some great ideas for communicating with your child. However, as you might expect, it has no place for spanking. Use it as a helpful side resource that supplements (but does not replace) Christian books on parenting.

CAREFUL Parenting with Love and Logic: Teaching Children Responsibility   Foster Cline and Jim Fay
This pseudo-Christian book has some great ideas for using consequences to help build responsibility with your child, but is lacking in other areas. Only as a helpful side resource that supplements (but does not replace) Christian books on parenting.

Pre-Teens

Between Us Girls   Trish Donohue (go through it with mother/mentor)
Girl Talk   Carolyn Mahaney & Nicole Mahaney Whitacre (go through it with mother/mentor)
CAREFUL   Parenting with Love and Logic: Teaching Children Responsibility   Foster Cline and Jim Fay
This pseudo-Christian book has some great ideas for using consequences to help build responsibility with your child, but is lacking in other areas. Only as a helpful side resource that supplements (but does not replace) Christian books on parenting.

Teens

Age of Opportunity   Paul Tripp
Between Us Girls   Trish Donohue (go through it with mother/mentor)
Girl Talk   Carolyn Mahaney & Nicole Mahaney Whitacre (go through it with mother/mentor)
Help! My Teen Is Rebellious Dave and Judi Coats
CAREFUL Parenting Teens with Love and Logic: Teaching Children Responsibility
          Foster Cline and Jim Fay
This pseudo-Christian book has some great ideas for using consequences to help build responsibility with your child, but is lacking in other areas. Only as a helpful side resource that supplements (but does not replace) Christian books on parenting.

Get Outta My Face! How to Reach Angry, Unmotivated Teens with Biblical Counsel   Horne, Rick
Get Offa My Case: Godly Parenting of an Angry Teen   Horne, Rick
Parenting Adolescents Kevin Huggins

All Ages

A Mother's Heart: A Look at Values, Vision and character for the Christian Mother   Jean Fleming
Child Proof Julie Lowe
Treasuring Christ When Your Hands Are Full: Gospel Meditations for Busy Moms   Gloria Furman
Your Child's Profession of Faith   Dennis Gundersen
Praying through the Bible for Your Kids Nancy Guthrie
Raising Kids in the Way of Grace   Bob Kelleman
Gospel-Centred Family: Becoming the Parents God Wants You to Be   Ed Moll, Tim Chester GBC
You Never Stop Being a Parent: Thriving in Relationship with Your Adult Child
      Jim Neuheiser Elyse Fitzpatrick
Parenting: 14 Gospel Principles That Can Radically Change Your Family   Paul Tripp
The Shepherd Leader at Home Timothy Z. Witmer
Raising Real Men: Surviving, Teaching and Appreciating Boys Hal and Melanie Young

---

Special Codes: **NC:** Non-Christian Book   **PC/AG:** Presumes Conversion/Add the Gospel

Theology

1, 2,3 The Garden, the Curtain and the Cross Laferton, Carl; Echeverri, Catalina
4,5 Visual Theology: Seeing and Understanding the Truth about God (w/Study Guide)
Challies, Tim; Byers, Josh
2,3,4 The Biggest Story Kevin DeYong
1,2,3 What Every Child Should Know About Prayer Guthrie, Nancy
1,2,3 God Is King MacKenzie
3,4 Indescribable 100 Devotions about God & Science Louie Giglio
1,2,3 My God Is So Big MacKenzie
2,3,4 The Ology: Ancient Truths Ever New Machowski, Marty (There's music, too)
1,2,3,4 Words about God: To Help You Worship Him Choy, Nicholas
1,2,3 God Is Better than Trucks Sarah Reju
1,2,3 God Is Better than Princesses Sarah Reju
4,5 Young Person's Guide to Knowing God St. John, Patricia
1,2,3 Everything a Child Should Know about God Taylor, Kenneth N.; Brake, Jenny
3,4, The Radical Book for Kids Champ Thornton

Made in the USA
Middletown, DE
19 September 2020